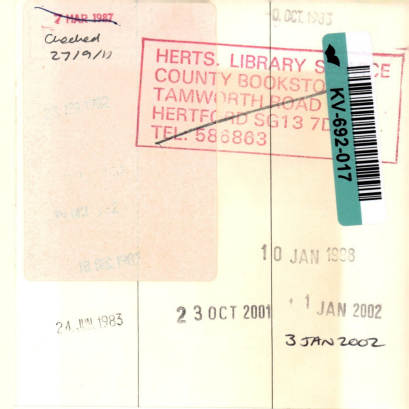
Please renew/return this item by the last date shown.

So that your telephone call is charged at local rate,
please call the numbers as set out below:

	From Area codes 01923 or 0208:	From the rest of Herts:
Renewals:	01923 471373	01438 737373
Enquiries:	01923 471333	01438 737333
Minicom:	01923 471599	01438 737599

L32b

STEAM LOCOMOTIVE

Midland Express on Settle-Carlisle line, pre-1914

STEAM
LOCOMOTIVE

The Unfinished Story

of

Steam Locomotives

and Steam Locomotive Men

on the

Railways of Great Britain

O. S. NOCK
B.Sc., F.I.C.E., F.I.Mech.E., M.I.Loco.E.

LONDON

GEORGE ALLEN & UNWIN LTD

RUSKIN HOUSE MUSEUM STREET

PRINTED IN GREAT BRITAIN
by Photolithography
UNWIN BROTHERS LIMITED
WOKING AND LONDON

PREFACE

THE announcement by the British Transport Commission of the great plan for modernization of British Railways, including the cessation of all building of new steam locomotives, served to give official countenance to a trend that many have felt inevitable for some time past. There is no arguing the fact that there are far more efficient ways of extracting the heat energy from coal than in the firebox of a steam locomotive. But the prospect of vast central power stations, control rooms with their tier upon tier of automatic recording instruments, and electrically hauled express trains does not conjure up those feelings of great human endeavour, of action, and of romance that have been aroused by steam. It is all so much more impersonal.

Despite the announcement of the PLAN, the end of the Age of Steam on railways, though possibly coming into sight, is not yet definitely at hand. Steam locomotives still have a great part to play in the transportation system of this country, and in the modernization of earlier designs there may well be some more surprises, and some further breaking of records before the last survivors of the breed are no more than museum pieces. Rather than carry the unfinished story down to the present day, and end in a welter of hopes, conjectures and fears, I have broken off at the year 1945, when so much that had been traditional of earlier days began to change.

In the writing of this book I have been fortunate in having the help of many friends, and in my publisher, Mr Philip Unwin, the advice and encouragement of one who is himself a railway enthusiast of the first water. It has been my privilege to know several of the Chief Mechanical Engineers of later days, including that great 'elder-statesman' of the locomotive world, Sir William Stanier. Through Mr H. G. Ivatt and two of his sisters I have had contacts with the Great Northern Railway of more than fifty years ago, while I have been equally fortunate in the friendship and help of Mr Matthew Robinson, son of the famous J. G. Robinson of the Great Central Railway. From the Historical Relics section of the British Transport Commission and from the various regions of British Railways I have had much help with the illustrations, and Mr C. R. H. Simpson of the Locomotive Publishing Co. Ltd. has been to particular trouble in looking out many special photographs of historic locomotives. To all of them my warmest thanks are due.

In addition, however, no present-day author of railway books could fail to record the help he has received from the various amateur 'enthusiast' societies. For these societies, by the numerous special trips they are organizing, are creating a new interest by the unusual locomotive workings sometimes involved. At the very moment of proof correction, for example, I have been watching one of the beautiful ex-SE&CR 'D' class 4-4-0s (Plate XVII*a*) making its way through the hills of Central Wales on a special from Shrewsbury to Towyn. A South-Eastern and Chatham express engine gliding down the Llanbrynmair bank! According to official views the steam locomotive may be on its way out, but interest is not likely to lessen while sights such as this are still to be seen. In any case it was enough to inspire two middle-aged business men to motor 360 miles between 8 a.m. and 8 p.m. of a September day, to follow the train, and photograph it nine times in the space of two and a half hours. I very much doubt if the diesels and electrics will move our descendants to similar exploits when, if ever, any of these ultra-modern locomotives reach the ripe age of fifty-five years!

O. S. NOCK
20 *Sion Hill*
Bath
March 1956

PREFACE TO THE SECOND EDITION

TEN years have passed since the first publication of this book—
ten of the most momentous years in the history of rail traction
in Great Britain. The last chapter of the first edition found me
writing of a St Martin's Summer of Steam. Today, except for
certain freight duties that are rapidly becoming less, steam has
virtually disappeared from regular main line service. In 1957 the
brief but intensely interesting episode of the British standard
steam locomotive stud was in the throes of its evolution, and in
the throes of its difficulties. We were too near to events, too
much involved in our daily travelling to be able to see the
episode in a reasonable perspective, and I therefore ended the
book at the year 1945. Now, when the products of the first wave
of British Railways motive power standardization are also going
to the scrap-heap, after very short lives, the story of steam
locomotives and steam locomotive men in Great Britain can be
brought nearer to completion.

The bulk of the book remains practically unchanged; but the
end has been revised, and I have added four new chapters to
bring the story up to the present time. Even so I have felt justified in leaving the original sub-title unchanged, because the story
is still unfinished. A high proportion of the illustrations are new,
though I have retained many of the original portraits, and added
others of engineers concerned with the final phase.

This new edition is being prepared at a time when interest in
the steam locomotive is, if anything, greater than ever, and
something of the genuine atmosphere has been re-created from
time to time by the running of celebrated engines of the past,
now privately owned and lovingly maintained. Long may they
continue to run, because we shall never see their like again!

In writing the last chapters of this book I have written of the
work of men who have become my personal friends, and it has
thus been an added pleasure to pay tribute to what they have

done. Although it was not done in an age of railway pre-eminence, when all engines—express, suburban and goods alike —were lovingly groomed and tended, the years from 1945 to 1965 represent an age of toil and achievement in locomotive engineering and performance that can rank with any two decades of an earlier period. All this made the summary end to the story all the more depressing, when the end did come.

Among those who have provided illustrations for this second edition I would like to thank particularly Mr W. Poultney, who put the collection of his father, the late Edward Cecil Poultney, at my disposal.

O. S. NOCK

Silver Cedars
High Bannerdown
Batheaston
Bath

January 1968

POSTSCRIPT

At the time of final proof correction, in August 1968, the use of steam traction has definitely ended in ordinary service on British Railways.

CONTENTS

PREFACE   *page* 5

PREFACE TO THE SECOND EDITION   3

I   Rainhill and Ten Years After   11

II   The Railway Financiers and their Influence   30

III   The Quest for Economy   52

IV   Artistry in Locomotive Design   74

V   Locomotive Men at Work   95

VI   The High Noon of Steam   118

VII   Momentous Years   141

VIII   In the Balance   162

IX   The Big Four   185

X   The End is Foreshadowed   207

XI   Nationalization   233

XII   St Martin's Summer   247

XIII   The Slaughter   259

XIV   The Survivors   261

ILLUSTRATIONS

PLATE

I   Midland Express on the Settle-Carlisle line,
pre-1914   *frontispiece*

II   THE TREVITHICKS, FATHER AND SON *facing page* 12

III (*a*) J. E. McConnell   13
    (*b*) Archibald Sturrock
    (*c*) Matthew Kirtley
    (*d*) Thos. W. Worsdell

IV   NORTH WESTERN DEVELOPMENTS   28
    (*a*) Long boilered 4-2-0 of 1847
    (*b*) A Ramsbottom 'Newton' 2-4-0
    (*c*) A Webb 3-cylinder compound

V   FURNESS, DOWN THE YEARS   29
    (*a*) 2-2-2 Sharp Stewart tank engine
    (*b*) 4-4-0 express passenger engine
    (*c*) 0-6-0 heavy mineral engine of 1920

VI   EAST COASTERS OF THE VICTORIAN AGE   44
    (*a*) One of Patrick Stirling's 8-foot bogie singles
    (*b*) One of Sturrock's heavy mineral 0-6-0s
    (*c*) A Fletcher '901' class 2-4-0
    (*d*) One of the framed NER 0-6-0s

VII   SOUTH EASTERN AND CHATHAM TYPES   45
    (*a*) One of the Cudworth 'mail' engines
    (*b*) A Cudworth 2-4-0 of 1875
    (*c*) One of the 0-4-2 'Small Scotchman' tank engines
    (*d*) James Stirling's 'B' class 4-4-0

VIII   NINETEENTH-CENTURY GREAT WESTERNS   60
    (*a*) One of Daniel Gooch's 8-foot broad gauge 4-4-2s
    (*b*) A typical narrow gauge 0-6-0
    (*c*) The second *Lord of the Isles*
    (*d*) One of the Dean 'Badminton' class 4-4-0s

IX   NORTH BRITISH RAILWAY   61
    (*a*) One of the two Drummond 7 ft. 2-2-2s
    (*b*) Holmes 4-4-0 of 1891 design
    (*c*) The preserved No. 256 *Glen Douglas*

X   GREAT CENTRAL PROGRESS   76
    (*a*) 5.40 p.m. Manchester express passing West
Hampstead
    (*b*) An early London-extension express
    (*c*) A Great Central 4-cylinder 4-6-0 on the up
Harrogate Pullman

PLATE

XI   LANCASHIRE AND YORKSHIRE   *facing page*   77
- (*a*) An Aspinall 7 ft. 3 in. 4-4-0 express engine
- (*b*) A Hughes superheater 2-4-2 tank engine
- (*c*) The tank engine derivation of the Hughes 4-cylinder 4-6-0

XII (*a*) F. W. Webb   92
- (*b*) Sir John A. F. Aspinall
- (*c*) S. W. Johnson
- (*d*) Wilson Worsdell

XIII   MIDLAND EXPRESS   93
- (*a*) West to North express topping the Lickey Incline
- (*b*) Train of Anglo-Scottish joint stock

XIV   TANK ENGINE VARIETY   108
- (*a*) Caledonian Railway: small wheeled 0-4-4
- (*b*) The fabulous Great Eastern 'Decapod'
- (*c*) Caledonian Railway, a Pickersgill 4-6-2 tank

XV   A NORTH WESTERN PAGEANT   109
- (*a*) A Webb 18 in. 0-6-0 express goods
- (*b*) The Whale 'Experiment' class of 1905
- (*c*) Bowen-Cooke's non-superheater 4-4-0
- (*d*) First of the post-war 'Claughtons'

XVI (*a*) Cecil W. Paget   124
- (*b*) C. J. Bowen-Cooke
- (*c*) Dugald Drummond
- (*d*) R. E. L. Maunsell

XVII   SOUTH COUNTRY EXPRESS TYPES   125
- (*a*) One of the beautiful Wainwright Class 'D'
- (*b*) A Drummond 4-cylinder 4-6-0
- (*c*) LSWR large express 4-4-0 class 'D.15'

XVIII   MIDLAND NON-SUPERHEATER 4-4-0S   140
- (*a*) A Johnson 7-footer
- (*b*) A Deeley rebuild of a Johnson 6 ft. 6 in. 4-4-0
- (*c*) A Deeley rebuild of a Johnson 7 ft. 4-4-0
- (*d*) Fowler rebuild

XIX   EAST COAST PASSENGER AND MIXED   141 ·
- (*a*) A Stirling 0-4-2 of 1875
- (*b*) First of the Ivatt superheater Atlantics
- (*c*) Worsdell's mixed traffic 4-6-0
- (*d*) W. M. Smith's four-cylinder compound Atlantic

XX   THE IVATTS, FATHER AND SON   156
- (*a*) H. A. Ivatt at his desk
- (*b*) The last Ivatt Atlantic to run

XXI   BRIGHTON ENGINES   157
- (*a*) One of R. J. Billinton's 'Scotchmen'
- (*b*) One of the first Marsh Atlantics
- (*c*) An L. B. Billinton 2-6-0 express goods engine

PLATE

XXII   EAST COAST FREIGHTERS   *facing page* 172
        (*a*) One of the Ivatt 'Long Tom' 0-8-0s
        (*b*) A Raven 3-cylinder 4-6-0 of Class 'S3'
        (*c*) GNR 3-cylinder 2-6-0 of Class 'K3'

XXIII   CALEDONIANS IN LMSR DAYS   173
        (*a*) A Pickersgill 4-4-0 No. 14498
        (*b*) A Pickersgill 4-6-0 No. 14637
        (*c*) A Pickersgill 3-cylinder 4-6-0 No. 14800
        (*d*) McIntoch's epoch-making 4-6-0 No. 49

XXIV   SOME TWENTIETH-CENTURY GREAT
        WESTERNS   188
        (*a*) Churchward's County class 4-4-0
        (*b*) A de Glehn compound of 1905 rebuilt
        (*c*) The Classic 'Castle': No. 5010
        (*d*) '72XX' class of 2-8-2 heavy main line tank engine

XXV   CMES OF THE SECOND WAR PERIOD   189
        (*a*) F. W. Hawksworth
        (*b*) O. V. S. Bulleid
        (*c*) Edward Thompson
        (*d*) H. G. Ivatt

XXVI   LOCOS. OF THE LMSR   204
        (*a*) 'Patriot' class 4-6-0 No. 5538
        (*b*) Beyer Garratt 2-6-0 + 0-6-2
        (*c*) The 'Princess-Coronation' class streamlined Pacific
        (*d*) Stanier Standard '8F' 2-8-0

XXVII   SOME LNER GIANTS   205
        (*a*) *The Cock o' the North*, pioneer 2-8-2 express engine
        (*b*) The final variety of 'A3' Pacific; No. 2500
        (*c*) The Gresley 'A4'
        (*d*) The Peppercorn 'A2' engine No. 525

XXVIII THE STANIER TRADITION   220
        (*a*) Sir William Stanier
        (*b*) R. A. Riddles
        (*c*) R. C. Bond
        (*d*) E. S. Cox

XXIX   BRITISH STANDARD LOCOMOTIVES   221
        (*a*) Action shot of a 'Britannia'
        (*b*) Class '6' Pacifics, No. 72009
        (*c*) Class '5' mixed traffic 4-6-0
        (*d*) '9F' 2-10-0 fitted with the Franco-Crosti boiler

XXX   EXPRESS TYPES OF THE SOUTHERN   236
        (*a*) 'Nelson' class 4-6-0 No. 856
        (*b*) 3-cylinder 4-4-0 No. 934
        (*c*) Bulleid air-smoothed Merchant Navy 4-6-2
        (*d*) One of the West Country 4-6-2s as rebuilt

PLATE

XXXI   THE SWINDON SUCCESSION   *facing page* 237
   (*a*) G. J. Churchward
   (*b*) C. B. Collett
   (*c*) K. J. Cook
   (*d*) R. A. Smeddle
XXXII (*a*) 'WD' Austerity 2-10-0 No. 73798   252
   (*b*) 'King' Class 4-6-0 No. 6015
   (*c*) Eastern 'A3' in its final form
XXXIII   PRESERVED ENGINES AT WORK   253
   (*a*) GNSR 4-4-0 *Gordon Highlander* and the Highland
   Jones Goods 4-6-0
   (*b*) The LNER streamlined 'A4' No. 4498

ACKNOWLEDGMENT

The author and publishers express their indebtedness to the following
sources from which illustrations have been obtained.

To British Railways for Plates III (*b*), (*c*) and (*d*), IV (*b*), V (*a*), V (*c*), VI (*b*)
and (*d*), VII (*d*), VIII (*a*), IX (*a*), XI (*a*), XII, XIII, XIV (*a*) and (*b*),
XV (*a*), (*c*), and (*d*), XVI, XVII (*b*) and (*c*), XVIII, XIX (*a*), (*b*), and (*d*),
XXI (*c*), XXII (*c*), XXIII, XIV (*b*) and (*c*) XXV (*a*), and (*c*), XXVI,
XXVII, XXVIII (*a*), XXIX, XXX, XXXI (*a*) and (*b*), XXXII (*b*) and
(*c*).

To Locomotive and General Railway Photographers for Plate X (*a*)
To the Locomotive Publishing Co. Ltd., for Plates IV (*a*) and (*c*), V (*a*),
VI (*a*) and (*c*), VII (*a*), (*b*) and (*c*). VIII (*b*) and (*d*)., IX (*b*), XVII (*a*),
XXI (*a*) and (*b*)
To the North British Locomotive Company for Plates XIV (*c*) and XXXII
   (*a*)
To the Council of the Institution of Civil Engineers for Plate II
To the Science and Art Institute, Wolverton for Plate III (*a*)
To R. C. Bond Esq., for Plate XXVIII (*c*)
To K. J. Cook Esq., for Plate XXXI (*c*)
To E. S. Cox Esq., for Plate XXVIII (*d*)
To Derek Cross Esq., for Plates IX (*c*) and XXXIII (*a*) and (*b*)
To H. G. Ivatt Esq., for Plates XX (*a*) and (*b*), XXV (*d*)
To K. H. Leech Esq., for Plates X (*b*) and (*c*), XXIV (*d*)
To E. Mason Esq., for Plates XI (*b*) and (*c*), SV (*b*)
To O. S. Nock Esq., for Plate XXII (*b*)
To the late W. J. Reynolds for Plates XXII (*a*), XXIV (*a*)
To R. A. Riddles Esq., for Plate XXVIII (*b*)
To Mrs. R. A. Smeddle, for plate XXXI (*d*)

CHAPTER ONE

RAINHILL AND TEN YEARS AFTER

THE opening of the Stockton and Darlington Railway, on September 27, 1825, the first public railway in the world to use steam traction, is now seen as a milestone in social history. It marks the first beginnings of the age of steam in transportation by land. And yet we can now see, all too clearly in retrospect, how narrowly the pioneer work on the Stockton and Darlington Railway missed becoming a mere flash in the pan. One need not dwell upon the widespread public hostility to the steam locomotive, that sprang alike from prejudice, vested interests and, in certain districts, to mass hysteria deliberately fomented. There were more serious and better founded objections. The locomotives of the Stockton and Darlington Railway were not reliable, and recourse had frequently to be made to horses in order to keep traffic on the move. While railways were being promoted in many parts of the country after the year 1825 the development of the steam locomotive hung by the most fragile of threads for several years. Yet to George Stephenson and his devoted band of young assistants railways without steam traction were scarcely to be considered.

The opponents of steam appeared to see the future only in the light of current engine performance on the Stockton and Darlington. Any swifter means of conveyance was considered impracticable, unnecessary, and subject to outright prohibition. The far-sightedness of George Stephenson was at this stage extraordinary —not merely in the possibilities for development latent in the steam locomotive, but in his vision of the way in which railway traffic would grow. In his view that traffic could be handled only by much faster running than they had on the Stockton and Darlington, and this requirement put clean out of court such alternatives as cable traction from stationary engines, and horses. But the years between 1825 and 1829 were critical beyond measure, and it is now time to bring into the picture the five young men who, beyond all others, helped to set the Age of Steam firmly on its way. The five men were: George Stephenson's own son, Robert; two of his pupils, Joseph Locke and John Dixon; Timothy Hackworth, the locomotive superintendent of the Stockton and Darlington Railway; and Henry Booth.

From the outset it was a controversy as much of men as of engineering principles, a controversy that grew in intensity once George Stephenson was appointed engineer to the Liverpool and Manchester Railway. There is no need, here, to recall the many moves and countermoves that took place before he won through to that much coveted post; or to recall how he and his friends outmanoeuvred the Rennies, and so earned their lifelong enmity. Opposition to George Stephenson boiled up in Liverpool itself. For construction of the line Stephenson naturally appointed as resident assistant engineers men who were well known to him, and no less naturally they all came from North-Eastern England. This caused no small offence in Lancashire, where it was felt that there were men just as good as Locke, John Dixon, and Allcard. The Northumbrian 'burr' of their voices was mocked and scorned; but as Hardman Earle, one of the Liverpool and Manchester directors, wrote in answer to a critic: 'Did it never occur to the Reviewer, that in novel and difficult undertakings, it may possibly be as wise a mode of proceeding to employ "workmen strangers to the soil" as labourers strangers to the work?' With some staunch backing from the majority of the Board George Stephenson rode out this particular storm without much difficulty but the question of locomotives was another matter altogether.

Stephenson was appointed Engineer-in-Chief in 1826, and for the next *three years* the method of traction hung in the balance. Two members of the Board in particular, Rathbone and James Cropper, came to the fore as implacable opponents of Stephenson, and nearly all he stood for. Reports as to the state of affairs on the Stockton and Darlington Railway were freely circulated in Liverpool, and matters proceeded to the length of a deputation going to Darlington to observe and report upon the working of that railway. Between 1826 and the visit of certain Liverpool and Man-

11 THE TREVITHICKS, FATHER AND SON

Reproduction of a Cuneo painting, from a sketch by F. W. Webb, showing the Penydaran engine of Richard Trevithick, and the LNWR

E. McConnell; Loco. Superintendent
NWR Southern Division 1847–1861.

Archibald Sturrock; Loco. Engineer, GN
1850–1866.

thew Kirtley: Loco. Superintendent
Midland Railway, 1844–1873.

Thos. W. Worsdell: Loco. Superinten
North Eastern Railway, 1885–1890.

chester directors to Darlington, however, two important events had taken place in the development of the steam locomotive. Timothy Hackworth, carrying on as best he could with the early Stephenson-built engines, deficient as they were both in steaming and tractive power for the loads offered, built the *Royal George*— a six-coupled mineral engine having not only enhanced hauling power, but a far greater capacity for sustained steaming. Instead of a single flue tube extending from firebox to the smokebox the *Royal George* had a flue that doubled back upon itself, and was roughly twice the length of the boiler barrel in consequence. A curious outcome of this arrangement was that the firebox was at the chimney end, and that the fireman had to ride in front on a small auxiliary tender.

The *Royal George* was put to work in November 1827. A little over six months earlier a Minute of a Liverpool and Manchester board meeting read: 'The Treasurer reported that he had discovered a method of producing Steam without Smoke, which he considered might be applied to Locomotive and other Engines; Mr Stephenson attended and having given his opinion that the Invention, if it succeeded on a large scale, would be highly important to the Company he was directed to make any experiments requisite to decide the real merits of the scheme, it being understood that an expenditure of £100 would be sufficient for the purpose.'

The Treasurer, afterwards appointed as the Secretary of the Company, was Henry Booth. He seems to have been a remarkable personality. Though not in any way trained as an engineer, he made two contributions to the technical equipment of railways that have been so widely adopted as to be ranked among the *principiae* of the art. It was he who suggested to the Directors of the Liverpool and Manchester Railway the multi-tubular boiler, as a means of producing, according to the minute, 'Steam without Smoke'. It was no mere random thought, tossed into the area for the engineer to make what he could of it; Booth and George Stephenson were in close consultation at the Liverpool end, while Robert Stephenson carried out the experimental work in the factory at Newcastle. At the same time Booth had lighted upon a far more effective method of making a boiler steam freely than the rather clumsy return flue of Timothy Hackworth. The use of a series of small flues going direct from the firebox to the smoke box greatly increased the area of hot surface in direct contact with the water; the tubes themselves could be made relatively short, which again would contribute to the maintenance of a good draught on the fire.

But while the experiment seemed very promising, and an order was given to Stephenson in January 1828 to build a locomotive incorporating such a boiler, the controversy about locomotives in general waxed so vigorously among the inner councils of the Liverpool and Manchester Railway that only four months after Stephenson had been given the order to go ahead it was decided to transfer the order to the Bolton and Leigh Railway Company. While the whole future of steam traction seemed to hang in the balance the Stephensons, father and son, were experiencing great difficulty in the manufacture of the new type boiler. George, very much involved in Liverpool and Manchester affairs, could do little but advise; but he wrote a multitude of letters to his son. The *Lancashire Witch*, as the engine was eventually named, did not have the modern form of multitubular boiler, but what may be called a faint prototype of that design. As originally schemed out she had a fairly large central flue, and two side ones of smaller size. At one time Booth suggested that two separate chimneys be fitted; but as actually constructed the subsidiary flues were bent at the front end to converge into one single chimney.

Even in the most critical days George Stephenson's sense of humour never left him. He lost no opportunity of emphasizing to his son the vital importance to steam traction of the *Lancashire Witch*, and the day after the board meeting in January 1828 authorizing its construction one finds him writing to Robert: 'You must calculate that this engine will be for all the engineers in the kingdom—nay, indeed, the world—to look at.' At a later stage he writes suggesting the double chimney arrangement; apparently Robert did not like this, and proposed joining the flues together at the front end. When it came to actual manufacture there were difficulties, which Robert described at some length in a letter to Liverpool. To this George replied somewhat drily: 'I am quite aware that the bent tubes are a complicated job to make, but after once in and well done it cannot be any complication in the working of the engine. This bent tube is a child of your own, which you stated to me in a former letter.' Although there was the deepest bond of affection between the Stephensons, father and son, one rather chuckles over this letter, with its 'well, you suggested it; you'd better make it' attitude on the part of Father! Make it they did, amd in July 1828 George was able to write to Timothy Hackworth: 'We have used the new locomotive engine at Bolton which works beautifully. There is not the least noise about it.' Although at the time that last sentence might have been thrown in casually, it was to have a deep significance in the future relations between Hackworth and the Stephensons.

The success of the *Lancashire Witch*, while giving the engineers concerned renewed confidence in themselves, did not alter the shaky reputation of the steam locomotive with the general public or with its principal opponents, and the ensuring months were a time of great anxiety. The proposal for working the Liverpool and Manchester Railway by stationary engines and cable traction seems fantastic to us today; but it was no fantasy in Stephenson's time. It was formally proposed as a result of a deputation visiting the Stockton and Darlington line, and he had to take the report, point by point, and set forth the objections detail by detail. It would have been no use saying the whole recommendation was just moonshine. But just look at it! There were to have been stationary engines at every mile along the line: a train of wagons would be attached to the rope, drawn along at 10 mph to the next engine station, disconnected from one rope and attached to the next; then a signal had to be sent to the engine-station ahead to start winding. A temporary defect in one engine would bring the whole line to a standstill, while progress under the most favourable conditions would be incredibly slow. Those responsible for such proposals obviously had no conception of the rate at which traffic was likely to develop.

While the controversy raged inside the councils of the Liverpool and Manchester Railway, the advocates of locomotives did what they could in the way of propaganda. Even after the Rainhill trials, to which we are leading up now, the future of the steam locomotive was by no means assured, and although it is carrying the story a year or so ahead Robert Stephenson and Joseph Locke felt it necessary to publish, in 1830, a pamphlet setting out the relative merits and de-merits of locomotive and cable traction. This pamphlet summarized the arguments George Stephenson had put to the Liverpool and Manchester board in previous years, and from the authorship of the pamphlet there seems no doubt that the crisp phraseology and lucid advocacy for steam put into those arguments bore the unmistakable stamp of the fluency of speech and facile pen of Joseph Locke. George Stephenson, while very far from being illiterate, was not at his best when expressing himself on paper, or when under cross-examination; and there seems no doubt that at this stage in locomotive history the talents of Locke in this respect must have been of great help to him. Robert Stephenson's great part, at this same stage, lay in the works at Newcastle; but already, like his father, he was viewing things on a far broader canvas than of a mere trading business in locomotives. On New Year's Day 1828 he had written to Michael Longridge, one of his partners in the firm:

'Since I came down from London, I have been talking a great deal to my father about endeavouring to reduce the size and ugliness of our travelling-engines, by applying the engine either on the side of the boiler or beneath it entirely, somewhat similarly to Gurney's steam coach. He has agreed to an alteration which I think will considerably reduce the quantity of material as well as the liability to mismanagement. Mr Jos. Pease writes my father that in their present complicated state they cannot be managed by "fools", therefore they must undergo some alteration or amendment. It is very true that the locomotive engine, or any other kind of engine, may be shaken to pieces; but such accidents are in a great measure under the control of enginemen, which are, by the by, not the most manageable class of beings. They perhaps want

16

improvement as much as the engines.' One could write pages in commentary upon this remarkably penetrating letter, and how, so far as simplicity and neatness of outline is concerned, the wheel has largely come full circle with the latest British locomotives. The machinery, which Stephenson thought it well to conceal as far back as 1830, is now out again in full view.

So we come to Rainhill. The directors of the Liverpool and Manchester Railway, still by no means unanimous on the form of motive power to be used, had offered a prize of £500 for the best engine to fulfil certain stipulated conditions for weight-haulage and speed. The contest aroused tremendous public interest, as the following extract from a contemporary newspaper shows:

'Meanwhile ladies and gentlemen, in great numbers, arrived from Liverpool and Warrington, St Helens and Manchester, as well as from the surrounding country, in vehicles of every description. Indeed all the roads presented on this occasion, scenes similar to those which roads leading to race-courses usually present during the days of sport. The pedestrians were extremely numerous, and crowded all the roads which conducted to the race-ground. The spectators lined both sides of the road, for the distance of a mile and a half; and, although the men employed on the line, amounting to nearly two hundred, acted as special constables, with orders to keep the crowd off the course, all their efforts to carry their orders into effect were rendered nugatory, by the people persisting in walking on the ground. It is difficult to form an estimate of the number of the individuals who had congregated to behold the experiment; but there could not, at a moderate calculation, be less than 10,000. Some gentlemen went so far as to compute them at 15,000.

'Never, perhaps, on any previous occasion, were so many scientific gentlemen and practical engineers together on one spot as there were on the Rail-Road yesterday. The interesting and important nature of the experiments to be tried had drawn them from all parts of the kingdom, to be present at this contest of Locomotive Carriages, as well as to witness an exhibition whose results may alter the whole system of our existing internal communications, many and important as they are, substituting an agency whose ultimate effects can scarcely be anticipated; for although the extraordinary change in our river and coast navigation, by steam-boats, may afford some rule of comparison, still the effects of wind and waves, and a resisting medium, combine in vessels to present obstructions to the full exercise of the gigantic power which will act on a Rail-way unaffected by the seasons, and unlimited but by the demand for its application.

'There were only one or two public-houses in the vicinity of the trial-ground. These were, of course, crowded with company as the day advanced, particularly the Rail-Road Tavern, which was literally crammed with company. The landlady had very prudently and providently reserved one room for the accommodation of the better class visitors. The good lady will, we imagine, have substantial reasons for remembering the trial of Locomotive Carriages. But there is nothing like making hay while the sun shines.'

Details of the locomotives entered by the three principal competitors are well known, so also are the circumstances in which the *Rocket* of Robert Stephenson's build won the prize. In his book *Timothy Hackworth and the Locomotive*, Robert Young emphasizes another side of the story and goes some way towards suggesting that the *Sans Pareil* did not get a square deal. Popular opinion during the actual contest was definitely against the *Rocket*, as can clearly be seen from an account in *The Mechanics Magazine*; 'The engine which made the first trial, was the "Rocket" of Mr Robert Stephenson (the son, we believe, of Mr George Stephenson, the engineer of the railway). It is a large and strongly built engine, and went with a velocity which, as long as the spectators had nothing to contrast it with, they thought surprising enough. ... The faults most perceptible in this engine, were a great inequality in its velocity, and a very partial fulfilment of the conditions that it should "effectually consume its own smoke".

'The next engine that exhibited its powers was "The Novelty" of Messrs Braithwaite and Ericsson. The great lightness of this engine (it is about one half lighter than Mr Stephenson's), its compactness, and its beautiful workmanship, excited universal admiration; a sentiment speedily changed into perfect wonder, by its truly marvellous performances. It was resolved to try first its speed merely; that is at what rate it would go, carrying only its complement of coke and water, with Messrs Braithwaite and Ericsson to manage it. Almost at once, it darted off at the amazing velocity of twenty-eight miles an hour, and it actually did one mile in the incredibly short space of one minute and 53 seconds! Neither did we observe any appreciable falling off in the rate of speed; it was uniform, steady, and continuous.'

As for the *Sans Pareil*, John Dixon gave a homely account of her adventures in a letter to his brother James, dated October 16, 1829. In this he wrote:

'Timothy has been very sadly out of temper ever since he came for he has been grobbing on day and night and nothing our men did for him was right, we could not please him with the Tender nor anything; he openly accused all G.S.'s people of conspiring to hinder him of which I do believe them innocent, however he got many trials but never got half of his 70 miles done without stopping. He burns nearly double the quantity of coke that the Rocket does and mumbles and roars and rolls about like an Empty Beer Butt on a rough Pavement and moreover weighs above $4\frac{1}{2}$ tons consequently should have six wheels and as for being on Springs I must confess I cannot find them out either going or standing neither can I perceive any effect they have. She is very ugly and the Boiler runs out very much, he had to feed her with more Meal and Malt Sprouts than would fatten a pig. . . .'

The Mechanics Magazine, in concluding its account of the trials, bestows a very half-hearted compliment upon the victor. After describing the failures of other competitors the article concludes: 'The course is thus left clear for Mr Stephenson; and we congratulate him, with much sincerity, on the probability of his being about to receive the reward of £500. This is due to him for the perfection to which he has brought the old-fashioned locomotive engine; but the grand prize of public opinion is the one which has been gained by Messrs Braithwaite and Ericsson, for

their decided improvement in the arrangement, the safety, simplicity and the smoothness and steadiness of a locomotive engine;
and however imperfect the present works of the machine may be,
it is beyond a doubt—and we believe we speak the opinion of
nine-tenths of the engineers and scientific men now in Liverpool
—that it is the principle and arrangement of this London engine
which will be followed in the construction of all future locomotives. . . .'

In contrast George Stephenson's opinion was brief and to the
point. As the *Novelty* passed on one of its runs he turned to Joseph
Locke and said in his broadest Doric: 'Eh mon, we needn't fear
yon thing, it's got no goots!' Guts! — that was the crux of the
whole question. Even in 1829 there were scientific men calling
the conventional steam locomotive old-fashioned; today the neophytes are chorusing to much the same refrain! But it was upon
the Stephensonian concept of robustness and simplicity that
British locomotive practice grew up and thrived, and provided
the railways of the whole world with the example upon which
motive power was based for a full hundred years. The Age of
Steam had truly begun with the triumph of the *Rocket* at Rainhill.

The capacity for speed displayed by the three principal competitors at Rainhill, sporadically by the *Novelty* and the *Sans
Pareil* and consistently by the *Rocket*, completed the discomfiture
of those who advocated cable, or horse traction for railways, and
brought a spate of orders to the locomotive works at Newcastle.
But within a very few years of their triumph the Stephensons—
and particularly Robert—were to experience not merely the
straightforward anxieties of pioneer engineering work on a vast
scale, but the more subtle, nerve-wracking anxieties arising from
the personal prejudice and intrigue of non-technical men who
sought interest and fortune in the building of railways. In those
early beginnings the engineers had been all important. It was a
case, no more and no less, of whether railways could or could not
be made, and run. The opening of the Liverpool and Manchester
Railway in 1830 provided the answer. The line had been cut at
great depth through Olive Mount; Edge Hill had been success-

fully tunnelled, and the line stood secure over Chat Moss. From Stephenson's Works at Newcastle had come already a series of excellent locomotives, and even though the arrangements for traffic working were primitive and led to chaos on the opening day, the management certainly had the tools for the job.

For George Stephenson the completion of the Liverpool and Manchester Railway was the consummation of his life's work. He built other railways afterwards, and his services as a consultant were in great demand, but in pioneer work on an ever-increasing scale the mantle passed to others—in particular to two of his most distinguished assistants, his own son, Robert, and Joseph Locke. Robert Stephenson very soon found himself in a difficult position due to his widening business interests. In 1833 he was appointed engineer for the construction of the London and Birmingham Railway, and there is no doubt that at first he felt that his connection should also provide some good business for the Newcastle works.

But the enmity that he and his father had incurred from a minority of the Liverpool and Manchester board during the controversy over locomotive and cable traction had gone deep. Messrs Rathbone and James Cropper had entered into an alliance with a certain Dr Dionysius Lardner, a pseudo-scientific man who had made something of a reputation by writing articles in the technical Press of the day. He certainly had the gift of a facile pen, and although the more specious of his arguments could be blown sky-high by anyone with real knowledge he did succeed in setting a great deal of damaging criticism on foot. Where railways were concerned he appears as the self-appointed critic of the established order. Isambard Kingdom Brunel, no less than the Stephensons, came under his adroitly aimed cross-fire. Neither was he a man whose opinions and writings could summarily be dismissed. He was called as an expert witness on many railway bills, including the Great Western, and on the latter line, after its completion, facilities were extended to him to conduct running tests with a train put at his disposal.

Business interests backing the London and Birmingham Railway were much interlinked with those of the Liverpool and Manchester, and of the Grand Junction, which would eventually connect the two; and at the London and Birmingham Board the anti-Stephenson campaign was waged by Edward Cropper, a brother of James. Like Rathbone, the Croppers belonged to a prominent Quaker family, reputedly great philanthropists; but in awkwardness Edward seemed to surpass his brother. So far as engine building was concerned, Robert Stephenson tells his own tale in a letter to Michael Longridge, one of his co-Directors in the firm of R. Stephenson and Company, written from London and dated January 26, 1835:

'Our enemies, viz. Rathbone and Cropper, are raising a hue and cry about our having an Engine to build at Newcastle—they say another article will be brought out by Lardner on the subject. They half intimate that I shall withdraw from the Railway or the Engine Building. *The revenge of these people is quite insatiable. This distresses me very much.* Can I withdraw temporarily from the Engine Building? I wish you would think this over *for the above named parties are annoying me all they can* by advancing Vignoles and his opposite opinions. The Directors support me, *but it makes sad uphill work.*'

Longridge replied in great sympathy, and after discussing the business implications, but without recommending any decision, concluded: 'Were you as case-hardened in these matters as myself I would set Messrs Cropper, Rathbone, Dr Lardner and all at defiance—but you have not yet attained sufficient philosophy to say "None of these things move me"—when you arrive at the sober age of Fifty you will bear these rubs better.'

Eventually after much indecision, Robert Stephenson did not give up his share in the locomotive building firm, though they did not supply any engines to the London and Birmingham till 1846.

While the Croppers, Rathbone and Dr Lardner were prepared to fight tooth and nail on a point of principle where Robert Stephenson was concerned their pious and philanthropic natures condoned, nay welcomed the appointment of another manufacturer as Locomotive Superintendent of the railway, and without blinking an eyelid allowed him to continue in his dual role for more than ten years. This was Edward Bury, a member of the Liverpool firm of Bury and Kennedy, which started business in 1829. During the thirties of last century there developed three schools of locomotive engineers in this country, headed respectively by Edward Bury, Timothy Hackworth, and Robert Stephenson. Bury was soon firmly established through his contact with the London and Birmingham, but while Hackworth had the contract for power on the Stockton and Darlington he was a man of wider ambitions, and his ill-luck at the Rainhill trials rankled sorely—one might indeed say for the rest of his life. The Liverpool and Manchester Railway purchased the *Sans Pareil* from him for £500, the same amount as they paid to Stephenson for the *Rocket*; but the relative usefulness to the company for revenue may be judged from the subsequent sale of both engines —the *Sans Pareil* for £110 after only three years' service, and the *Rocket* for £300 after nearly seven. There was no sentiment in either sale; they were sold as outdated 'hacks', as ordinary business propositions.

Before the Bury era ended on the London and Birmingham Railway there must have been many among the less prejudiced members of the Board who regretted the manoeuvres that deprived Robert Stephenson of any share in the provision of motive power for the line. It was not that the Bury engines were unsatisfactory in themselves. Their workmanship, finish, and reliability were alike excellent; but they were far too small for the traffic as it developed, and many trains were powered by two, and even three engines. This was hardly an economical way of working, but curiously enough the trait persisted on the London and North Western railway for more than fifty years after Bury's time. Even today the London Midland Region of British Railways is more partial to double-heading than any of the other regions. But before proceeding any further it will be as well to look at the basic design features of the Bury, Hackworth and Stephenson types of locomotives.

Bury set his standard with the 0-4-0 engine *Liverpool*, completed in 1830. She had bar frames inside the wheels; the cylinders were inside and immediately beneath the smokebox, and the firebox was D-shaped in plan with a hemispherical top—commonly termed 'haystack'. Although this general type has always been known as the 'Bury', the detailed design was almost entirely due to his partner, James Kennedy. Bury himself, as we see later, was the business man of the firm. On the London and Birmingham, down to 1845, the goods engines were of the 0-4-0 type and the passenger engines were of the 2-2-0 type. While in 1830 the *Liverpool* had represented a considerable advance in design over the *Rocket* the continuance of such small proportions well into the 'forties resulted in the later engines turned out by the firm being quite outclassed in weight haulage capacity.

Hackworth, with his activities largely confined to mineral haulage on the Stockton and Darlington, persisted in the use of steeply inclined, or vertical cylinders for some years. It was this feature that contributed not a little to the unsteadiness of the *Sans Pareil* at Rainhill, so amusingly described in John Dixon's letter to his brother. This unsteadiness would not show itself to any extent in any slow, hard slogging coal engine, though even in these conditions Hackworth had to provide a counterweight at the opposite end of the engine to contribute some damping effect to counteract the unbalanced forces set up by the motion of the pistons. This type of locomotive, with firedoor at the chimney end, and tenders both fore and aft, was built by Hackworth at the Shildon works as late as 1838.

While Hackworth and Bury clung obstinately to their conception of 1830 the firm of Robert Stephenson and Co. forged rapidly ahead. The 'Patent' engine of 1837 was almost as prominent a milestone in locomotive development as the *Rocket* itself. As the speed of travel and the power of engines on the Liverpool and Manchester Railway increased it was found that the original permanent way was proving too light; the riding of the larger four-wheeled engines was rough and generally unpleasant, and to obviate such troubles Stephenson built a locomotive with an additional pair of wheels at the firebox end. She was intended for passenger service and had the 2-2-2 wheel arrangement. As originally built the additional pair of wheels at the rear end were intended not so much to relieve weight on the driving wheels as to check the pitching of the engine, once that unpleasant action had started. With the big locomotives of today having at least ten, and often twelve wheels, pitching is practically non-existent on the well-lain permanent way of our main lines; but on some small six-wheeled engines of 1875 to 1890 vintage I have experienced a galloping action, which could suddenly include a sickening pitch, when, as one driver expressed it, 'the engine fell into a hole in the road!' But to appreciate more fully what Robert Stephenson and his contemporaries were up against as speeds increased, one has to ride some of the small four-wheeled steam locomotives still operating in remote quarries and industrial railways.

In studying the design of the *Patentee*, as Stephenson's 2-2-2 engine of 1837 was named, it is remarkable indeed to see how many features of lasting quality in British locomotives were incorporated. In mentioning the problem of bad riding it is important at this stage to appreciate how the entity of the steam locomotive is made up. The boiler must necessarily be a rigid structure; were any flexing to be applied it would not be long before joints began to give way and the engine would fail. But the frame is another matter. While any unevenness of the track can be allowed for in the springing of the wheels it must provide for smooth riding on curves. In 1837 we had not reached the stage of bogie engines, and to give a degree of lateral flexibility without undue sideplay in the axleboxes Stephenson adopted the so-called sandwich frame, which he had originally used in the 2-2-0 engine *Planet* of 1830. The frames were built up of timber planking, usually either oak or ash, and re-inforced both outside and inside by wrought iron plates. The boiler was mounted upon the frames by a series of brackets, which from the study of contemporary drawings seem relatively light, and which were themselves probably intended to flex a little, on curves.

The cylinders were attached, not to the frame at all but the boiler; while this went some way towards ensuring that the more precise machinery, particularly the valves, worked in housings that were rigid and not subject to stresses set up by the inequalities and misalignment of the road, the running gear—connecting rods, valve rods and so on—formed a link between one set of working parts which operate in a fixed position, and the wheels and axles, which have considerable latitude in movement. This feature is, of course, still a characteristic of the steam locomotive today, though with all-round improvement in the quality of permanent way, and in constructional technique the whole locomotive is much more nearly a machine of precision. A curious feature of the *Patentee* were the drag links by which the engine was attached to its tender; these were attached to the firebox, and not to the frames, and thus, to use a colloquialism, 'pulled through its firebox'. While there were, of course, many improvements in detail in after years, engines of this general type—2-2-2 with outside frames—were built for express passenger service in this country down to the year 1892. This in itself is a marvellous tribute to Robert Stephenson's qualities as a locomotive engineer.

At the time the *Patentee* was built, and indeed for many years afterwards, opinion was sharply divided among locomotive men as to the best position for the cylinders. Stephenson, with the rough-riding of the *Rocket* in mind, disposed them very neatly beneath the smokebox in the *Planet* and the *Patentee*; but this meant that the main driving axle had to be cranked. The craft of forging crankshafts was then in a very primitive stage, and fractures were apt to occur with disconcerting frequency. George Forrester of Liverpool had the contract for building engines for the Dublin and Kingstown Railway in 1834. He produced a 2-2-0 in keeping, so far as wheel arrangement was concerned, with the fashion of the times; but to make the cylinders and running gear more accessible he mounted them outside. The cylinders were attached to a system of outside plate framing, with the slide bars ensconced in a slot in the frame. As such they were the first locomotives to have horizontal outside cylinders. The disadvantage of inclined or vertical cylinders had been sufficiently demonstrated at Rainhill. But while Forrester secured accessibility and the definite advantage of a straight driving axle, the considerable lateral width apart of the cylinder centre lines gave rise to severe swaying when the engines worked up to speed; they were nicknamed 'boxers' and were later fitted with a pair of trailing wheels behind the firebox to check this unpleasant motion.

The mere existence of this problem of unsteadiness of locomotives, however, serves to underline the 'hit or miss' principles on which the development of design was proceeding in those relatively early days. Then, there were no 'back-room boys', who could settle down in comparative seclusion and work out, stage by stage, the full theory of the locomotive. The swaying motion that developed with speed was due to the unbalancing effect of the reciprocating pistons and rods, and it was naturally worse the further the cylinders were placed. But Robert Stephenson and his contemporaries do not at first seem to have realized the importance of this effect. In all probability they were so busy and harassed by the immediate problems of the day in their various spheres that they had little time to think quietly over such finer points as engine balancing. It may well have been the growing unsteadiness of locomotives that caused Robert Stephenson to clamp down on any appreciable increases in speed from the 1840's onwards.

In the meantime however, other engineers with more restricted responsibilities were working on the problem. There are two factors contributing to the balance or unbalance of a locomotive while running; there are revolving masses, such as the big-ends and crank pins, and reciprocating parts, while members like the the connecting rods contribute an unbalancing effect that is partly revolving and partly reciprocating. An early as 1837 some engineers, notably Braithwaite on the Eastern Counties Railway, had fitted weights in the driving wheels opposite to the cranks, to balance the big ends and cranks pins. Braithwaite had, of course, been Ericsson's partner in the running of the *Novelty* in the Rainhill trials; as a practising civil engineer he had built the Eastern Counties Railway, and it is probably no mere coincidence that he was concerned in some of the first attempts to balance locomotives. The Eastern Counties was not one of the richest of the early railway companies; by comparison with the Great Western and the London and Birmingham it was built 'on the cheap', and there is every probability that the road bed was 'delicate', if not necessarily unstable in places. The swaying action of early locomotives was therefore likely to be more pronounced and serious there than on the London and Birmingham, and measures to counteract it might, one could imagine, have become a matter of urgent necessity.

The first attempt to deal with the unbalancing effect of the reciprocating parts seems to have come from a certain John G. Bodmer who patented a rather complicated arrangement of two pistons moving in opposite directions in the same cylinder! But the complete solution came from an engineer who strangely enough is very little known today, William Fernihough; it is perhaps significant that he, too, was Locomotive Superintendent of the Eastern Counties Railway from 1843 onwards. Previous to this appointment he had been with Edward Bury, not on the London and Birmingham Railway, but in the engine manufactory at Liverpool. Still more significantly he had served his apprenticeship with Forrester of Liverpool, and had been there when the notorious outside cylindered 2-2-0's for the Dublin and Kingstown Railway were built.

Fernihough seems to have been a remarkable man, and although his superintendency on the Eastern Counties was his first railway appointment he brought to it not only a sound practical knowledge of locomotive construction, powers of clear theoretical reasoning, and lucid exposition of a technical point, but a mature and balanced judgment. His evidence before the Gauge Commissioners in 1845 was a model on which more illustrious witnesses might well have pondered. It was in that evidence that he described his method of balancing the reciprocating parts of the engine by adding weights in the driving wheels. It is a method that is now universal—not theoretically perfect, but a judicious compromise between the mathematically exact and the practical minimum. By Fernihough's method, and used with success on the

Long boilered 4-2-0 Southern Division 1847.

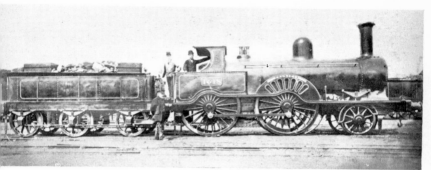

A Ramsbottom 'Newton' class 2-4-0 of 1866, as modernized by Webb.

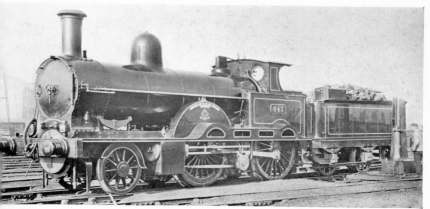

A Webb 3-cylinder compound, 'Dreadnought' class of 1885, No. 643 *Raven*.

2-2-2 Sharp Stewart tank engine of 1866, for the Coniston branch.

4-4-0 express passenger engine No. 120, one of a class of 4 built by Sharp, Stewart 1890, and nicknamed 'Seagulls'.

0-6-0 heavy mineral engine of 1920, built by North British Locomotive Co. Ltd

Eastern Counties Railway, the weights added in the driving wheels balanced the whole of the revolving masses and a portion of the reciprocating masses too. The Gauge Commissioners were immediately impressed by this exposition, so much so that Fernihough was interrupted in his evidence and asked whether he would report independently on certain aspects of Daniel Gooch's evidence! But in referring thus to the Gauge Commission and to Daniel Gooch I have drawn somewhat ahead of the general theme of this chapter; but having made his outstanding contribution to locomotive constructional practice Fernihough drops completely out of the picture.

CHAPTER TWO

THE RAILWAY FINANCIERS AND THEIR INFLUENCE

THE business manoeuvres that succeeded in ousting Robert Stephenson from any share in the locomotive working on the London and Birmingham Railway were a mild foretaste of what was to come in the 1840's. From certain aspects of this ferment engineers cannot be held entirely free from blame. It is natural enough that there should be differences of opinion among technical men, indeed a healthy rivalry keeps all parties on their toes. Considerable difficulties arose in civil engineering work between George Stephenson and Joseph Locke; C. B. Vignoles, with the formidable shadow of the Rennies behind him, was for ever a thorn in the side of Robert Stephenson, and in locomotive design the practice and precepts of Hackworth, Bury and Stephenson were divergent. But then there was Brunel. The challenge he flung down by his championship of the Broad Gauge was something far more profound than the professional rivalries of other engineers of the day. The establishment of the Broad Gauge automatically set up railway frontiers, and at all such frontiers a practical barrier to the interflow of traffic with other railways.

One can believe that Brunel took his stand in all sincerity, on technical grounds. He was the most upright of men, and one can well imagine he saw clearly enough that the path of duty led him to no other course than to recommend the best he knew. In this, for a fast running trunk line like the Great Western, he was right—unquestionably and absolutely right. In his idealism he had no room for compromise, and there is no doubt he felt that once the advantages of the broad gauge were demonstrated other lines would be converted. In this his judgment was at fault; instead his policy, and that of the Great Western in general tended to unite all the narrow gauge lines into a confederacy. The Great Western sought to advance the frontiers of the broad gauge empire. The business men, the administrators and the financiers bid against each other for control of smaller railways lying between the Great Western main line to Bristol and the London and Birmingham main line, and a high time was had by all.

The Bristol and Gloucester, though independent, was built to the broad gauge under Great Western auspices, while the Birmingham and Gloucester—narrow gauge—advanced southwards to meet it. The situation was critical. Starting from the two extremities the odds were fifty-fifty, and both sides sought to obtain control throughout from Birmingham to Bristol. If the Great Western could get into Birmingham in this way their position would be tolerably secure—for a time; but if the narrow gauge got to Bristol it would be as a gun pointing at the heart of the Great Western. The engineers were powerless. It was a battle of financiers, with the Great Western and Midland Boards successively tempting the proprietors of the Bristol and Gloucester Railway. The prospects offered by both the larger companies were extremely rosy, but eventually the Great Western felt they had reached the limit of what could honestly be promised; John Ellis, the Midland Chairman, went one better and he won the day. Although control had been secured, the line, however, remained for some years in a state of betwixt and between, narrow gauge from Birmingham to Gloucester, and broad gauge onwards to the south. The difficulties in working were extreme, and one is inclined to wonder what the original proprietors came to think of the Midland ownership.

I would not dwell upon the episode of the Bristol-Birmingham line unduly were it not for the personality of the Locomotive Superintendent in those break-of-gauge days—James Edward McConnell. Originally he was in charge of the Birmingham and Gloucester Railway, and took over the locomotive superintendency of the whole line after the amalgamation of 1845. Before that he had been employed in Bury's works at Liverpool. For the first months of the amalgamation McConnell was in a curious position. His responsibility did not extend to the broad gauge portion of the line, but he took special care to become thoroughly acquainted with the workings. The locomotive power was then under contract to the firm of Messrs Stothert and Slaughter, who built the locomotives and supplied many broad gauge engines to the Great Western. McConnell was also on most friendly terms with Daniel Gooch at Swindon, and thus armed with a good deal of first hand information about broad gauge engines he set out very deliberately to show what could be done on the narrow gauge.

By the year of the amalgamation, however, the thoughts of the public were turned far away from any technical considerations in the operation of railways. The novelty of travel at 45 or even 50 mph was gone; the steam locomotive was no longer the wonder of the age. All the nobility of pioneer engineering work, the great contributions to the national economy envisaged many years earlier by George Stephenson, were obscured in the flood tide of railway promotion, and wild speculation that culminated in the Mania of 1845. For a time the gigantic personality of George Hudson dominated the scene. There is no need here to go into the reasons for his eventual crash from power. At the time of his greatest influence and prosperity he virtually controlled all the existing lines between Rugby and Newcastle; his administration was shrewd and extremely energetic, though in combating opposition he was very apt to make statements of a technical kind that the engineers of his various concerns would have the greatest difficulty in substantiating. He was an inveterate showman and publicist, and with his rise into prominence the status of engineers was already beginning to decline.

The controversy over the broad gauge was brewing up some years before the sitting of the Gauge Commission in 1845. The Great Western shareholders were by no means confident of ultimate success, and doubts were frequently expressed as to the wisdom of the original decision. The Management consistently looked to Brunel for vindication, and his locomotive superintendent—young Daniel Gooch—was pressed harder than would otherwise have been the case to reach some spectacular results. A lesser man might have easily gone down under the strain, but

Gooch, though still in his twenties, stood firm and with the aid of his brilliant design assistant, T. R. Crampton, produced some first rate engines. It was a strange reversal of poetic justice that the principles embodied in Robert Stephenson's *Patentee* engine of 1837 should find their most successful application, up to that time, in a locomotive design that threatened the narrow gauge interests most seriously. Daniel Gooch's new locomotive *Firefly*, put into service in 1840, was based both in principle and detail upon Stephenson's patent 2-2-2. From the outset she did splendid work; many more were ordered from various makers, and on the opening of the broad gauge line throughout from London to Exeter in May 1844, one of these engines ran through to Exeter and back, 387 miles in the one day, at an overall average of more than 40 mph.

Nothing on the narrow gauge could touch such a performance at the time, and on the northern lines magnates and engineers alike continued in stigmatising any further increases in speed as unsafe. No wonder they wanted to stem the advance of the broad gauge. During the sitting of the Gauge Commission George Hudson made one of his characteristically reckless statements: 'We have, on the York and North Midland, carried from 700 to 800 tons with one engine.' Whether that extraordinary remark carried any weight with the commissioners it is hard to say, but in response to a further question about the nature of the line Hudson said: 'It is a line of remarkably easy gradients, in open country, which is not subject to those fogs which arise in deep cuttings.' A load of 700 to 800 tons would be considered heavy today over that same stretch of line; in 1845 it would be fantastic, and with their lords and masters making such statements it is not unnatural that engineers tended to drop out of the picture, so far as the general public was concerned.

McConnell gave evidence before the Gauge Commission, and with a certain amount of sly humour told of an exploit on the Bristol and Birmingham line that brought broad and narrow gauge engines into direct comparison. An extremely heavy special was ordered at short notice from Bristol, a gross load to be hauled of

235 tons. Over the broad gauge section of the line one of Slaughter's largest goods engines was used, together with an assistant engine up the steep initial incline from Bristol to Staple Hill; the $37\frac{1}{2}$ miles to Gloucester were covered in 4 hr 13 min inclusive of four stops. At Gloucester all the freight had to be transhipped into narrow gauge wagons, and they went forward with a load of 254 tons. McConnell himself rode on the engine, and with six stops and rear-end assistance upon the Lickey Incline they covered the 51 miles from Gloucester to Camp Hill station, Birmingham, in 3 hr. 55 min. Taken overall, the average speeds were $8\frac{3}{4}$ m.p.h. on the broad gauge and 13 m.p.h. on the narrow. This, of course, does not prove anything very conclusive, except that McConnell himself took good care to make a first-class run. He was to make an outstanding reputation for himself as an engine designer before many years were out.

The Lickey Incline, which came within McConnell's sphere of activity, has always presented a challenge to locomotive engineers. Here, against northbound trains is a gradient of 1 in 37 for 2 miles from Bromsgrove to the crest of the hills at Blackwell. If one were to believe the verbose Dr Dionysius Lardner it would be impossible to operate. In his *Pneumatics and Heat* he wrote: 'An acclivity which rises at the rate of not more than one foot in a hundred presents a serious impediment to the Locomotive and an acclivity of 1 in 50 renders its use almost impracticable.' Against this McConnell told the Gauge Commissioners that the Lickey Incline had always been worked by Locomotives, and for some time prior to 1845 some curious little 4-2-0s built by Norris of Philadelphia had been used for assisting northbound trains.

Apart from McConnell's impromptu and quite unofficial contest with the broad gauge the controversy centred upon three main points. Of these one was a case of practical politics, the second was financial, and only the third was one of pure engineering. The difficulty of interchange between broad and narrow gauge was very much one of practical politics. However ingenious might be the devices for facilitating the transfer, however smartly they were made, the transhipment could not be other than a great nuisance. Then granted that a 'break of gauge' was undesirable one was faced with the accomplished fact that in 1845 the proportion of narrow gauge mileage to broad was in the region of 8 to 1. Financially it was almost unthinkable that the higher proportion should be converted, unless the technical advantages of the broad gauge were so completely overwhelming as to outweigh every other consideration. In one vital respect Brunel's own case was weakened, by the example of the Taff Vale Railway, which had been built to the narrow gauge. This fact was recorded, quite justifiably, as evidence from Brunel himself that the broad gauge was not suitable for universal application.

On technical grounds, and particularly as far as motive power was concerned, the broad gauge was in a strong position. Daniel Gooch's 'Firefly' class 2-2-2s were without much doubt the fastest and most powerful engines in the country at that time, but the features that gave them that superiority were not inherently due to the broad gauge. Following the design of the *Patentee*, which Gooch had exploited so thoroughly in the *Firefly*, Stephenson had, figuratively—and sometimes literally too!—got off the rails in following his later conception of the 'long-boiler' design. By the year 1840 his interests were so wide, and his activities so intense, that locomotive design in connection with the Forth Street Works of R. Stephenson and Co. had to be attended to largely on a long-range basis from London. He could no longer personally follow up the working of engines on the road. And as the Mania period approached the time of all civil engineers became occupied to such an incredible extent with considerations of new railway Bills that one can well imagine everything else was pushed aside. The mechanics, as one might term them, had to carry on. Where the broad and mature experiences of men like Locke and Stephenson himself would have been invaluable in guiding the younger men in their day-to-day problems, they were so tied up in the financial maelstrom that they were just not available. Out of this critical period a number of first-rate locomotive engineers emerged, but before coming to them I must tell of the vicissitudes of Stephenson's 'long-boilered type'.

In the late 'thirties concern had arisen over two features of locomotives working, the tendency to rolling and oscillation, and the amount of heat wasted through the chimney. To reduce oscillation, which as we know now was caused as much by the unbalancing effects of the moving parts, the early engineers endeavoured to keep the centre of gravity as low as possible and to do this, and at the same time to secure a higher boiler efficiency Robert Stephenson conceived the idea of the long-boiler engine. Instead of a short relatively fat barrel, as on the earlier engines, the barrel was made long and narrow. It provided approximately the same heating surface, but by giving the hot gases a longer passage through the flue tubes from the firebox to the chimney it was hoped to utilize more of the heat in those gases for evaporation of the water. Furthermore by placing all wheels ahead of the firebox the boiler itself would be set at a low level, and thus help in providing a low centre of gravity of the locomotive as a whole.

There is no doubt that in the early 'forties the 'long-boiler' principle 'caught on'—to use a colloquialism—to a considerable extent in this country. In many quarters Stephenson's name carried a good deal of weight in the introduction of any new idea; but in actual practice the long-boilered engines were the very antithesis of success in passenger traffic. The low centre of gravity did nothing to alleviate rough riding; the short wheelbase aggravated the tendency to swing, and the long boilers themselves were not free in steaming. It is, indeed, strange that Stephenson having produced in 1837 such a carefully thought out, well-proportioned engine as the *Patentee* should have proceeded so soon afterwards to misshapen, oddly proportioned 4-2-0 long boilered engines like the *Great A* of the Great North of England Railway, or the notorious *White Horse of Kent*, which seemed to spend more time off the road than on it.

But in all fairness to Stephenson one must record that the long-boilered engines were entirely successful in goods traffic. This success arose from rather different reasons from those in mind when the idea was first propounded. First of all the goods were

36

mostly six-coupled, and were required to run only at slow speeds. Any tendency to rough riding would thus be small, and in this class of traffic the long boiler came into its own. Heavy mineral trains then, as now, rarely get a long uninterrupted run; more often than not they stand, sometimes for an hour or more, in a siding or loop awaiting the passage of faster traffic. Then you get a run, to the next chosen place for side-tracking. Service of this kind favoured the long boiler and small firebox. While standing a good head of steam could be worked up, for which the long boiler acted as a reservoir, and while standing the amount of fuel used in the small firebox would be relatively small, and although there was not capacity for a long-sustained hard effort, there was always plenty of steam ready to get a heavy train smartly under way. On the Stockton and Darlington line the long-boilered goods engines were built new down to the year 1875, and the last of them were still in service as recently as 1923.

T. R. Crampton, at one time an assistant to Daniel Gooch at Swindon, and later working more or less as a free-lance inventor, carried the low centre of gravity theory still further by putting the driving axle *behind* the firebox. A number of large and picturesque engines on this novel principle were built, a few for this country, but the majority for abroad; while there is reason to believe they were steadier engines than Stephenson's they did not solve the riding problem, for their action was harsh and their effect on the track severe. The Cramptons introduced on to the London and Birmingham line and to the South Eastern were too late to take any part in the trials of broad and narrow gauge engines arranged for the benefit of the Gauge Commissioners. Stephenson's *Great A* was the selected narrow gauge champion, but she was no match for Gooch's broad gauge *Ixion*, a later engine of the 2-2-2 'Firefly' class. But despite the obvious superiority in locomotive performance it was practically inevitable that the decision should go against the broad gauge.

While locomotive engineers soldiered steadily on, with varying success, the financial background to railways generally became more and more alarming and insecure. The Mania years, leading up to the crash of 1848, were such as to read like a fairy tale now-adays: the torrent of speculation, the millions of people who were lured on to invest their all in spurious schemes, the colossal mani-pulations of George Hudson—all cause the imagination to boggle! When the inevitable disaster did come, and so much that was spe-cious fell like so many packs of cards, there was also a rush to sell out from even the soundest of concerns, and a great slump de-scended upon the whole railway stock market. Those shareholders who did hang on were critical and suspicious; in the public eye the novelty of railways was gone for ever. They had become an insti-tution—an institution full of frailties and shortcomings, an insti-tution to be used for business, pleasure or profit, and therefore to be taken for granted when all went well, and roundly abused at the slightest *contretemps*. There were one or two final touches of romance, as when Stephenson built the Britannia Tubular Bridge, and Brunel built the Royal Albert Bridge at Saltash; but from the public point of view the romantic age of railways was over. The Mania and its aftermath had seen to that.

From that time onwards the majority of engineers were very largely in leading strings. It was not a question of technical achiev-ment, but what could be afforded. At the same time the status of engineers on the railways was in process of rapid change. In the pioneer days a leading personality such as Locke, Vignoles, or Cubitt would be appointed as Engineer-in-Chief to a new railway; he would be not merely responsible for construction of the line but would continue in office after the traffic had begun to flow. Locke, for example, was Engineer to the Grand Junction while building lines in France, and while being consulted on hundreds of new schemes in the Mania days. Once the railway network was beginning to be established in this country it was obvious that this early situation could not continue, and out of the madness of the Mania the specialist railway engineers began to emerge. These men had a single well-knit command. Cases like that of Edward Bury, with a locomotive building business on one hand, and re-sponsibility for motive power on a large railway on the other, ceased to exist; and the attention of the locomotive superintendents began to extend from repair and running to more specific design, and construction in their own shops.

At this stage it is interesting to reflect upon the situation that had existed almost from the inception of the Great Western Railway. Daniel Gooch in title had no greater status than men like Fernihough on the Eastern Counties, Buddicom on the Grand Junction, or McConnell on the Bristol and Birmingham; but his mandate was on a far greater scale, and he had the ability and authority to prepare engine designs in full detail himself, and avoid any reliance on the ideas or whims of contractors. He fulfilled expectations to such an extent that he came to enjoy a status with his Board far ahead of any of his contemporaries, and he paved the way in this respect for three successors who in turn fully maintained the lustre of the office he had created. His work down to the year 1864 was wholly for the Great Western and its associated broad gauge companies.

The simple, straightforward organization that the Great Western set in motion with the appointment of Gooch took some time to develop on other railways due to the piecemeal way in which they were built up by amalgamation. Of this the London and North Western Railway provides a striking example. This line was an amalgamation of the Liverpool and Manchester, the Grand Junction, and the London and Birmingham, and prior to the merger the respective locomotive departments were under Edward Woods, Joseph Locke, and Edward Bury. Both Woods and Locke were primarily civil engineers, but Locke in particular had paid considerable attention to locomotive design, and certain principles worked out in the Grand Junction shops at Edge Hill, Liverpool, were carried far and wide on lines with which he was connected. Locke certainly had a vast number of irons in the fire. When the Grand Junction absorbed the Liverpool and Manchester, in 1845, he became engineer to the enlarged company. He was also engineer to most of the associated northern lines, such as the Preston and Lancaster, and the Lancaster and Carlisle. Then there was the Caledonian, and its nothern extensions, the Manchester and Sheffield, the London and South Western, not to mention the Paris and Rouen, and the Rouen and Havre! Had he been less involved elsewhere he would have seemed the obvious choice for chief engineer of the London and North Western, but for the first years of the amalgamation the constituents were operated as separate entities.

When a big amalgamation of highly individual concerns takes place it is rare that a clear-cut organization can be put straightway into effect. Account has to be taken of personalities, and personalities were certainly involved in the Locomotive departments of the London and North Western. In the south Edward Bury had managed to maintain his hold, and until his resignation, in 1846, there was not an engine of any other design on the line although there were some made by different manufacturers. He certainly went to inordinate lengths to ensure that this happy state of affairs should continue so. In his role as Locomotive superintendent he needed new engines, so in his role as a manufacturer he wrote to the Board thus:

'It would afford me great satisfaction to fix such a price for the Engines now wanted by the London and Birmingham Railway Company which would ensure the order falling into my hands as in the last Engines of the same size great care and pains have been taken to arrive at perfection as possible, and I do not assert too much when I state that the Mail Engines are without exception the best yet set to work on any line of railway—and though other makers might copy No. 45 with great exactness yet there are numerous points which all require to be correctly adjusted to produce the greatest effect and which experience alone can furnish the necessary guide for. I have no doubt the Board will take all these matters into consideration and that they will look favourably to my tender which is at the rate of £1,300 for each of the six Engines wanted.'

The Board evidently did not respond at once, for in a fortnight Bury wrote again:

'The discussion relative to the order for six new Mail Engines will no doubt be resumed the next Board meeting in Birmingham and although the price I before offered them at is a reasonable and by no means high price, yet to meet the question, I am quite willing rather than not have the order, to take the contract at £1,250 feeling quite assured that the system of uniformity cannot possibly be carried out by having Engines made by different individuals however anxious they may be to adhere strictly to drawings and specifications.'

That was certainly one way of pleading the cause of standardization; but in certain circumstances standardization is only another name for stagnation, and so it certainly was in the Locomotive department of the London and Birmingham Railway. By the year 1845 Bury's 2-2-0 passenger engines were hopelessly undersized for the job; a typical variety weighed $12\frac{1}{4}$ tons without its tender, in contrast to the 'Fireflies' on the Great Western which weighed 24 tons. More than this: Gooch's big engines dated from 1840, and in 1846 he built the 30-ton *Great Western* at Swindon works. It is probable that the business manoeuvres that first put Bury into the saddle on the London and Birmingham continued to keep him there, though it became more and more obvious that his small engines were not up to the job. Eventually, the story goes, an ultimatum was put to him to design some larger and more suitable engines, or resign. Whatever the truth or otherwise of this story he did resign at the time of amalgamation in 1846. Instead of handing over the whole line to Locke, the Board appointed J. E. McConnell, of the Bristol and Birmingham Railway, to take over what was in future known as the Southern Division. In a very few years he had transformed the whole situation, to such an extent indeed that his brilliant success and growing prestige became a source of embarrassment in the more sedate and conservative Northern Division.

At the time of the amalgamation the Grand Junction locomotive superintendent was Francis Trevithick, son of the great Cornish pioneer; but he seems to have left strikingly little impress of his personality upon railway affairs in general. The real power behind the throne at Edge Hill for some time had been Alexander Allan, officially styled Foreman of Locomotives. He had held the same position under Trevithick's predecessor, W. B. Buddicom,

and it was during this earlier partnership that Allan laid the foundation of locomotive practice on the Northern Division of the
L&NWR which was to last until 1858. When he joined the Grand
Junction Railway there was a good deal of trouble with broken
crank axles, some of which was attributed to the strains set up in
rounding the sharp curve on to the Liverpool and Manchester line
at Earlestown. The GJR used inside cylinder engines at the time,
and having thought over the problem Allan put forward a novel
solution. Like Fernihough he had been with Forrester's in Liverpool at the time the Dublin and Kingstown Railway 2-2-0 outside
cylindered engines were built; but while Fernihough developed
his theories of balancing from that unfortunate episode Allan
profited by the experience in quite a different way.

Far from eschewing outside cylinders Allan took the front-end
arrangement of the Forester 'boxers' and built a larger and more
substantial version of it. The outside cylinders were snugly and
very massively ensconced between inside and outside frames; there
was plenty of guiding effect in rear of the driving wheels, and a
degree of balancing was applied. The ensemble was one of the
neatest and most effective locomotives to be run on British metals
up to that time. Joseph Locke was very taken with the design, and
used it as a powerful argument for the narrow gauge in his evidence before the Gauge Commissioners.

'Speaking of the North Midland Railway', he said, 'where
engines of enormous power have been constructed principally for
the purpose of carrying heavy trains of minerals, I may say that
in the early construction of engines much inconvenience was felt
from the want of space between the wheels and boilers; and I must
say that I believe that the first impression of want of width in the
gauge arose from the complexity of the machinery under the
boiler, and the necessity for having some more space, by which
not only the parts could be made stronger, but that they might be
got at and repaired, oiled, and cleaned with more facility; and I
believe that the slight change of gauge on the Eastern Counties,
from 4 feet 8½ to 5 feet, arose from that circumstance; the engineer
finding when he came to design his engines, that if he had a little

more space for the application of his cranked axles and his eccentrics, he would make a better engine than by being confined to the narrow space of 4 feet 8½. Now, I felt, as engineer of the Grand Junction, also the same inconvenience; but, instead of directing my attention to a change of gauge, I directed my attention to simplifying the engine itself, and the result of that was that, instead of wanting space under the boiler, we now have no machinery there at all, except the eccentrics. We now place the cylinder outside the engine; we have got rid of a very great deal of complexity in the machinery itself, and the complexity which remains is on the outside of the engine, and not under the boiler. In that way we have obtained what we wanted—space for our machinery without going to the much greater and much more extraordinary expense of increasing the gauge.'

Whether Locke himself was the prime mover in that interesting change of design is a moot point. Certainly he took the ultimate responsibility for it, and through his interest Buddicom resigned his position on the Grand Junction, and became locomotive superintendent of the Paris and Rouen Railway. There, large numbers of locomotives of the basic Allan design were put to work. One of them, built by Buddicom and preserved to this day, was exhibited at the Festival of Britain exhibition in London in 1951. At home the Grand Junction works were moved to Crewe in 1843, and there, in 1845, the first new engine of Allan design was built. These 'Old Crewe' engines, as they are known to historians, were of two general types: 2-2-2 for passenger, and 2-4-0 for goods. Many locomotives of the same general design were built elsewhere, for service in Scotland, on the lines to which Locke's influence extended.

These Allan locomotives were relatively small machines—albeit very good—at the time of their introduction. As such they came to suit the managerial policy of the London and North Western Railway very well. In complete contrast James McConnell on the Southern Division of the line went all-out to reverse the small-engine policy previously pursued by Edward Bury, and seemed determined to out-do the Great Western in the realm of engine power and speed. In may well seem strange that two such different policies were allowed to develop in the two divisions of the same railway; but for some time after the amalgamation there was quite a definite line of demarcation. Furthermore McConnell had a much freer hand. In the Northern Division Francis Trevithick seems to have been little more than a titular head, and a very pale shade of his illustrious and dynamic father; and Allan, however capable, was never much more than a glorified works manager. It was inevitable that given half a chance McConnell would outshine his contemporaries at Crewe.

Apart from the actual job of engine designing McConnell was a man of great personality and force of character, a natural leader of men, a fine speaker with more than a dash of his native Irish eloquence and fire. He was the moving spirit in the formation of the Institution of Mechanical Engineers. The story has been told before, but it is worth re-telling. In 1845 the only association of professional engineers in this country was the Institution of Civil Engineers. As the madness of the Railway Mania developed and many men connected with spurious projects styled themselves 'engineers' that body saw the danger of a serious lowering of the standards necessary for qualification of bona-fide civil engineers, and duly tightened up its regulations regarding the election of its members. Among new requirements was a clause requiring each application to submit a thesis on some engineering subject as proof of his eligibility. Just at this time George Stephenson, the great 'elder statesman' of railway construction, chose to apply for membership, and through some shocking blunder he, of all men, was told to submit a thesis! The president of that time, Sir John Rennie, chose to let the letter of the law stand, and Stephenson naturally declined to bow to the indignity.

Engineers all over the country were naturally furious at the slight cast upon one who had done so much for the advancement of railways; but as usual while some merely talked others acted. One day on the Bristol and Birmingham line, during locomotive trials on the Lickey Incline, McConnell and his associates were driven to take shelter from a heavy rainstorm. They foregathered

One of Patrick Stirling's 8-foot bogie singles: Engine No. 550, of 1878, then fitted with Smith's non-automatic vacuum brake.

One of Sturrock's heavy mineral 0-6-0s, No. 465 of 1866, with tender designed for steam propulsion.

A Fletcher '901' class 2-4-0 of 1872: crack express engines of the NER for many years.

One of the '13' class outside-framed NER 0-6-0s dating originally from the 1860s.

One of the Cudworth 'mail' engines of 1865, South Eastern Railway.

A Cudworth 2-4-0 of 1875, as rebuilt by James Stirling.

LC&DR One of the 0-4-2 'Small Scotchman' suburban tank engines of 1866.

South Eastern Railway: James Stirling's 'B' class 4-4-0 of 1898.

in a plate-layer's hut, and before the deluge had ceased they had fallen to discussing the action of the Institution of Civil Engineers. McConnell and his friends felt that mechanical engineers should have an institution of their own. The outcome was a meeting at McConnell's own house, at the foot of the Lickey Incline, to discuss the matter further. In addition to McConnell there were two other locomotive engineers present, namely Charles Beyer, of Messrs Sharp Brothers, and Richard Peacock, of the Manchester and Sheffield Railway. The other three present at that historic gathering were two Birmingham tube manufacturers, and a banker. As a result of this informal meeting a circular was sent out to the profession, and what was, in effect, the first meeting of the new Institution was held in Birmingham under McConnell's chairmanship on October 7, 1846. The formal founding of the Institution of Mechanical Engineers took place in January 1847, and George Stephenson was unanimously elected the first president. This event was indeed a triumph for McConnell's initiative and energy, and by that time he himself had been appointed locomotive superintendent of the Southern Division of the London and North Western Railway.

I have dealt with the leading personnel of the locomotive department of the L&NWR to show how infinitely more complicated the set-up was than that of the Great Western. It was not surprising that for many years there was a strong diversity in practice between north and south, and intense rivalry between the works at Crewe and Wolverton. But McConnell's splendid engines belong to a later chapter of this story, and we must retrace steps a little to notice some further engineers and engine designs that emerged more or less from the Mania period. As always it was the simplest and most straightforward types that won the day. There might be experiments with the 'Atmospheric' in South Devon, on the Croydon Railway and in Ireland; there were Cramptons, long-boilered Stephensons, and the fantastic *Cornwall*, with the boiler placed below the driving axle. To try to get a better balance with the long-boilered passenger engines Stephensons tried using three cylinders. But the engines that stand out at this period are the simple 2-2-2s, and the 0-6-0 goods with Stephenson's long boiler.

Four varieties of 2-2-2 express engine deserve special mention: the North Midland 'mail' engines of 1840; R & W. Hawthorn's type, exemplified by the *Plews* of the York, Newcastle and Berwick Railway; Daniel Gooch's *Great Western*, of 1846, and the *Jenny Lind*, built by E. B. Wilson's of Leeds. The first three of these were basically of Stephenson's *Patentee* type, with outside frames to all wheels; but the *Jenny Lind* had inside bearings only for the driving wheels. Gooch's *Great Western* was a very much enlarged development of the 'Firefly' class—a most handsome and imposing engine, with sandwich type frames and an enormous 'haystack' of a firebox. She proved to be too heavy at the front end, and Gooch added a second pair of carrying wheels, turning her virtually into a 4-2-2. But although the two pairs of leading wheels had a compensated suspension they did not constitute a bogie. It is rather sad to recall that broad gauge express passenger motive power had virtually reached its climax in 1847, and that no further development took place in the remaining 45 years before the gauge was finally converted. More of this, however, in the next chapter.

The most interesting of all the standard 2-2-2s of the 'forties was, of course, the *Jenny Lind*, not only for its good design and excellent performance but through the delightful personality of its designer, David Joy. Rarely can an engineer have had a more appropriate surname, for all through his earlier years among railways and locomotives Joy seems to have had the time of his life. He left school in 1841, at the age of 16, and although it was a time when very young men shouldered big responsibilities few can have done so earlier in life than David Joy. For after two years of general apprenticeship, and a year as a drawing office apprentice at the Railway Foundry, Leeds, he became manager of the drawing office at that firm in 1844—at the age of 19. He threw himself into everything appertaining to locomotives with immense zest, and in 1845, in unexpected circumstances, he had his first ride on an engine. He wrote afterwards: 'We used to frequent the railway station very much, and one afternoon, watching the 4 p.m. York express start, the driver, Sid Watkins, asked me if I would like a ride. (Will a duck swim? Rather.) No coat, nothing on, I popped on to the engine, and away we went, so jolly. This was my first fair run on an engine with a train; only to Castleford, still it was fine. I had many another like it.' It provided a special thrill for Joy, for the engine was none other than Stephenson's 'Great A' that ran in the gauge trials.

The circumstances in which the *Jenny Lind* was designed will find a sympathetic echo in the breasts of many engineering draughtsmen today, and in every age, when conflicting interests and the experience of experimental work cause many a promising design to be laid aside and a clean sheet of drawing paper to be stretched over the board. Well, in 1847 the Brighton Railway ordered some new express engines from E. B. Wilson and Co. David Joy was sent to see John Gray, then the locomotive superintendent. The chief was not immediately available when Joy arrived, and so, to give him an insight into Brighton running conditions, he was given a footplate pass to go anywhere on the line. Joy 'had a go' on practically every engine, and took particular fancy to a Hackworth 2-2-2, with inside bearings to the driving wheels, but otherwise like a Stephenson 'Patentee'. Joy began to make drawings of this engine on the spot, but then the Brighton authorities countermanded the earlier instruction given to Joy, and sent him home, with orders that Wilson's could supply any type they liked.

A few days later there was a conference at Leeds around Joy's drawing board. Wilson naturally favoured a design similar to that which they were building at the time, a long-boilered type with outside cylinders. Drawings were made on this, and then Fenton, another of the directors, countermanded this instruction, and said he wanted an engine with inside cylinders, 15 in. by 20 in. and 6 ft. driving wheels. Joy, who had journeyed to Brighton in such enthusiasm and eagerness, was now thoroughly 'browned off'—to use a modern colloquialism; and the day being Saturday he went home in great ill-humour, intending to forget all about Wilson's, the Brighton Railway, and locomotives in general till the following Monday morning. But once into the quiet of his home, where he always kept a drawing board, he looked at the problem afresh; he began to sketch, and by Sunday evening the 2-2-2 engine that became famous as the *Jenny Lind* was designed—in broad outline of course. Joy took in his sketches on the following day; Wilson and Fenton were delighted, and construction of the engine was authorized forthwith. In service on the Brighton line and elsewhere the engines proved so successful that at one period Wilson's were turning out 'Jenny's' at the rate of one a week.

In 1850 Messrs E. B. Wilson of the Railway Foundry secured the contract for providing motive power on the Nottingham and Grantham Railway, and Joy was appointed their resident locomotive superintendent. In his diary he wrote: 'One of the funs of the place was its being a new line, everybody and everything was strange to the engines.

'People used to come and get on to the line at the road crossing gates and wave their umbrellas at us to stop as if we were an old stage coach.

'We didn't!

'Then the game, and the cows and sheep used to stare. We picked up lots of game, especially at night when they ran at the lights.'

Joy continued in a reminiscent mood:

'Anyway, this life was very lively, and I learnt every practical dodge going, and could drive as well as a driver, indeed better. Thus I caught one of my drivers alone on the engine one night at Ratcliff, his stoker had gone to prig coal to whip up the fire, which was dead and the steam slack. I felt I must do the normal thing, so sent the coal back, and told the man I would take the engine. Well, somehow or other, I wheedled her, got steam up, crawled through the tunnel, and, that over (the summit) slipped down the bank to Grantham like anything, and then told the man "Do that next time." But I did win those men to care for me, and to believe in me.

'I had one very clever fellow from Brighton, Bob Wilkes. I learnt heaps from him.'

48

Seeing that Joy was no more than 25 when he was appointed to the Nottingham and Grantham Railway his personality and qualities of leadership must have been remarkable. All this very practical experience was to stand him in good stead in later life when his work changed from the job of running a railway to that of a prolific inventor. But Joy's work on the Nottingham and Grantham Railway was no more than typical of railway conditions everywhere at the time. It was a glorious opportunity for the adventurous young spirits of the age. Before traffic working regulations became systemized there was always an element of excitement and danger about the job of running a train. Even in those early days, on a comparative by-way, Joy was getting speeds of nearly 70 m.p.h., and in 1851 he enters a few laconic comments about some engine trials on the North Midland Railway.

'The trains consisted of about ten ordinary carriages, say 60 tons. Kept time fairly. Then went to Normanton to let her fly. In those days an engine could not go too fast for me.'

For the next forty or fifty years it was, generally speaking, men brought up in the rough and tumble of practical railway life that carried the main responsibilities of locomotive engineering in this country; at the mid-way point of the nineteenth century, when the British railways were passing out of the formative and Mania years into one of the critical periods of their history, one looks back with interest to see the status then attained by some of the great personalities of the Age of Steam. There was Matthew Kirtley of the Midland, for example: he was then 37 years of age, but already had 24 years of tough railway experience behind him. At 13 he had begun work on the Stockton and Darlington Railway; then he was a fireman on the London and Birmingham. By 1850 he had been locomotive superintendent of the Midland for six years—since its formation in fact—and as such was head of the rapidly expanding works at Derby.

Kirtley was not alone in having been a regular engine driver. There was William Stroudley, who came near to immortalising the nineteenth century locomotives of the Brighton Railway; there was Edward Fletcher of the North Eastern, and at a much later date, John F. McIntosh of the Caledonian. Fletcher, like Kirtley, had been 'in' at the very start of steam locomotion on railways. He was a pupil of Robert Stephenson, and assisted in the trials of the *Rocket* on the Killingworth Colliery railway before that famous engine went to the Rainhill competition; he drove the *Invicta* at the opening of the Canterbury and Whitstable Railway and eventually reigned as locomotive superintendent of the North Eastern Railway for nearly 30 years. Men like Kirtley and Fletcher, no less than McConnell and Daniel Gooch, were out-and-out locomotive men. They were of the same race as the drivers and firemen; they had grown up amongst them, and shared their troubles and triumphs on the road. McConnell in experimenting to get higher efficiency built one or two isolated freaks, but his principal designs were first-rate, while of Fletcher and Kirtley I cannot recall a single bad engine built in the long years of their superintendence.

But the magnificent pioneer spirit of the Age of Steam was not to be found only on the larger railways. The coal carrying lines of the Welsh valleys, and their long and severe gradients provided tasks worthy of the finest of engines; though while the Taff Vale was a wealthy enough concern there were others in very straitened circumstances in their early days. Such a line was the Brecon and Merthyr. Even in those early days some of the working in South Wales was hair-raising, in its disregard of precautionary measures, to those men coming from the trunk lines of England. Some of the downhill running seemed absolutely reckless, but it was necessary to gain momentum for the next ascent steep. Sometimes a heavy train would get completely out of control and come careering downhill pushing its helpless engine before it—helpless even though that engine was in full reverse with steam on! Sometimes a wild run ending in disaster with the train completely wrecked, and its crew killed.

To be locomotive superintendent of a railway like that, and to carry the job successfully, needed outstanding qualities. To be capable, with the vast resources and ample material of a huge railway, is one thing; it is quite another to meet difficulty, to adapt, to contrive, and to improvise, with next to nothing in the way of large machinery. On the Rhymney Railway, a very brilliant young engineer, John Kendal by name, was at one time locomotive superintendent. He was a native of the Stephenson country in Northumberland, and had all the amazing capacity for work, the enthusiasm, the inventiveness of the Stephensons crammed into his vivid personality. He lived on the railway, for the railway, and from the great promise of his early life might well have become one of the greatest locomotive engineers of the day with a distinguished position on one of the largest English railways. But the hazards of railway life were not confined to trains on the move in those days. John Kendal had accepted the invitation of his fellow superintendent, Simpson, of the Brecon and Merthyr, to witness the trials of a rebuilt engine, and at Maesycwmmer the boiler burst. Simpson, Kendal and several others were killed on the spot.

The hard, vigorous, open air life of locomotive running came to possess men, from superintendents down to the youngest firemen. The spirit of the footplate is something that even today still captures and enthralls, and in my own travels I have met many young men who revel in the robust life. and would change it for no other. When the control and direction of railways had passed from the engineers to the business men it was the new-born race, the race of locomotive men, who carried on the job of running the trains, often with much discouragement, often with many setbacks. In later years we read of superintendents whose tenure of office was shaky, if not disastrous; such periods were those usually associated with men who, though original thinkers and clever scientists in themselves, never really got to grips with the practical problems of day-to-day running. If ever there was a task requiring complete team work it is the designing, building and repairing of steam locomotives.

CHAPTER THREE

THE QUEST FOR ECONOMY

AFTER the rapid developments that followed Rainhill, and the brilliant promise of the early 'forties the railways of this country were, by the year 1850, fairly on the defensive. There were brave exceptions, like the newly-completed Great Northern, but for the rest the times dictated a policy of retrenchment. In world history it was a time of violent unrest. Europe was just emerging from a series of revolutions; deep concern at events in the Balkans led to military and naval 'precautions', and eventually to war in the Crimea. The Indian Mutiny followed, and then the American Civil War, over which feelings ran high in this country. The gradual process of social evolution in this country followed its thorny and controversial way, and with the manifold troubles and distractions of the age it is hardly likely that railway development would follow a steady and uniform course. The railway managers sought every means of economizing in both new works and maintenance, and the stubborn reluctance of some to adopt fundamental safety measures may well be traced to a parsimony based on the stringent economic circumstances of the day.

For many engineers, it may well be imagined, it was a time of frustration, but to no one more than Daniel Gooch. He above all locomotive men had shown a foresight and ability to plan far ahead of the immediate needs of the day. The *Great Western*, of 1846, built in a race against time, was by far the largest and most powerful engine of the period, and the *Iron Duke* which followed in 1847 was the first of the standard 4-2-2 express locomotives that were to serve the GWR for the rest of the broad gauge era— forty-five years in all. They were huge engines for the period, weighing 35 tons without their tenders, and they were intended for really fast running. Gooch was no half-hearted supporter of Brunel's original conception of high speed travel, and some almost legendary tales of great exploits have been handed down through many generations of locomotive men. One is that of the engine *Great Britain*, which is reputed to have run from Paddington to Didcot at an average speed from start to stop of 67 m.p.h. One of the best known of the class was the *Lord of the Isles*, built in 1851, and exhibited in Hyde Park at the Great Exhibition of that year. That exhibition, for which the original suggestion came from the Prince Consort, was to have been the rallying point and steadying influence among all the seething emotions of the day; but the hopes of the Prince were crashed in ruins within three years, when all hopes of peace in the Balkans faded and the British and French forces sailed for the Crimea. Seven new engines of the 'Iron Duke' class were built during the war years and were named appropriately *Alma, Balaklava, Crimea, Eupatoria, Inkerman* and *Sebastopol*.

But the broad gauge express trains, once the wonder of the railway world, had perforce to be decelerated. The tremendous project had passed its zenith, and Brunel, whose restless energy would hardly be content with the more prosaic problem of engineering maintenance on the Great Western Railway, turned his attention to the development of steamships. In 1860 Gooch also became a director of the Great Eastern Steamship Company. In 1859 Brunel died, utterly worn out by the anxieties of his later projects, but no less by the tremendous pace at which he had lived throughout his professional life. Gooch resigned in 1864, in order to devote the whole of his time to the laying of the Atlantic cable; but Great Western finances were then in a bad way, and in no more than a year, at the pressing invitation of the Board, he returned, this time to the illustrious office of Chairman of the Company. As locomotive superintendent the Great Western was fortunate in having a very able successor in Joseph Armstrong, and in mentioning him it is an appropriate point to break away from the locomotives and trains to some of the social implications of the Age of Steam as it particularly affected railway administrations.

Of the railway towns that grew up in the nineteenth century there is no more striking example than New Swindon, as it was first known to distinguish it from the old market town clustered high upon the hill to the south of the railway. In his diary Daniel Gooch tells how he came to select the place. Brunel laid out the line for high speed, and to get the alignment he needed meant avoiding the Kennet Valley and the towns. Instead of following the Bath Road and going through Newbury, Hungerford, and Marlborough, with a possibility of tapping Devizes, Trowbridge and Bradford-on-Avon farther west, he took the line up the Vale of the White Horse. To touch the towns that lay near this route would have meant diversions, so Wallingford, Abingdon, Wantage, and Faringdon were all by-passed. On the direct route there was not a place of any size between Reading and the ancient borough of Chippenham, 58 miles. Gooch wrote:

'1840. During this year further portions of the Great Western were opened and agreements were made for leasing the Bristol and Exeter and the Swindon and Cheltenham Railways, and it became necessary to furnish large works for the repair, etc., of our stock. I was called upon to report on the best situation to build these works, and on full consideration I reported in favour of Swindon, it being the junction with the Cheltenham branch and also a convenient division of the Great Western line for the engine working. Mr Brunel and I went to look at the ground, then only green fields, and he agreed with me as to its being the best place.'

The establishment of the works in such a rural community made it necessary to build what was virtually a new town for the accommodation of the workmen and their families, and with the works rising on the north side of the line, in the 'vee' between the main line and the branch, the Great Western initiated a veritably model example of town planning on the south side. They made an arrangement with a local firm of building contractors, who were to build the station itself and 300 workmen's cottages at their own expense. In return the company were to lease the refreshment rooms to the contractor for a period of 99 years, and to stop all trains for a period of at least ten minutes to enable passengers to buy refreshments. The houses were tastefully built in stone, to harmonize, as it were, with the buildings of the works and the station, and in addition financial support was given by the Great

Western Railway for the building of St Mark's Church just beside the line, to serve the spiritual needs of the new community. Not only this, but the Company paid the stipend of the clergyman, and the salaries of the teachers in the new schools.

In all this social welfare work the Locomotive, Carriage and Wagon Superintendent came to play a leading part. He was by far and away the most senior of all Great Western officers in the neighbourhood, and in due course successive holders of the office came to exercise a wider influence on local affairs as Justices of the Peace, and in some cases as borough councillors. The present author recalls mentioning to a former chief at Swindon this traditional interest, and the calls on his spare time that it must have made. He waved it aside with a smiling comment: 'Oh, it just went with the job.' But how well it was done may be gauged by the respect and in some cases sheer affection in which the Great Western Locomotive, Carriage and Wagon Superintendent was held. Those who imagine that the duties of such an office are confined wholly to engineering matters might indeed be surprised at the monthly round of one like Joseph Armstrong or George Jackson Churchward.

At Swindon, in Gooch's time, a Medical Fund Society was established, in 1847, to provide medical and surgical attendance and medicine for the railway employees and their families. Here was established under private industrial enterprise a health service that was closely studied a hundred years later by the Ministry of Health, and which virtually became the pattern on which the operations of the National Health Service under the Act of 1948 were based. The service eventually provided by the GWR Medical Fund Society was extraordinarily comprehensive, so that it needed the full time services not only of the superintendent medical officer and his deputy but of eight medical officers, and a number of specialist consultants. The Society had its own hospital, and an extensive block of buildings, consulting room, dispensary, and numerous facilities for rendering every kind of attention that could be required. It was, indeed, an almost perfect prototype in miniature of the National Health Service. And it was established in 1847!

So far as the Great Western Railway was concerned, while the period from 1850 onwards did not witness any immediate advance in locomotive design, or any exciting exploits on the road, the work of the locomotive department at Swindon in its multifarious activities was steadily growing and building up those traditions that were to prove invaluable when the time for locomotive development arrived once again. In 1850 Swindon made the second of her many contributions to British locomotive practice outside the Great Western Railway, when Archibald Sturrock left to become locomotive superintendent of the Great Northern Railway—then not completed. Previous to that T. R. Crampton had left to develop his fascinating rear-driver express locomotive, which had such a remarkable run of success on the Continent; but Sturrock left a deeper impression at home. Like Gooch himself he was an indefatigable worker and a first-rate engineer, but in character he had much of the dash and fire of Brunel. He was, in fact, the very man for the Great Northern.

All the earliest of our main line railways met with great opposition when the Bills were introduced into Parliament; but whereas opposition at first came from landowners, and vested interests in canals, coaches and suchlike, the Great Northern came late enough upon the scene to incur heavy opposition from existing railways. George Hudson, for example, was building up a compact railway 'empire' extending from the most southerly extensions of the Midland to the group of lines eventually merged into the North Eastern Railway. Traffic between London, York and Newcastle travelled from Euston to Rugby, and thence over the Midland line. Any direct and independent railway from London to York would cut right across Hudson's interests, and he used every means, fair and foul, from intrigue to recklessly spoken threats to try to prevent the very inception of the rival route. But he more than met his match in Edmund Dennison, though the long story of the fight to establish the Great Northern is another story. The outcome of this opposition was that when the line was eventually built it had to fight every inch of the way to secure traffic. There was only one way to do it—by speed. While the older companies, in deference to economic conditions and the mood of cautiousness that set in after the Hudson financial 'crash', were tending to decelerate their services, the Great Northern had, at all costs, to show a handsome lead over the Euston–Rugby–Derby–Normanton route from London to York.

Before Sturrock arrived on the scene a miscellaneous collection of engines had been purchased; but new engines to his own design were already at work in 1851, and these bore the unmistakable imprint of Swindon: domeless boilers; the firebox raised above the level of the boiler to provide more steam in the hottest part; and above all the high boiler pressure for that period of 150 lb. per sq. in. Most engineers of the day were using 100 to 120 lb. pressure, even including Daniel Gooch. These first Sturrock engines were 2-4-0s, but in the following year the famous 'Large Hawthorns' were put on the road—twelve handsome 2-2-2 'singles', which as their *soubriquet* suggests were built by Messrs R. & W. Hawthorn. Three of these engines had domeless boilers, but the remainder had the huge, rather aggressive dome that characterized most Hawthorn locomotives of that period. The use of such a greatly enhanced boiler pressure reflects great credit on Sturrock's design and the craftsmanship in the boiler shop at Hawthorns. Such an advance is not secured by a mere stroke of the pen, and at a time when manufacturing technique was still in the stage of evolution it needed no small amount of courage to take such a big step. Many years afterwards Sturrock himself wrote:

'The success of the GNR was nearly entirely due to the introduction of fireboxes of about double the area of those in use on the narrow gauges in 1850, and the raising of the steam pressure from 80 lb. to 150 lb. Engines, like horses, go well in many shapes, sizes, and colours, but no variations such as position and diameter of a wheel or diameter of a cylinder are worth anything unless there be plenty of steam *at a high pressure*, which gives economy by expansion. The finest gun is no use unless there be plenty of powder.'

In this letter, while stressing the importance of high pressure, Sturrock shows that he was not seeking power at any price, and the expansive working of steam was a feature that was to claim the attention of many engineers in the ensuing fifty years. Sturrock tells an amusing story against himself over this question of high steam pressures: 'Mr Brunel, who took an interest in me, told me he thought I was right, but advised me to keep the proposed advance to myself, as if I let it be known that I was about to build engines with such dimensions and pressure, I should be considered a dangerous man, and one to be shunned.'

The spirit of the Great Northern in those early days is magnificently shown by the story of the hair-raising episode on Retford level crossing, in which one of the 'Large Hawthorns', No. 210, was involved. I am bound to confess that the affair takes some believing, though at that time most goods wagons were of extremely light construction. Anyway here is the tale, as described by Michael Reynolds: 'The down Scotch express was going down Retford bank, signals all clear, when Oliver Hindley saw a train going east from Sheffield to Lincoln, which would meet him on the level crossing. He could not stop, and with that clear mind that is so marked in Englishmen in time of danger, he put on full steam, and sent Mr Sturrock's beautiful express engine clean through the goods train, scattering the trucks like match splinters. and carrying all safe. When asked about the matter Hindley said he could not keep clear so he would clear away his obstruction. There is no doubt that, had he hesitated or feared, many lives would have been sacrificed. No. 210 engine carried the dents and scars like an old warrior, and looked handsomer than ever for this brush with the enemy of express trains.'

One can well imagine that Driver Hindley was a man after Sturrock's heart, for he too was prepared to stop at nothing. He had been at Swindon in those thrilling days when the Gooch 'Fireflies' were proving their worth, and when the *Great Western* was built, and now he was urging the Great Northern on to faster and faster running. In 1853 he not merely proposed an 8-hour service from King's Cross to Edinburgh by the East Coast route, but actually built an engine to demonstrate the practicability of doing the Great Northern share of such a service. This was the very celebrated 215, a 4-2-2 modelled in many ways on Daniel Gooch's 'Iron Duke' class, but more powerful. But as Sturrock himself said: 'This service was not carried out, because there was no demand by travellers for, nor competition amongst the railways to give the public such accommodation.' Speed enterprise at that time was certainly confined to the Great Northern. With Hudson gone the one-time alliance between the Midland and the North Eastern was broken for good and all, so far as through Anglo-Scottish traffic was concerned, and the North Eastern showed no inclination to emulate the Great Northern enthusiasm for speed.

When Archibald Sturrock went from Swindon to Doncaster he was 34 years of age. Had he remained in railway service for more of his long and vigorous life there is no knowing what enterprises he might have pioneered; but after sixteen years on the Great Northern he retired to enjoy the less exacting life of an English country squire. His retirement lasted for no less than *forty-two years*! He outlived his successor, and at the age of 91 was still hale and hearty enough to give an interview to the Editor of *The Railway Magazine*. But before he retired from the Great Northern he had made two more major contributions to the development of British locomotive practice. The first was the notable design of 2-2-2 express passenger engine of 1860-1, numbered from 229 to 240. They were an enlargement of the earlier Hawthorns, and carried all the principles of Sturrock's practice a stage further, particularly in the very large and long fireboxes, in which the 'mid-feather' then usually fitted was longitudinal instead of transversely, as in the earlier engines. The mid-feather was a device used to promote more complete combustion, at a time when the railways were changing over from coke to coal, as a locomotive fuel, and will be discussed more fully at a later stage.

But of all Sturrock's innovations that of the steam tender will perhaps be best remembered. At a very early stage in Great Northern history the coal traffic into London was growing rapidly. Having built boilers that were very free in steaming Sturrock conceived the idea of getting additional power by fitting an auxiliary engine in the tender. A series of 0-6-0 goods engines were built from 1863 onwards having 16 in. by 24 in. cylinders, with an auxiliary engine, also 0-6-0 on the tender. In this latter the cylinders were 12 in. by 17 in., and provided an augment of 40 per cent in the tractive power. This ingenious arrangement was in some ways a prototype of the modern articulated locomotives of the Beyer-Garratt type, in which two engine units are supplied with steam from one boiler. One had the power of a double headed train, hauled by one large and one small locomotive, without the expense of two sets of enginemen. But it was on this very count that the steam tenders proved unpopular. There is much in evidence to the effect that the men thought they were being asked to do too much; the units proved heavy on maintenance, possibly because the enginemen left undone many little jobs that they would have done on a normal locomotive. As a result, although 50 steam-tender units were put on the road their life was short, and Sturrock's successor dismantled the engine mechanisms.

Sturrock had a very energetic and enterprising counterpart in J. E. McConnell, of the London and North Western, Just as Sturrock was proposing to run from King's Cross to Edinburgh in eight hours so McConnell was proposing two-hour trains between Euston and Birmingham in 1852. The forty 2-2-2 express locomotives with 7 ft. driving wheels put on the road between 1851 and 1862 were among the finest of the day. They were fast and powerful, and rode well—just a simple, straightforward machine with a good boiler, high pressure and well-designed engine machinery. There are many stories as to how these engines got the nickname of 'Bloomers'. In contrast to the great majority of locomotives of the day all the bearings were inside the wheels. The Stephenson *Patentee* and its derivatives had a considerable amount of shrouding from the outside frames, and even in the *Jenny Lind* there were outside frames to the leading and trailing wheels. But on the 'Bloomers' there was none, and in all probability this absence of a 'skirt', and exposure of the works—coinciding with certain attempts at female dress reform by Mrs Amelia Bloomer—gave rise to the name. At all events, in subsequent

One of Daniel Gooch's 8-foot broad gauge 4-2-2s.

A typical narrow gauge 0-6-0: built 1864, rebuilt at Wolverhampton, by G. Armstrong 1880.

The second *Lord of the Isles*, W. Dean's 7ft. 8in. narrow gauge 4-2-2 of 1892 carrying the historic name of Gooch's 8-footer of 1851.

The Churchward influence beginning: one of the Dean 'Badminton' class 4-4-0s of 1899, No. 3310 *Waterford* with domeless boiler and Belpaire firebox.

One of the two Drummond 7ft. 2-2-2s built in 1876 for the Edinburgh–Glasgow expresses. This engine, No. 474, was originally named *Glasgow*.

Holmes 4-4-0 of 1891 design, for the express services over the newly-opened Forth Bridge.

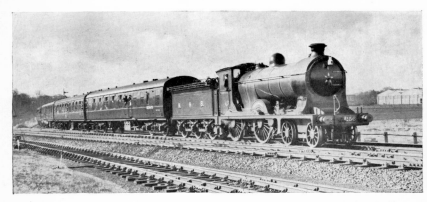

The preserved No. 256 *Glen Douglas* working an enthusiasts' special at Dalmeny in 1963.

literature, technical and otherwise, McConnell's 2-2-2s have never been known by any other name.

McConnell, like Sturrock, was experimenting with midfeathers in his fireboxes. From the earliest days coke had been used as a locomotive fuel, partly to reduce to a minimum the emission of smoke. But as railways developed and the consumption of fuel went up by leaps and bounds—and with it, of course, the cost— more attention came to be given to the use of coal instead of coke. The trouble at first was to get good combustion. The sharp blast drew large quantities of small particles from the fire, and threw it out of the chimney as 'black smoke'. The traverse midfeathers in the firebox acted as a baffle, and went some way to prevent the direct effect of the draught on the fire; but these were expensive to make and maintain. The eventual solution was obtained on the Midland Railway as a result of a long series of experiments carried out by an engineer named Charles Markham, working under the direction of Matthew Kirtley. Like all great inventions Markham's device was extremely simple, and consisted of an arch of firebrick built across the firebox at the leading end. Air for combustion entering through the dampers had to pass backwards over the fire-bed before it could be drawn round the rear end of the arch and go straight to the flue tubes. With proper proportioning of the dampers and a suitable length of firebrick arch it was found that good combustion of coal could be obtained, and a largely colour-less exhaust from the chimney. Though some inventors persisted for a time with other devices the brick arch eventually became standard practice on all steam locomotives and the saving in fuel costs resulting from the change from coke to coal was very welcome.

As McConnell's bold and successful locomotive policy pro-ceeded on the Southern Division of the L&NWR it became in-creasingly clear that this policy was poles apart from that of Crewe. The Allan 2-2-2s were tiny engines in comparison with the 'Bloomers', and when Francis Trevithick was succeeded by John Ramsbottom in 1857 it was soon evident that the 'small-engine' policy was to continue. That is not to say it was reactionary or unenterprising. Throughout the entire span of the Age of Steam Ramsbottom stands out as a veritable giant, as inventor and administrator, and one having a genius for the layout and development of a large engineering works. While some sought economy by slow running, and coal saving, Ramsbottom achieved still more spectacular results by standardization, not only of engine classes, but by designing so that many detail parts were interchangeable on many engine classes, and by systemizing the entire works procedure. Ramsbottom's pioneer work at Crewe is the pattern on which later large-scale standardization schemes have been based, not least that which was applied to the British railways as a whole after nationalization in 1948.

The works practices introduced by Ramsbottom, combined with the great simplicity of the constructional details, made it possible to build locomotives very cheaply at Crewe. While, for example, the Great Northern main line engines of the day were costing between £3,000 and £4,000 apiece it is astonishing to realize that their counterparts on the North Western were costing less than £2,000. The boiler pressures were low, the frames were lightly built, and the whole process of construction was, to use a modern phrase, streamlined throughout. The management came to regard overall speeds of 40 m.p.h. as the hall mark of express travel, and senior officers about to attend inter-railway conferences were briefed to oppose, tooth and nail, any accelerations. The small-engine policy of Crewe fitted admirably with this outlook, and as time went on McConnell and his big, powerful engines tended to fall more and more out of favour.

There was a significant, but rather amusing instance of this during the American Civil War in 1862, when the 'Trent' incident led to very strained relations between this country and the Northern States, and arrangements were made to convey an anxiously awaited dispatch from the British Ambassador in Washington to London with the utmost speed. With the aid of the newly-introduced water-troughs one of Ramsbottom's dainty little 2-2-2 'singles' of the 'Lady of the Lake' class ran the 130½ miles from Holyhead to Stafford non-stop in 144 minutes, an average speed of 54½ m.p.h. The general 'ballyhoo' that followed this excellent achievement savoured almost of some modern publicity tactics one can think of; but at the same time it was scarcely mentioned that at Stafford the Ramsbottom engine was relieved by a McConnell 'Extra Large Bloomer', and that the 133 miles to Euston were covered in 139 minutes, despite fully 10 minutes lost by fog south of Rugby. The respective average speeds over almost the same distance were 54½ m.p.h. with the aid of water troughs, and 57 m.p.h. without water troughs, and with fog on the way. Such a disparity was just what one would expect from a comparison of the proportions of the two engines concerned.

McConnell had actually retired before this run took place. He was still relatively young, and took up a practice as a consultant. But before that remarkable man passes from the railway scene there is a story to be told of McConnell, Sturrock, and David Joy. Since its opening in 1852 the Oxford, Worcester and Wolverhampton Railway had been worked by a contractor named Williams, to whom Messrs E. B. Wilson of the Railway Foundry, Leeds, had supplied the motive power. As on the Nottingham and Grantham line at an earlier date Joy was resident locomotive superintendent, but after three years the railway company wished to terminate the contract and make arrangements for either the Great Western or the London and North Western to work the line. The locomotive stock had to be valued, and arbitrators were appointed: McConnell for the Oxford, Worcester and Wolverhampton Railway, and Archibald Sturrock for the contractors. McConnell tried all he knew to write down the value of each item; various practical tests were carried out but Joy was ready for him at each point, and Sturrock, in his element in this battle, backed up Joy for all he was worth. Joy records the result in his diary in a somewhat unconventional balance sheet:

The result that while Williams' invoice prices for all the plant were	£160,296
The valuation by the arbitrators was	£183,205
Hurrah	£22,909

A good bargain indeed, seeing that Joy had got three years work out of all the plant, since it was purchased—and all second hand at that!

While Kirtley obtained economies in working through the successful use of coal, and while Ramsbottom reduced manufacturing costs to an absolute minimum, Joseph Beattie of the London and South Western was possessed of that fascinating but nevertheless dangerous attribute of a 'gadget mind'. That he was also possessed of a volcanic temper is beside the point. His engines, generally of handsome proportions, were crowded with patent devices. Some carried what looked like a slender additional chimney in front of the main chimney; on others there was a triple pipe erection. There was a flywheel affair between the driving wheel splashers, but withal the engines were very smartly and tastefully finished in a chocolate livery with much adornment in the way of polished brass and copper. Beattie must have designed patent fireboxes by the score; the erections on the boiler were parts of a system of feed water heating, all of which was intended to economize in the use of fuel, and in those fancy fireboxes he burned coal instead of coke. But while Beattie's engines were institutions south of the Thames, in their day, none of his gadgets survived the test of time; his engines did some good work on the road, but for all their complications nothing better, if so good, as the simple, straightforward 2-4-os of Matthew Kirtley on the Midland, of the McConnell 'Bloomers', or of Sturrock's 2-2-2s on the Great Northern. Around 1870 the best engines of the day were the simplest, engines like Edward Fletcher's '901' class on the North Eastern, or those splendid little engines, the North Western 'Precedents', designed by Ramsbottom's successor Francis W. Webb. In the ensuing 30 years the North Western was, indeed, to read the lesson of simplicity *versus* complexity in letters of fire!

We must now turn for a moment to the question of valve gears. After the early experiments that led to the designing of the Stephenson link motion in 1844 that portion of the mechanism had laid outside the realm of new invention for a time, and in the quest for economy efforts were concentrated on the methods of steam raising. The interest in valve gear was revived in 1879 when David Joy patented his radial valve gear. It was an extremely clever mechanism, providing for a very 'slick' steam flow into and out of the cylinders. Joy was one of the first engineers to point out that economies could be effected by reducing the back pressure caused by restrictions to the flow of steam; but his valve gear became very popular for a time for quite a different reason. It was driven directly from the connecting rod; no eccentrics were needed on the driving axle, and this meant that larger bearings than otherwise could be used for the axles. F. W. Webb of the London and North Western not only adopted it for his new express goods engines of 1880, but arranged to exhibit one of these engines at the Summer Meeting of the Institution of Mechanical Engineers, which in that year was held at Barrow-in-Furness. Joy was invited to read a paper on his valve gear, and from that moment onwards the gear was definitely on the map.

That particular period of the nineteenth century had some interesting parallels to the immediate present. The continent of Europe was beginning to revive from the effects of a long period of war, revolution, and general unrest, and British business men and engineers were feeling the unpleasant experience of strong foreign competition. The President of the Institution, Mr Edward A. Cowper, in referring to this, and to the 'very great and general depression in trade that has now held its dull course for years', called for a supreme effort to develop the latent capacity in the British engineering industry; in the course of the Barrow meeting, the ingenuity of the Joy valve gear and Webb's readiness to put so promising a device to practical test were hailed as examples of the forward-looking spirit that was generally necessary if Englishmen were to hold their own as the leading engineers of the world.

On the railway stage, towards the latter end of the nineteenth century, there were some great characters among the locomotive superintendents; men who had grown up amid the rough and tumble of early footplate work, who knew their men, and who steered a middle course between the technical perfection of Ramsbottom, the scientific novelties of Beattie, and the ruthless, stop-at-nothing egotism of a man like John Chester Craven, on the Brighton Railway. One of the most interesting of these 'characters' was Edward Fletcher, locomotive superintendent of the North Eastern Railway. In cold print the policy he pursued over a period of thirty years appears haphazard, often illogical, and hopelessly uneconomic. In contrast to the standardization of Crewe Fletcher seemed at times to go deliberately in divergent directions. Contractors were allowed to incorporate their own fittings on what was supposed to be a uniform class of engine, and the four works, at Leeds, York, Darlington and Gateshead, were allowed their own styles of painting on repaired locomotives. The divisional officers did their work well; the line was relatively prosperous, so—one could imagine Fletcher argued—why interfere?

But while adopting a benevolent go-as-you-please kind of policy Fletcher contrived to become a formidable power in the land. His engines, despite their individual variations, were economical and did their work well; and 'the Old Mon', as the men affectionately called him, became the symbol of all that was right and proper in locomotive construction. He became, in fact, something of a legend in his own chieftainship. The extent of his hold upon the locomotive department of the North Eastern Railway was scarcely realized until he retired, and the directors appointed in his place Alexander McDonnell, an Irishman, whose early training was very different from Fletcher's. He made his first bow to the world at the age of 22 when he emerged from Dublin University with a brilliant degree, and his training continued for several years more as an engineering pupil. Then after varied experience at home and abroad he was appointed locomotive superintendent of the Great Southern and Western Railway, with headquarters in his own native Dublin. There he carried out a very difficult task with distinct success, bringing something of the standardization policy of Crewe to a then impecunious Irish Railway, and laying the foundations of the excellent design and constructional tradition of Inchicore works that was to serve the

GS&WR well, and in due course to provide England with three of her most distinguished locomotive engineers.

And then McDonnell moved over to Gateshead. To one with a neat and orderly mind the state of affairs existing on the North Eastern might well have seemed appalling. Reform was, perhaps, overdue, and one can well understand the eagerness of the new broom to get to work; but McDonnell seems to have committed every conceivable error of tactlessness and ill-judgment it was possible to make. Locomotive enginemen as a body are extraordinarily conservative where their machines are concerned. On the North Eastern it might have been another matter if the engines were not masters of their work; but the men resolutely believed they had the finest on earth, and on the main line certainly they were not far wrong in 1875-80. When McDonnell not only built engines that were different in every way, but started altering some of the most cherished features of the Fletchers, the men just rose in revolt. Some of the alterations were in the way of technical detail, but a very sore point was the moving of the driver from the right to the left-hand side of the cab. Now while it is true to say that this stance is a matter of what one is used to, tradition does play a big part. Today, with colour light signalling the left-hand corner is undoubtedly correct; but with tall semaphores opinion used to be very much divided on the railways of this country, and one side was as good as the other. McDonnell had followed London and North Western practice, and when he carried out his summary change on the North Eastern Tyneside was soon aflame with protest! The opposition might have melted if the new McDonnell engines had proved eventually superior; but they definitely did not, and after a mere eighteen months McDonnell bowed to the storm and resigned.

McDonnell undoubtedly intended to pursue a policy of standardization on the North Eastern, on the Crewe style; but the policy was stillborn, and instead the company was faced with an urgent need for larger and more powerful engines, and no locomotive superintendent to design them. That particular year, 1884, marked an interesting and critical time in locomotive development. The need for economy in working was still keenly felt, and yet there was need for increasingly large locomotives. Traffic was on the increase, and there was a growing demand—highly distasteful to many managements—for greater comfort and amenity in travel. This latter trait meant, of course, larger and heavier coaches, and while the passengers were thus given more for their money, the locomotive superintendents endeavoured to do something in redressing the balance by getting more power out of every ton of coal they burnt. At this stage the work of Francis W. Webb at Crewe began to attract world-wide notice. This was partly due to his exalted position on the London and North Western Railway, then carrying the heaviest traffic to be found anywhere in the world; he was able to conduct his experiments on a vast scale, and above all he was an excellent though perhaps unintentional publicity agent. Though personally of a retiring disposition, a lonely and austere bachelor, Webb took a prominent part in the proceedings of the Institutions of Civil and Mechanical Engineers, and he kept the engineering world well informed of every stage of his developments.

Webb sought increased efficiency by trying to realize in practice the theoretical advantages of a long range of expansion of the steam. Instead of confining this range to what had then been achieved in one stage, he adopted the 'compound' principle, whereby steam is partly expanded in one cylinder or pair of cylinders, then passes to an intermediate receiver, and finally completes the process in a second pair of cylinders, or single cylinder as the case may be. Two-stage and even three-stage compound engines were by that time in use for stationary and marine purposes, and were giving good results, and there was every chance of equal success in railway locomotives. As might be expected the Webb compounds had many shortcomings at first; it was only natural that the working out of a novel arrangement, not free from complexity, would meet with teething troubles. But the greatest difficulties arose not with the engines themselves, but from the personality of Mr Webb himself. He was a man of immense self-confidence, and once having adopted the compound principle he was entirely convinced that compounds must, of necessity, be superior to single-expansion engines of comparable dimensions. In his severely autocratic way he would accept no views to the contrary. One cannot think that a man of his engineering skill would have left untouched several relatively simple defects that dogged the prowess of his three-cylinder compound locomotives; but by that time in his career he had become such a dictator that one fancies no one would dare to tell him of practical troubles on the line! As a result the great majority of his compound engines were sluggish in running, and considerably heavier on coal than the best single expansion engine working elsewhere in the country.

In the general quest for economy compound locomotives were tried on various other British railways, though nowhere on the same scale as that of Crewe; but in general the most successful locomotives were the simplest, in which the principal working parts were well proportioned, and in which careful design had provided for plenty of air for combustion in the firebox, for a good, though not too fierce draught, and for a free flow of steam into and out of the cylinders. Engines built on these simple but fundamental bases proved far more reliable and efficient in service than complicated compounds and gadget-infested creations of men like Joseph Beattie. It is perhaps significant that some locomotives with the cleanest, simplest and most handsome external appearance were the most effective.

The quest for economy took an interesting turn in a very different direction in the 1860's. Among the mountains of Snowdonia a line laid to the very narrow gauge of 1 ft. $11\frac{1}{2}$ in. had been built to convey slates from the quarries of Festiniog to the coast at Portmadoc. The line was opened for traffic in 1836, but at that time there was no question of locomotive haulage. The line was single tracked; on it the loaded trains descended by gravity, and the empties were hauled up to the quarries by horses. But with the growth of industry elsewhere the demand for slates exceeded all expectations, and in 1863 four little 0-4-0 steam engines were put to work. The situation was certainly relieved, but engines of considerably greater power were needed in order to haul longer trains up the incline, and so avoid the congestion that at one time seemed inevitable. Charles Easton Spooner, the engineer of the line, then made the historic decision to adopt Robert Fairlie's patent double-bogie double-boilered locomotive. It was virtually two engines in one, though worked by a single crew stationed amidships. The articulated arrangement enabled the engine to negotiate sharp curves, of which there were many on the Festiniog, and the greatly increased loads taken by the Fairlie engines avoided the necessity for doubling the line.

The success of the Fairlie engines on the Festiniog Railway led to a great amount of narrow gauge railway building both at home and abroad. The first cost of such railways was vastly less than that of standard gauge lines; they could be taken on sharp curves, through difficult country, though curiously enough no other British narrow gauge line adopted the Fairlie type of locomotive. None had anything like the traffic carried by the Festiniog, and there was no need for such power on one train. Fairlie himself waged a tremendous campaign in favour of the very narrow gauge in what he termed a new 'battle of the gauges'. In his view, so far as many new lines were concerned, it was a case of narrow gauge or nothing. As a short term policy he was probably right, though the coming of road transport has sounded the death knell of many picturesque little narrow gauge lines running out into the back-of-beyond. Today the Festiniog itself is being re-opened, stage by stage, after a period in which traffic was entirely suspended, and further down the Welsh coast the Talyllyn continues as a classic example of the small, isolated, narrow-gauge railway of last century. This also would have closed but for the efforts of the Talyllyn Railway Preservation Society.

Before closing this chapter, however, I must refer to the extraordinary situation that developed here during the seventies and eighties of last century on the subject of brakes. At this lapse of time it is difficult to pin down any direct evidence that this situation arose in the interests of economy; but on the other hand it is hard to conceive of men whose business depended upon

the safe conveyance of countless passengers being apparently so
blind to the need for safety precautions, and being so outspoken
on the subject, if the underlying reason had not been their desire
to avoid, or at least to postpone for a long time the expenditure
involved in providing the necessary equipment. Until the 'seventies, while the development of locomotive power had gone
steadily forward, very little had been done to improve brake
power. In Great Britain arrangements were primitive, and there
were frequent accidents due to trains being unable to stop in time.
Brakes were provided on the locomotives and in the guards' vans,
and if a driver wanted the brakes applied he made a pre-arranged
signal by whistle to his guard. Far greater brake power could be
obtained by having brakes on every vehicle; but at first there were
difficulties, and some of the first English attempts to do this were
crude and ineffective.

A very simple and effective solution to the problem was obtained by an American, the famous George Westinghouse, and
he travelled to Europe and discussed his invention with many
British and Continental engineers. He provided a brake that was
not merely continuous throughout the train, but which was
applied automatically to both parts of a train in the event of a
breakaway. This latter feature was included at the suggestion of
the English technical journal *Engineering*. After trials, the North
Eastern and the London, Brighton and South Coast adopted the
Westinghouse brake, but among other administrations any suggestions of an automatic brake seemed repugnant to the last
degree. I think there was undoubtedly some 'sales resistance',
purely on the grounds that it was American, while the Midland
Railway, experimenting with the Westinghouse brake, strove
tooth and nail to produce an alternative way of doing the same
thing. Out of their endeavours arose the automatic vacuum brake.

Prior to that, in 1877, the Board of Trade had sent a circular
to all the railways of this country impressing on them the necessity of fitting all their passenger engines with automatic continuous brakes. In this circular were laid down all the commonsense
essentials of a good brake—all of which were eventually accepted.

At that time, however, no legal power existed to enforce these recommendations, and for a time certain companies seemed to delight in flaunting them, Lord Colville, for example, the Chairman of the Great Northern Railway, once told the shareholders 'that Smith's vacuum brake was held in very high esteem; it was not automatic and did not meet what the Board of Trade wished' —as though that was a big point in its favour! Then Smith's Vacuum Brake Company issued two circulars attacking the Board of Trade, and called its conditions 'unnecessary' and 'inconsistent'. The railway inspecting officers of the Board had a very difficult time of it; they could and *did* address very strong words to the recalcitrant companies—and that meant some of the largest and most influential—but without legislation to back them, there could be no enforcement. Following a double collision at Birmingham, Colonel Rich said:

'The many collisions that have occurred on the London and North Western Railway in past years from defective brake power should convince the directors of the *insufficiency and inferiority* of their various systems, and induce them to adopt at once one of the systems that fulfil the requirements of the Board of Trade, and which all other large railway companies in the kingdom have adopted or are adopting.' Yet the Chairman told the shareholders 'we believe the simple vacuum brake is the best. We are putting it on to a very great extent—forty-two a week. We should object to legislation.'

The London and North Western version of the simple vacuum was designed by Francis W. Webb, and his recommendation may have been based on an incomplete knowledge of its failings, as in the case of his compound locomotives. At that time, however, implicit trust was placed in him by the Board, and the remarkable statements made from time to time by the Chairman, Sir Richard Moon, may well have been based entirely on the advice given to them by Mr Webb. As indicating something of the status he enjoyed this chapter may be concluded by a story of the Edinburgh Exhibition of 1890. One day a gentleman connected with the forthcoming exhibition called upon Mr Webb by appointment at Crewe. He was received by the usual rather stiff courtesy, and after some preliminary remarks said:

'Mr Webb I wonder if your Directors would consider exhibiting an engine . . .' at which stage Webb cut in, with an extremely curt: 'I beg your pardon?'

The visitor began again:

'I wonder if your Directors . . .'

But even earlier came the query

'I beg your pardon?'

For the third time the emissary of the Exhibition tried to explain, but Webb waved him aside with a regal gesture:

'*I* shall be very pleased to exhibit an engine.' And that was that!

CHAPTER FOUR

ARTISTRY IN LOCOMOTIVE DESIGN

IN the approach from the Lawn to the Great Western Royal
Hotel at Paddington there is a model locomotive in a glass case.
To a casual present-day onlooker it is clearly nothing more than a
hopelessly old-fashioned 'Puffing Billy'; a long chimney, an
absurdly small boiler, and only a single pair of driving wheels—
how stupid! To railway enthusiasts of almost any age she would
be recognizable at once from the many photographs that have
been published of her kind, even if they had never been fortunate
enough to see one in full action. But at first I want to consider
that beautiful engine, William Dean's 7 ft. 8 in. single No. 3048
Majestic, not as a locomotive at all, but as an *objet d'art*. Today, in
the dust and turmoil of workaday conditions one thinks more
prosaically of locomotives, but in a period of some fifty years before the First World War there was time and opportunity to keep
locomotives really clean, and some designs stand out in the truly
artistic beauty of their proportions.

Now I realize that in coming to discuss such a subject as artistry
in locomotive design I am at once on controversial and delicate
ground. Most enthusiasts in middle age have their favourite
among older locomotives. The reason for their preference may be
past associations, quality of performance, or some strange,
though quite definite attraction that an individual may have for a
particular locomotive. But the enthusiasts will most certainly
regard locomotives as locomotives—not as *objets d'art*; and this
means that some types that are—I say it with bated breath—less
artistic than others are regarded as great favourites. It was the
words of Brunel, in one of his more expansive moments, that put
this into my mind. In the very early days of the Great Western he
wrote: 'We have a splendid engine of Stephenson's; it would have
been a beautiful ornament in the most elegant drawing room'.
An ornament—that is exactly how one could describe William

Dean's *Majestic;* and in looking through the records of contemporary locomotives there are quite a few that one could pick out in the same category. Just as models and paintings help to document the age of sail on the high seas, and men have grown to love and cherish the memories of some of the greatest and most beautiful ships, so it should be also with the age of steam on railways. The parallel is a close one. For just as it was in the 'middle ages' of sail, in Tudor and Stuart days, that the sailing ship reached the height of its beauty, so it was in the late nineteenth century, roughly half-way between Rainhill and the nationalization of British railways, that the steam locomotive touched its greatest heights of elegance and beauty.

The sceptic returning to the old-fashioned 'Puffing Billy' in the glass case at Paddington could well retort, 'what constitutes a handsome locomotive, handsome that is, as a work of art; they all look much the same to me'. And that naturally pulls the enthusiast up sharp, and he begins to analyse the points of locomotives, one by one. There must be symmetry in the *ensemble*, no clashing of styles, no indiscriminate mixing of sharp corners with flowing curves, no abrupt breaks in the flowing lines. In many cases the boiler mountings were veritable ornaments in themselves, but that is not enough. Their massed effect on the line of the boiler must be pleasing to the eye, tapering in height from the chimney rearwards, and blending no less with the height of the cab roof. Then there is the spacing of the wheels: with bogie engines the finest effect is obtained with the chimney on the bogie centre line. As an *objet d'art* a locomotive should have most of its 'works' and machinery hidden, leaving the simple grace of the large driving wheels and the more discreetly placed carrying wheels only in view.

Those with a practical turn of mind may well be thinking by now that in claiming some of these old locomotives as 'period' ornaments I am forgetting their prime purpose, and giving prominence to points that have no importance whatever so far as the functioning of the locomotive was concerned. In any case, the critic might continue, how could you expect that men brought up

in the rough and tumble of early railways days could possibly pay
any attention to such things. They were concerned with building
a practical machine that would do the job. But the astonishing
fact remains that many of these men did succeed, incredibly, brilliantly, in producing locomotives that not only did a grand job of
work on the line, but which were in every way works of art.
These men succeeded not once but throughout their careers. They
produced a style that pervaded all their designs, so that whether
the engines were for goods, shunting, or express passenger work
the style of the designer was evident. Naturally, express locomotives with their large wheels gave the greatest scope for artistry,
but with such men the handling of the theme was no less carefully
done with the lesser lights.

It is interesting to try to trace this remarkable trait to its
source. Daniel Gooch came very near to a classic with his *Great
Western* of 1846; but subsequent engines of the same general
design required an extra pair of carrying wheels at the front end
and the beautiful effect was lost. Sturrock came a little nearer with
his 'Large Hawthorns' on the Great Northern, in 1852, and
Matthew Kirtley's 2-2-2 for the Midland in 1865 nearer still. In
studying scores of photographs of locomotives of this period it
seems that the influence of William Stroudley was pre-eminent.
Through men who were at some time associated with him variations upon the Stroudley style spread eventually to four out of the
five Scottish railways and to the London and South Western,
while in a less direct way it came to have a slight bearing upon the
looks of Midland engines for a time. It was from the fount of Stroudley's inspiration that the Drummond Brothers developed their
own original style: David Jones had his own variation, on the
Highland, while perhaps the greatest stylist of all, Samuel Waite
Johnson, showed at one stage of his long career that he too was
not unmindful of Stroudley. Then there was Edward Fletcher,
the veteran superintendent of the North Eastern Railway, who,
while not attaining the unity of a Johnson, or Drummond design,
certainly achieved a very characteristic style of his own, and above
all Patrick Stirling, who through sheer austerity of line on the

Shortly after the London opening: 5.40 p.m. Manchester express passing West Hampstead hauled by a Pollitt 4-2-2 No. 967.

An early London-extension express, hauled by 3-cylinder compound 4-4-2 No. 365 *Sir William Pollitt*.

After grouping: a Great Central 4-cylinder 4-6-0 on the up Harrogate Pullman (GNR Line) near Potters Bar.

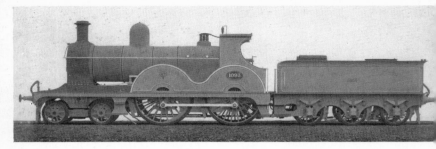

An Aspinall 7ft. 3in. 4-4-0 express engine, derived from his earlier Irish designs.
Built Horwich 1891.

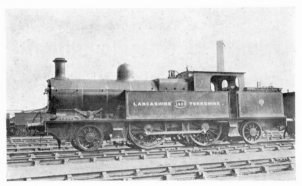

A Hughes superheater 2-4-2 tank engine.

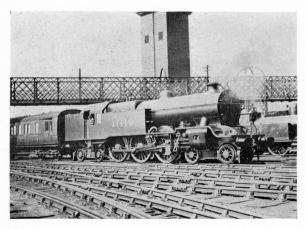

The tank engine derivation of the Hughes 4-cylinder
4-6-0: one of the 4-cylinder 4-6-4 tanks built for the
LMSR just after grouping.

boiler carved for himself a very special niche in this art gallery of fame.

It is curious after so dashing and promising a start that the Great Western should have dropped out of the picture for so many years. Almost without exception the broad gauge stud was ugly and awkward-looking, and although there were some quite pleasing express engines running on the narrow gauge sections of the line, it was hardly likely that a definite individual style would develop while the great problem of the conversion of the gauge on the rest of the line remained to be solved. For a time, also, things became infinitely worse from the aesthetic point of view, as several new types were built as 'convertibles'—to run first on the broad gauge and afterwards be readily convertible to run on the narrow. In their hybrid state these engines were some of the ugliest ever run in Great Britain, though the ultimate transformation, like the pantomime act from bent and wizened crone to fairy godmother, was almost breathtaking. However, more of this anon. We must now return to Mr Stroudley.

In 1865 the Highland Railway Company was formed by an amalgamation of the Inverness and Perth and the Inverness and Aberdeen Railways, and Stroudley was appointed locomotive superintendent. The influence of Joseph Locke had been strong on most of the early Scottish railways, and despite the severe gradients of the Perth line, crossing the Grampians at the 1,484 ft. altitude of Druimuachdar summit, locomotives had originally been of the basic Allan design, as built by the London and North Western at Crewe for so many years: 2-2-2 for passenger, and 2-4-0 for goods. In retrospect one could hardly imagine anything quite so unsuitable for a line like the Highland, but in the five years he was at Inverness, Stroudley had to carry on with them as best he could. Finances were very low, and anything new was out of the question. But during his time at Inverness Stroudley did give one glimpse of his hand, when he received authority to re-build two of the Allan 'singles' as 2-4-0 express engines.

The 'Old Crewe' types, as they became generally known, had an air of the primitive about them. Their finish was plain, if not necessarily rough, and the cab side sheets, extending no more than waist high, were rectangular. At that time no one thought of 'pampering' the enginemen to the extent of providing cabs! The old drivers of stage coach days were fully exposed to the weather, and so it was originally on the railways. But the Highland was another matter, and Stroudley's predecessor, W. Barclay, had built above the rectangular side sheets of the 'Old Crewe' engines one of the earliest cabs to be seen on British Railways. It was a plain rather angular erection, built for utility rather than appearance. But in rebuilding the 2-2-2 engines as 2-4-0s Stroudley at once showed his artistry; the cab was handsomely fashioned, and where others put a large rectangular splasher for the trailing pair of coupled wheels Stroudley blended the curving splasher into the cab-front, and continued the lining-out in such a way as to give a sweep and balance to the whole design. Moreover the engine was beautifully finished in a livery that was gay yet dignified. The basis colour was known officially as 'Stroudley's improved engine green', yet actually it was little removed from a pure yellow ochre; the underframes were of a deep carmine red. This livery can be seen to perfection today on the Brighton engine *Gladstone*, which is preserved in the railway museum at York.

But Stroudley's artistry in line and finish was merely the outward manifestation of his skill and devotion to detail in all matters of engineering design. He was a first-rate practical mechanic himself, and an experienced engine driver; but he was no mere follower of existing practice. He took office on the Brighton Railway in 1870, when there were signs in many quarters that locomotive engineering was dropping into something of a groove; but Stroudley took every detail, thought it out for himself afresh, and if necessary broke clean away from existing practice. Like many of his predecessors he was a tough customer, having a self-assurance that bordered on pugnacity, and some of his new ideas took some forcing through. He allowed not the slightest latitude to contractors. Engine building firms who incorporated features of their own for Edward Fletcher on the North Eastern were bound hip and thigh when dealing with Stroudley. Both by contractors and at Brighton works engines had to be BUILT. Everything had to be exactly fitted, with little or no allowance for initial play, and just as there were no jingling side rods, or clinking big-ends, so externally there were no projecting rivets, or crudely-placed bolt-heads. Likewise in running the engines in traffic the economical use of coal was almost a fetish: a harsh exhaust or fire-throwing from the chimney was almost unheard-of on the Brighton. It is true that train speeds were not high by comparison with some of the other railways, but there is more than a grain of truth in the jocular statement of a Brighton driver after he had ridden on a severely-thrashed North Western 2-4-0 from Rugby to Willesden: 'Honestly I think we could have run on what she threw out of the chimney!'

Stroudley was in command at Brighton from 1870 till his death in 1889, and during that time the 'yellow' engines became an institution and a legend. Among the express designs the dainty little 'G' class 2-2-2 singles and the front-coupled 'Gladstones' have a sure place among the immortals of the locomotive world, though the 'Gladstones', handsome appearance apart, caused a great deal of comment in engineering circles at the time, by having the coupled wheels at the leading end. Stroudley gave a lucid exposition of his reasons for this radical departure from orthodoxy in a paper read before the Institution of Civil Engineers in March 1885. He placed the coupled wheels where the greatest weight was, and explained: 'The leading wheels pass round curves without shock or oscillations, owing to the small weight on the trailing wheels, as it is the trailing wheels that have the most influence in forcing the leading flanges up to the outside of the curve.' Certainly the 'Gladstone' engines rode very well, and long after Stroudley's death they continued to be used in fast traffic on the Brighton line when some trains at any rate were considerably faster than at the time the engines were originally built. One of these engines, No. 189 *Edward Blount*, was shown at the Paris Exhibition of 1889, where it was very much admired. Following the exhibition it was tested on the main line of the Paris, Lyons and Mediterranean Railway between Paris and Laroche. As might be expected Stroudley took a great personal interest in the working of his engine in France, but unfortunately in the course of the trials he caught a chill, and died in Paris in December of that year.

The fruits of his works flourished long after he had passed from the scene, through the immense personality of Dugald Drummond, and of his younger brother, Peter. The older Drummond had been foreman erector under Stroudley at Inverness, and was, until 1875, works manager at Brighton. One would hardly expect there to be many aesthetic leanings in the make-up of so rugged, so forthright, so omnipotent a character as Dugald Drummond. Certainly little suggestion of it has emerged from the stories of his career handed down by those who had close contact with him. Yet he and his brother produced a whole range of very handsome engines. With the Drummonds, beauty was derived from simplicity of line, and an entire absence of gadgets, externally at any rate. As the two brothers moved, as was the fashion among locomotive engineers of the nineteenth century, from one railway to another, so the basic 4-4-0 express engine, with its evidences of Stroudley influence, appeared in many individual colours: in the bright gamboge and style of painting that Dugald Drummond took from Brighton to the North British; in the 'Prussian Blue' of the Caledonian; in the apple green, that Peter Drummond found in vogue when he first went to the Highland, and lastly in the pleasing yellow green of the London and South Western.

How then was it that such men came to incorporate such artistry, such harmony into the external appearance of their locomotives? The Drummond 4-4-0 during the first 25 years of its production was in essentials an extremely simple machine, but it was also one of the fastest, most powerful and most ecomomical in the country. The machinery was simple; the valves were placed between the cylinders, and driven by the most direct form of the Stephenson link motion; the steam ports were large, and direct; there were no complications. Where other designers hampered their engines by restricted passages for the steam Dugald Drummond went almost to the opposite extreme. The result was that his engines ran very freely. The chimney was not perhaps so ornate as some others, but it was finely proportioned; the safety valves on top of the dome gave a touch of distinction, and to the plain Stroudleyesque styling of the cab and splashers was added the smokebox 'wings', giving a poise, dignity and balance to the whole ensemble.

The type made its first bow on the North British, in 1876; large powerful engines were needed for hauling the Anglo-Scottish expresses worked in conjunction with the Midland Railway over the heavily graded line between Edinburgh and Carlisle. The Drummond 4-4-os built for this job were among the most powerful of the day. Following Brighton practice they were all named after celebrated places on the route. There was not much opportunity for high speed between Edinburgh and Carlisle, for the line is sharply curved for much of the way; but after Drummond had left the North British to become Locomotive Superintendent of the Caledonian, and had introduced the same type, with slight variations, on the latter line, it was not long before the whole world became aware of what they could do. In the great railway race of 1895 Drummond's Caledonian 4-4-os hauled the West Coast sleeping car express north of Carlisle, and night after night the $117\frac{3}{4}$ miles to Stirling were run in very little over two hours, even though the train had to climb from a few feet above sea level at the Solway Firth to an altitude of 1,014 ft. at Beattock summit. On the last night of the race engine No. 90 ran non-stop from Carlisle to Perth, negotiating a second major summit, Gleneagles, in the process, and covered the $150\frac{3}{4}$ miles in 150 minutes.

Peter Drummond was ten years younger than his brother, and in his early career he followed him, as junior partner, at Brighton, on the North British, and on the Caledonian. But in 1896, he was appointed locomotive superintendent of the Highland Railway, just before Dugald secured the important office of locomotive superintendent of the London and South Western Railway. And before the end of the century two further variations of the basic Drummond 4-4-0 were at work, the 'Small Ben' class on the Highland, and the very celebrated 'T9' on the South Western. In the

latter engines were embodied all the best of the Drummond tradition up to that date, and their capacity for load haulage and speed
was astonishing. In the early 1900's in hauling West of England
expresses between Salisbury and Exeter, it was not unusual for
these engines to run up to well over 80 m.p.h. in four or five
different places on that hilly road. It was not merely a case of
'Handsome is as handsome does'; the Drummond 4-4-0s were
handsome on any count, and their splendid performance on the
line earned them a place among the immortals.

While the Stroudley influence can be readily traced in Scotland, and on the London and South Western through the work of
one or another of the Drummond brothers, there has always
seemed to be a solid *bloc* of railways in Midland and Northern
England that lay outside the pale of this particular 'magic'. But
among the locomotive superintendents of those railways there
was Samuel Waite Johnson, of the Midland. Born in 1831 near
Leeds, he was apprenticed to E. B. Wilson & Co. at the Railway
Foundry; there he met David Joy, and helped in the making of
the drawings of the *Jenny Lind*. After that he served on the Manchester, Sheffield and Lincolnshire, on the Edinburgh and Glasgow, and on the Great Eastern, and it was while he was on the
latter line that he showed that he was not unmindful of Stroudley.
He rebuilt two of the quaint 2-2-2 singles of Robert Sinclair's
design, as 4-2-2s, and turned them into quite elegant engines; in so
doing, however, he painted them in Stroudley's Brighton 'yellow'!
He then went from the Great Eastern to the Midland, to develop
perhaps the most beautiful locomotive style ever seen. It did not
rely, as did Drummond's, on good proportions and simplicity of
detail; Johnson's style was full of sweeping curves, the wheel
splashers lavishly adorned with brass beading, the chimney, dome,
and safely valve cover each a little masterpiece in itself. At first
Midland engines continued in the medium green of Matthew
Kirtley's day, but then Johnson changed to the deep crimson lake
—the ever memorable 'Derby Red'—which continued as an
express locomotive livery on the LMSR until the austerities of the
Second World War compelled a change to black. Thus adorned,

82

a Midland express engine in Johnson's day was indeed a 'sight for the gods'.

For perfect symmetry of line Johnson touched the heights in his 2-4-0s, and his 4-4-0s of the middle period. The 4-2-2 'singles', known affectionately and with good reason as the 'Spinners', had a miniature version of the old traditional square rear splasher; although this one detail looked incongruous, the engines were otherwise so beautifully proportioned that one could hardly say it detracted from a superb design. The broad brass band over the great driving wheel splasher, the elaborate coat-of-arms, and the huge polished brass of the driving axle-box combined to give a wonderfully impressive effect. Added to all this, the engines were not merely kept 'clean'; the 'singles' in their prime had little short of an exhibition finish as a matter of course. No wonder their drivers and firemen took a pride in them! The Johnson style, and standard of finish were not confined to express engines. Just as much care in detail design and finish was lavished on the main line 0-6-0 goods engines, while the 0-4-4 suburban passenger tanks were equally recognizable as of the same family. Some of these latter engines have survived with practically no alteration until the present day; and despite their black paint, and usually—alas! —a coating of grime, the Johnson style is there for all to see, as they skate along across the Somerset marshlands maybe, from Evercreech through Glastonbury to Highbridge, or on that very rural branch from Ashchurch to Tewkesbury and Malvern.

The London and North Western engines suffered greatly by comparison with those of the Midland. In 1873 their colour was changed from green to black by order of the General Manager, as an economy measure; and although the workmanship put into the machinery was always first-class at Crewe nothing was spent on adornments, still less on such luxuries as countersunk bolts and rivets. For this reason North Western engines tended to look a rough job. The passenger classes, simple and compound, were well-proportioned, though the large rectangular rear splasher remained as a characteristic feature. But the Crewe express engines had a vitality and character that, to the mind of at least one enthu-

siast, exceeded all others; that character was given to them by
their names. It is true that many other railways of that period had
named engines. Stroudley named everything on the line except
the goods engines and the shunting tanks; but the names were
devoid of inspiration, since the vast majority were of towns, vil-
lages and hamlets served by the line, not forgetting the slum districts of east and south-east London. One could hardly get enthusiastic over *Shadwell*, *Shoreditch*, and *Wapping*, which latter, by
the way, bore little reference to the size of the engine. The heights
of unconscious humour were reached however, when one of the
Brighton engines was named *Crawley*!

But both inspiration and artistry were shown in the North
Western names, with much of the felicity characteristic of ship-
names in the Royal Navy. They were varied, without being far-
fetched; they were euphonious, as names. Here are a dozen, taken
at random from the 'Precedent', 'Whitworth' and 'Dreadnought'
classes: *Ariadne*, *Lucknow*, *Newcomen*, *The Queen*, *Greystoke*,
Luck of Edenhall, *Sister Dora*, *Wizard*, *Charles Dickens*, *Thun-
derer*, *Alchymist*, *Marchioness of Stafford*. If the engines themselves
went in black, it was a very glossy, gleaming black, and the brass
nameplates on the splashers were polished till they shone like
gold. The unusual names among those quoted above naturally
arouse curiosity: what, for example, was the Luck of Edenhall,
and again who was Sister Dora? There was, indeed, a story behind
every engine name, some tragic, some gay, and one or two extremely funny. It was this character, this personality among the
Crewe engines that made them so popular among the connoisseurs, even though their artistic qualities were not so high as those
of their contemporaries on the Midland.

It is impossible while considering the artistic aspect of locomotives to neglect the appeal they make to the emotions when running at speed. But here again there were great differences to be
noted between the individual railways: the beauty of a Stroudley
'single', *Fairlight*, *Hurstmonceux*, or *St Lawrence* gliding downhill
under the lightest of reins, in the mellow light of a summer evening, had the pastoral charm of the Sussex countryside. Compare

with this the sound and fury of *Merrie Carlisle* and *Leviathan* together thundering up among the Westmorland Fells with a Scotch express: exhausts roaring, fire flying thick and high from their chimneys, and one felt like shouting with joy in a mad exhilaration, 'harder, harder'. In face of such a spectacle the slender grace of a 'Stroudley' or an early 'Johnson' counts for nought; visions of economy are cast to the winds at sight of those two fire-spitting chimneys tearing by in the dusk. Here is all the thrill of intense human effort.

In his delightful book *Highways and Byways in Derbyshire*, Mr J. B. Firth recalls what he describes as 'the incoherent ravings' of Ruskin at the building of the railway through Bakewell. Yet see how an author of fifty years ago, an author of great sensitivity and poetic feeling, reacted to the Midland Railway in Derbyshire:

'Remembering', he writes 'what Ruskin had written of this railway I purposely waited, high above the tunnel mouth, till a train should pass. Soon I heard the shrill of a far-off whistle and the rushing sound of a distant train. Then silence again. The train had entered the tunnel on the Ashford side of the hill. A little while and a rumbling began growing in intensity every second until, with an exultant roar, the express came out from the hill below me, crossed the bridge, and swung round the bend of the embankment towards Monsal Dale station. The engine was straining up the incline, working hard, putting forth obvious effort, and addressing itself to its task. In a few moments another train came gliding down in the opposite direction, not conscious of her load. She flew down the embankment like a skater with the wind behind him, holding her breath in enjoyment of the pace. The sight might have startled Ruskin's goddesses "walking in fair procession on the lawns"; but do they always "walk in fair procession"? I will be bound that the thousand Oreades who formed Diana's troop of nymphs on the banks of the Eurotas or the crags of Cynthus would clap their hands with glee if they could see an express flying down Monsal Dale, and would halloo to the scared driver in his cab and bid him go faster still.'

The engines Mr Firth saw would have been the most beautiful

of the small Johnson 4-4-0s. Had there been a fire-throwing championship held for the nineteenth century engines I fancy those of the Great Northern would have been hot—very hot!—favourites. While F. W. Webb's North Western engines threw sparks by the myriad most of Patrick Stirling's express, mixed-traffic, and suburban tanks alike, gave a passable imitation of a volcano in eruption. At night their exhausts showed a solid column of flame, punctuated frequently by quite sizeable lumps of white hot coal! This was all the more extraordinary, because a Stirling engine *passant* was a stately thing of pale green, with much lovingly polished brass, giving no hint of the fearsome animal it became when the regulator was opened. With some locomotive engineers a 'style' developed, and sometimes changed radically in the course of the designer's career; but there was little change with Patrick Stirling. His first important post was in his native Kilmarnock, where he became locomotive superintendent of the Glasgow and South Western Railway, at the age of 33; and for the next 43 years, whether at Kilmarnock or Doncaster there was no mistaking a Patrick Stirling engine. The Scottish ones had much the same pyrotechnic qualities, and an old driver after making a hard run with a special was heard to remark next day: 'Some of the sparks are no' doon yet!'

But fireworks from the chimney have little to do with artistry in locomotive design, and in one respect Patrick Stirling's work shows some interesting inconsistencies. His first express engine was a 2-2-2 built at Kilmarnock in 1857; it had outside cylinders, all the bearings were inside, and the running plate was carried upward in a graceful sweeping curve over the driving wheels boss, so that the connecting rod was never concealed. The first engines of this type had domed boilers; but the design in later years became a very familiar one in England, for in general outline and style John Ramsbottom copied it very faithfully in his 'Lady of the Lake' class on the London and North Western Railway. So far as the latter designer and railway was concerned this class remained an oddity. All his other locomotives had inside cylinders, and were of a more or less conventional style. With Stirling, however, that early Glasgow and South Western design was developed on the Great Northern into the magnificent 8-foot bogie singles—again outside cylinders, again that tremendous sweep of the running plates; but instead of the rather stumpy appearance of the Scottish 2-2-2s, and Ramsbottom's copy of them, the Great Northern 4-2-2s had the greater dignity and poise given by a leading bogie. They stood alone among the many beautiful engine designs Stirling made for the Great Northern, as all others had inside cylinders, and no bogies.

The great unifying feature of all Stirling's engines, other than the very first G&SWR 2-2-2s, was the domeless boiler, and the beautifully fashioned brass safety-valve casing over the firebox. While Sturrock had used the raised firebox to give additional steam space over the crown, Stirling had one unbroken line from chimney to cab. This chapter is not really concerned with technicalities, but one must point out that Stirling's very graceful lines were accompanied by a considerable reduction in that most important attribute of a locomotive, the capacity to *burn* coal. The last Sturrock engines, his 2-4-0s of 1866-7, had a firebox heating surface of 121 sq. ft. and a grate area of 19.7 sq. ft. while Patrick Stirling in the great majority of his bogie 'singles' used 109 sq. ft. of firebox heating surface, and a grate of $17\frac{3}{4}$ sq. ft. These engines had to do much heavier work than anything set to the Sturrock's and with such relatively small boilers and fireboxes they had to be well and truly thrashed—hence the firework displays! All Stirling's engines were the same. The 0-4-2 and 2-4-0 mixed traffic types, and the austerely-beautiful 2-2-2s, with inside cylinders and 7 ft. 7 in. driving wheels threw fire sky-high. The train timings were certainly hard. The semi-fast and stopping trains had to go hard between stations, while the main line expresses were the fastest in England at the time.

Patrick Stirling was very proud of his engines and had a keen regard for appearance. In 1882 a great deal of interest was being shown everywhere in the Joy valve gear, as a means of improving steam distribution and consequently providing freer running and lower coal consumption. But Joy made the following very revealing entry in his diary: 'Pat Stirling (Great Northern Railway) sent me blue prints of his big 8-footer (his pet engine) to arrange valve gear. It was awfully difficult—no room between the wheel and the motion plate; still there it was very neat and compact, and then the old man said, after all my trouble: "Naa, mon, I canna spile my grand engine with the likes o' that machinery outside o' her."' The Joy was one of the neatest of valve gears, with a minimum of rods and no eccentrics; and on the 8-footer it made an excellent design. In view of Stirling's objection, however, one hesitates to describe some later arrangements, perpetrated in the cause of accessibility, during our own times.

Stirling's younger brother, James, followed immediately in his footsteps at Kilmarnock. There is, indeed, something of a parallel between these two brothers and Dugald and Peter Drummond in this respect, though James Stirling never copied his brother's practice to the same extent as did Peter Drummond. He followed the cult of the domeless boiler, and took it to the South Eastern Railway when he went to Ashford in 1877. But the domeless-boilered engines of James Stirling on both the G&SWR and SER had not the perfectly-balanced symmetry and grace of Patrick's Great Northern types. The safety valve columns and their springs and balance lever were open and placed on the centre of the boiler; its height was insignificant in relation to the chimney and cab, and there were other features that detracted from the general appearance of the locomotives, from the artistic point of view. The South Eastern 'F' class 4-4-0s of 1891 were the most graceful of James Stirling's design, but one would not place them among the classics of locomotive artistry.

The old argument between inside and outside cylinders was swinging decidedly in favour of 'inside', by the eighties of last century. The use of steel instead of wrought iron, and improved methods of manufacture had largely eliminated the early troubles experienced with cranked axles, but there were nevertheless some very fine outside-cylinder locomotives built for express work between 1875 and 1900. For many years after the direct influence of Alexander Allan passed from the neighbourhood of the Highland Railway his very characteristic arrangement of the front-end framing persisted on 4-4-0 passenger engines. The locomotive superintendent, David Jones, was in some ways a disciple of Stroudley, whom he succeeded at Inverness, and in his 'Bruce' class of 1874 and the 'Straths' of 1892 many features of the Stroudley style, including the cab, were combined with the Allan style of front-end framing. These were engines of great character, strongly suggestive of the wild and rugged country they traversed. They were all named, and while many were no more than topographical, such as *Strathcarron*, *Glenbruar*, and *Morayshire*, others had the true ring of the Highland about them, such as *Auchtertyre*, *Aultwharrie*, and the sonorous *Clachnacuddin*. It rather spoils the illusion, however, to add that the last mentioned name means nothing more romantic than 'the stone of the tubs', the stone where, by tradition, the housewives of Inverness rested their wash-tubs on returning from the river bank!

In his last design of main line passenger engine for the Highland Railway, the 4-4-0 class of 1896 named after Lochs, David Jones abandoned the Allan style of framing at the front-end, and while something of the distinctive Highland character was lost thereby, the design considered by itself had more unity of style. It still included several of those delightful individual touches that so marked the railways of pre-grouping era, where a superintendent had no more than a few hundreds, instead of thousands of locomotives in his charge. The Highland 'Lochs' had a Stroudleyesque cab, together with two of Jones's particular specialities: the two safety valves were placed athwartships, as it were, instead of in line ahead, and there was that curious louvred chimney. There were really two chimneys, one inside the other; the real chimney was the inner one, and the louvres led into the annular space between the two. The idea was to induce a strong upward current of air at the back of the real chimney that would lift the exhaust steam, and prevent it beating down and obscuring the driver's look-out. Whether it was effective I cannot say. Peter Drummond discontinued it the moment he took over at Inverness, but the Jones engines ran with their louvred chimneys for many years afterwards—and many still retained them in the late nineteen-twenties.

Another group of locomotives having a marked individual character were those designed by Charles Sacré for the Manchester, Sheffield and Lincolnshire Railway. He was a confirmed believer in double-frames, and in a group of 4-4-0 engines built in 1877 he carried the slotted outside frame forward to the front footsteps, even though this reinforcement had no connection with the bogie. These 4-4-0 engines were used on the heavily graded main line over the Pennines between Sheffield and Manchester, but at that time this railway was in partnership with the Great Northern, running a very fast service between King's Cross and Manchester, via Sheffield and Retford, and the MSL provided the engine power as far south as Grantham. The trains were light, and the speed required was high, particularly over the Great Northern main line between Retford and Grantham, and Mr Sacré built a new class of 2-2-2 'single' express locomotives for this service in 1883. It would barely have seemed possible, at this relatively late stage in nineteenth century locomotive history, to crowd more distinctive features on to a new engine. They bore the imprint of a personality: outside cylinders; a new version of the Allan framing; slotted splashers; raised firebox, with a huge brass band accentuating the transition; oval side windows in the cab—but in any case the photograph speaks for itself! One can call them nothing more than charming little period pieces.

Stove-pipe chimneys came into vogue later on the Manchester, Sheffield and Lincolnshire Railway, in Mr Parker's time, and the appearance of the Sacré engines was not improved when the new style was impressed upon older engines. Remembering how much the chimney plays its part in setting the seal on a handsome design one would imagine any engine with a stove pipe chimney would be beyond the pale, so far as artistry was concerned. But then there is the case of William Adams, on the London and South Western. It was the fashion among nineteenth-century engineers to move fairly freely from job to job, but among railway personalities few could claim a more varied career than Adams. Marine engines, docks, engineer to the Sardinian Navy in 1848, railway surveying in the Isle of Wight, design of railway workshops—all these he had taken in his stride before he was forty years of age. He did not touch locomotive work at all in these early years, until, indeed, he went to the North London Railway in the early 'fifties. From the North London he went to the Great Eastern, in 1873, and finally to the London and South Western in 1878. There at Nine Elms works he built two series of outside-cylinder 4-4-0 express engines, that from both the aesthetic and the engineering point of view were as near masterpieces as any locomotives running in the nineteenth century.

In outward appearance these locomotives, when analysed piece by piece, were simple enough; but there was a specious elegance about them, and the lengthy wheel-base of the bogie gave them a striding effect. There was no mistaking the intentions of the designer: they were obviously express passenger engines. Curiously enough the stove pipe chimney suited them admirably. At a later date many of them received new chimneys of Drummond design, and with these chimneys something of the original character of the Adams 4-4-0s was lost. They were finished in the very attractive pale yellow green then standard on the London and South Western Railway, and by the happiest of inspirations one of these engines, still in service in 1945, was restored to its original glory to mark the centenary of Waterloo station, and it is now preserved by the British Transport Commission.

These Adams 4-4-0s were not merely ornamental. In his encyclopaedic work *A Manual of Locomotive Engineering* published in 1899, W. F. Pettigrew described them as 'among the most powerful and economical engines in the world', a statement amply confirmed by a series of very successful trials carried out on the L&SWR in 1891. Pettigrew, friend, confidant, and a one-time assistant to Adams, was himself a railway engineer in the front rank, and was later Engineer-in-Chief of the Furness Railway, embracing all the civil engineering, docks, dock machinery—all in addition to locomotives, carriages, wagons, and signalling. In his book of 1899 the trials of the Adams 4-4-0 locomotive are very fully reported. The coal consumption was low; the rate of steam production was high in relation to the coal burnt, and the running of the engine was very free. The detailed design of the valve gear allowed the engine to be run with a very long range of expansion of the steam, and this in itself contributed in no small measure to the high working efficiency. The significance of this will be discussed later when I come to the Great Western development from 1903 onwards; but at this stage it is pleasant to record that so elegantly-handsome an example of a Victorian locomotive should have been such an excellent one in service.

Before the nineteenth century had come to a close there were already signs of a 'new look' in British locomotive styling. Attempts to provide something better than the scantiest of cabs had met with opposition from the drivers and firemen, who said that such erections interfered with the look-out. But after the McDonnell storm on the North Eastern, the new chief T. W. Wordsell introduced a cab with a roof extending backwards over the shovelling plate, and having two windows in the side sheets. This was in 1886, but although this type at once became standard on the North Eastern Railway another 36 years were to pass before it was seriously followed elsewhere. There were one or two isolated examples, it is true, but these were in the nature of 'feelers' rather than indications of a definite policy. The North Eastern developed a handsome style incorporating these 'canopy' cabs; the coupled wheel splashers were blended into one, and the outline continued, by a sweep of the lining, across the face of the side sheet.

In the five years he was on the Great Eastern William Adams started a tradition of stove-pipe chimneys that was continued by his successors, Massey Bromley, T. W. Worsdell and James Holden. On this line the later engines of our period were distinguished more by the very handsome dark-blue livery than by any special features of design. Express locomotives built in Holden's time were neat and compact; excellent workmanship was put into them, and no better proof of this could be found than the continuing in service today of a number of the mixed traffic 2-4-0s built in 1891-1902. But with many engines of the period a feature

Webb, Chief Mechanical Engineer, LNWR, 1871–1903.

Sir John A. F. Aspinall, Chief Mechanical Engineer, and later General Manager, Lancashire and Yorkshire Railway.

Johnson, Locomotive Superintendent, Midland Railway, 1873–1902.

Wilson Worsdell, Chief Mechanical Engineer, North Eastern Railway, 1890–1910.

West to North express topping the Lickey Incline and passing Blackwell hauled by a Class '3' Johnson Belpaire 4-4-0 No. 779 and a 2-4-0.

Train of Anglo-Scottish joint stock 'M&GSW' posed for photographing near Millers Dale Junction, and headed by 2-4-0 No. 102.

instantly recognizable was the placing of the dome relatively close behind the chimney. The dome naturally must be placed in the centre of one of the boiler rings, and at that time the Great Eastern was using many 2-ring barrels. Holden put the dome on the forward rather than the after-ring, and thus gave rise to the distinctive effect.

And so we come back in concluding this chapter to the Great Western, and in some way to the culmination of the nineteenth century vogue for embellishment and adornment of locomotives. When fully developed into their narrow gauge form the Dean 7 ft. 8 in. singles were perhaps the most gorgeously arrayed of any express engines of the day. The basic colour was no more than the Brunswick green that had reigned supreme at Swindon from the days of Daniel Gooch till now, and is today the standard British Railways colour for the largest express engines; but in 1894 the under-frames and wheel-splashers were crimson lake, and the narrow rearward splashers fitted below the frames to all engine wheels were tipped with polished brass. To add that the chimney was copper-capped and that the safety valve cover was polished brass goes without saying on the Great Western; but then there was that huge dome. They used powdered soot to 'get up' those domes, and it was not good enough to get them up and leave it at that. In moving off the shed they might be splashed or spotted by ejections from other engines, or by the first movement of their own; and so after cleaning, sacks were put over them, and kept there till the engine was actually moving out from the yard. Then a young cleaner would climb up to the running plate, remove the sack, and the dome would embark upon the main line literally spotless.

Many of these engines took names from the old broad gauge 'singles', such as *Amazon, Courier, Rover, Lord of the Isles*, But there were far more of these Dean 7 ft. 8 in. 4-2-2s than of Gooch's old flyers, and some of the additional names had a wonderfully appropriate flavour of the West Country: *White Horse, Westward Ho!, Sir Richard Grenville, Devonia, Stormy Petrel* and *Lorna Doone*. There were also such traditional—one might almost say inevitable—Great Western names like *Flying Dutchman* and *North Star*. These engines were no mere decorative show pieces, no delicate ornaments to be treated with care; they did a great deal of hard work on the road, and can claim one outstanding record. By the turn of the century there were many engines in this country capable of running at 80, or even 85 m.p.h.; but the Dean 4-2-2s did that almost as a matter of course on the really fast trains. It was another matter to keep up such a speed for any length of time, and on May 9, 1904, one of the 'Deans', No. 3065 *Duke of Connaught* running an Ocean Mail special, covered the 70¼ miles from Shrivenham to Westbourne Park in 52¾ minutes—an *average* speed for this entire distance of *exactly eighty miles an hour*.

CHAPTER FIVE

LOCOMOTIVE MEN AT WORK

BY the end of the nineteenth century the railway network of this country as we know it today was practically complete, and by various amalgamations the sixteen large railways of pre-grouping days—eleven English and five Scottish—had assumed their final form. Further than this, the locomotive department had, all over the country, come to take a generally similar pattern in organization; and from considerations of high policy, of engine design, and of such outward manifestations as artistry we can well turn to take a look at the locomotive department in action, from the superintendent himself right down to the drivers and firemen. On all railways the organization that had developed was rather different from that existing today. The change is not merely one of historic interest; it is a fundamental change, and one fraught with a deep significance.

Sixty years ago, carrying the title of Locomotive Superintendent, the chief was responsible for everything appertaining to locomotives on the whole line; usually, too, he included carriages and wagons. He had to provide engines to work the traffic, to keep the existing stock in good repair, to replace obsolete types with new ones, to design locomotives of enhanced power when they were needed, and above all to run the trains. The engine sheds, and all the equipment for day-to-day servicing were his responsibility and the drivers and firemen came under his command. The chief and his leading assistants were well-known figures up and down the line, keeping in touch with running conditions by frequent journeyings. The bigger the railway the less intimate could be the contact, however, and on lines like the Great Western, the North Western, and the Midland the task of liaison between headquarters and actual working lay more with the locomotive running inspectors. Naturally, of course, the degree of liaison varied enormously with personalities; I have already written of Francis W. Webb of the London and North Western, who was one of the most unapproachable of men. But in the years immediately preceeding the high-noon of steam most locomotive departments were closely knit, fully integrated teams.

The most prominent superintendents of the day, men like Dean, of the Great Western, S. W. Johnson, the younger Worsdell on the North Eastern, Dugald Drummond, and of course, F. W. Webb, enjoyed an extremely high status on the railway; some regularly attended Board meetings, and their responsibility to the General Manager of the railway was a mere formality. Their freedom of action, which would be envied by a modern locomotive engineer, sometimes led them into high-handed courses; some were courtly-mannered, others remained 'rough diamonds' all their lives, but all were alike in their utter devotion to the railway service. In a spacious age some of them became rich men, and spent their days of leisure fishing, shooting or deerstalking; Wilson Worsdell, indeed, kept a shooting box in Norway.

Some of the most remarkable men of the day were the seconds-in-command, and of these George Whale of the London and North Western was outstanding. As Running Superintendent he had the terrific task of keeping the traffic going at a time when Webb was building nought but compounds, and engines that were neither reliable nor fast enough for the job. He bore the brunt of it both ways, in keeping things 'sweet' with Webb—no easy task at the best of times—and in dealing as best he could with the day-to-day troubles in running the traffic. One does not like to think of him as a hard, embittered man, though his portraits tend to give that impression; and of all men he needed a hide like a rhinocerous. But no running superintendent was more completely at one with the footplate men, in practical mastery of their job, and in understanding of their needs.

Every year Queen Victoria travelled from Windsor to Balmoral for her autumn holiday, and the route lay first over the Great Western, and then from Wolverhampton onwards over the London and North Western. The Locomotive Running Superintendent would be travelling on the Royal Train in any case; but merely to 'travel' was not good enough for Whale. He must be on the engine and drive it himself. It was in those days that the London and North Western was passing through its inglorious episode of the brakes, when Webb at first persisted with the 'Heath Robinson' contraption of the chain brake, and engine driving was sometimes a hazardous business. Stops were sometimes very jerky and harsh, and one can imagine that with a rough stop in the middle of the night Queen Victoria would not be amused! But G. P. Neele, who was Superintendent of the Line during this period, has recorded in his reminiscences that Whale was the most expert of drivers, and always gave them a beautifully steady run. At one time it would seem that he would work out the whole of his railway career as a second-in-command, but at the age of 61 he was called upon to succeed Webb, as Chief Mechanical Engineer, and his subsequent work, as told in a later chapter, forms one of the most dramatic episodes in British locomotive history.

At that time there were considerable variations in the way staff and the footplatemen were treated, and where the locomotives of different companies worked into the same stations or depots friction arose. On the Midland, for example, discipline was very strict, and relations between the Company and its men at times severely strained. On the other hand Charles Sacré of the Manchester, Sheffield and Lincolnshire handled his men on a very light rein. He knew all the express drivers personally, and treated them with a brusque comradeship that made him very popular. He was known jocularly as 'Hell fire Jack'—one would imagine from his sheer enjoyment of speed on the footplate. Of course there were some who took advantage of his kind and warmhearted ways, and there was a certain amount of slackness, both in working and in personal habits by men of the MS&L. Nevertheless, one is drawn instinctively to Charles Sacré. He resigned not long after the terrible accident at Penistone in 1884. The primary cause was the breaking of a crank axle on one of his engines; but the results would have been relatively mild, had not a coupling broken, and all the carriages crashed down a steep embankment. The train was fitted with the very dangerous earlier form of vacuum brake that was non-automatic, and although the engine and tender stayed upright on the embankment the breaking of the coupling left the whole train without any form of control. Sacré took the disaster very much to heart; it was not many years before it was evident that his mind was affected, and this great-hearted man died in 1889 at the early age of 58.

Dugald Drummond in his London and South Western days went further, perhaps, than any other superintendent in trying to co-ordinate footplate work with his principles of design. From his long experience on a number of important railways he went to Nine Elms with very definite ideas as to how locomotives should be built and how they should be run. He was essentially a practical man, and his theories worked out satisfactorily. He was frequently on the footplate, and gave a series of lectures on the management of locomotives at all important centres on the system. Discipline was strict. Every Monday morning Drummond held what he himself called a *levée* at his office, at which drivers responsible for breaches of regulations found themselves very much 'on the mat'; he constantly stressed 'the great inconvenience to the public by any neglect of the strict observation of the time-table', but in all his dealings with the men, tough customer though he was, he was scrupulously fair. He was not merely respected and admired, but liked, so much so that many enginemen who had known him in his Scottish days came south and joined the London and South Western. It was not unusual to hear the driver of a West of England express at Waterloo say: 'He's a gr-r-reat mon is Mr Dr-r-rummond, and I've a guid opeenion of his engines too!' Many of the design and works staff, too, were Scotsmen.

One always regards locomotive enginemen as the very salt of the railway service, but a modern writer knowing many of the splendid fellows who are on the job today is naturally intrigued by the sight of the men who have been photographed on and alongside some of the famous engines of the past. Pride in the job and immense character shine out of their faces; tremendous bearded men, standing with the air and authority of a supreme commander, with the fireman alert and respectful alongside. The running they made, often in exposed and difficult conditions, was often incredible. Mr David L. Smith has told of a terrible night in Galloway, and how the last train got through before the line from Stranraer to Ayr was completely blocked with snow-drifts. It was the 4.15 p.m. up, on a December night in pitch darkness and a raging blizzard. Two engines were put on, but the leading one scooped the snow into her ashpan wherever drifts were forming and before very long she was not much use in hauling the train. But she was clearing the way for the second engine, one of James Stirling's 0-4-2 mixed traffic class, driven by a man named Bob Cuthbertson and fired by 'Geordie' Thomson. How they got through, despite the snow and disabled leading engine, is best described in Smith's own words: 'Cuthbertson, flailing that engine till he was like to rive her in pieces, put them through everything, and *lay over the side all the way*. Verily a Man of Iron!' In those days cabs were made narrow, so that the men could 'lay over' all the time without fear of their heads striking bridges and other objects at the lineside.

C. J. Bowen-Cooke, who later became Chief Mechanical Engineer of the London and North Western, tells of the courage of a driver and fireman in a different kind of emergency. It concerns Webb's 'Precedent' class 2-4-0 express engine *Hardwicke*, named after the architect of the Great Hall at Euston. 'On May 27, 1892,' Bowen-Cooke writes, 'when working the 2.10 p.m. train from Euston it was run into by another company's train at Derby Junction, and pushed completely over the viaduct into the street below, a depth of some 40 ft. The engine pitched over on its side, the tender turned a complete somersault, and landed upside down at the chimney end of the engine.

'Strange to say, the driver and fireman, who went over the viaduct on the footplate, lived to tell their experiences. The driver remembered distinctly the left leading wheel of the engine striking the ground first, while he stood in his position in the corner of the cab as the engine was making its downward plunge. He was stunned by the fall, but without knowing what he was doing, he crept out of the ruins, and although regaining consciousness for a moment, he knew nothing of what had happened until several weeks afterwards. After being off duty some months, he started work again on local passenger trains, and one would think his experiences would have made him content to remain on such work but not so, he was never satisfied until he got back again on to his old job on express trains, where he remained until he left the Company's service of his own accord some time afterwards. The fireman is still at work at Bushbury'—that was in 1899.

Accidents, though hair-raising at the time, are not always such desperate affairs as the collision outside Stoke-on-Trent, so vividly described above by Mr Bowen-Cooke. They can have a comical side, especially when there is an eyewitness present with so rich a sense of humour as the late Ernest L. Ahrons. In 1886 Swindon built an experimental four-cylinder compound 2-4-0 engine on the broad gauge; she was a bit troublesome in her first days, but then authority was sufficiently confident to try her out as assistant engine on the 3 p.m. express from Bristol to Paddington. It was always a heavy train and required two engines from Bath to Swindon to negotiate the steep gradient up through the Box tunnel. The train engine on this occasion was an old but trusty 2-4-0, the *Acheron*, in charge of a taciturn and slightly cynical old driver named Jones; and when the new compound engine coupled on ahead of him at Bath he could ill conceal his disgust, especially when those on the trial engine told him to give the *Acheron* just enough steam to keep it going. 'We'll haul the train,' they told him.

Ahrons was one of the party on the footplate of the compound, and the rest of the story can well be left to him. 'For about 5 miles all went well, until we reached a point about 10 yards outside the western end of Box Tunnel, when two loud explosions were heard, and amidst the roar of escaping steam we entered the tunnel. It was pitch dark, and a rain of fragments of cast iron mixed with large gun metal nuts was projected against the roof of the tunnel, from which they rebounded like shrapnel on to the foot-plate. The position was distinctly uncomfortable; no one could tell what had happened, but the driver dare not shut off steam or the train would have "stuck" on the 1 in 100 rise, for had this occurred all the efforts of Mr Jones and the *Acheron* would have been useless.

'As a matter of fact, No. 8 had smashed to bits three of her four pistons and cylinder covers, the fragments and nuts from which had broken the ports and been blown out of the chimney. Luckily no one was hurt, but one or two of us were hit on the shoulders by gun metal nuts. The fourth piston—one of the high pressure ones—was fortunately intact, and by keeping steam on we just managed to crawl out of the Corsham end of the tunnel, the *Acheron* keeping the train moving. At Chippenham we were pulled off by a goods engine that happened to be there, and after taking down the motion, we were ignominiously towed home to Swindon about supper time. As the train emerged from Box Tunnel I happened to look back at the other engine, and to this day can recall to mind the pained expression depicted on the features of *Acheron's* driver, as he hung over the side of his cab. Mr Jones was, as a rule, a very taciturn individual, and on this occasion thought a good deal more than he said, but I was after-wards told that "Jones on compound engines" was worth hearing if only on account of its extreme pungency of expression.'

This episode brings home the rather scanty protection pro-vided for the men, right up to the end of the nineteenth century. Many of them disliked anything in the way of an extensive roof over their heads, and when Patrick Stirling, newly arrived at Doncaster from the Glasgow and South Western Railway, built his first new engines with cabs in which the hitherto waist-high side sheets were continued straight 'up and over', with only a cir-cular hole in each side, the men expressed feelings akin to claustro-phobia and petitioned him to cut some of the sides and roof away. I was never more conscious of the lack of cover provided by the cabs of the Webb engines than when I was making some runs on the footplates of the old '18-inch' 0-6-0 express goods engines in quite recent years. These locomotives, however, notable as being the first main line class to have the Joy valve gear, were working in the last days over the mountainous line from Workington, through Keswick, to Penrith. There was not a great deal of room in their cabs, and for the most part I stood well back, so as not to get in the way of driver or fireman. All was well until we began the long and steeply-graded ascent past Troutbeck; we were not making more than about 20 m.p.h., the engine was being pounded hard, and I quickly became conscious of a rain of cinders falling on my head!

It is sometimes assumed that with the old locomotives anything approaching high speed gave their crews an extremely rough ride. Certainly there are circumstances in which a small engine may dance and pitch more readily than a large one, but rough riding is, in the majority of cases, a matter of maintenance more than anything else. It is true that there have been some classes that included features of design that made them inherently uncomfortable; but these are the exception rather than the rule, and the smaller engines running at the turn of the century were mostly very good riders. Roughness develops as wear increases the play in bearings, increases the side play on guides, and the 'slogger' in reciprocating parts. With stringent maintenance such signs of roughness can be eliminated, but sometimes the preoccupation of workshops with other things results in locomotives running with more slack in bearings, and so on, than is desirable for sweet action. It is not a case of danger, and no suspicion of roughness reaches the passengers. Naturally when any maintenance jobs are postponed it is the older engines, mostly engaged on lighter duties, that suffer, and some who make their acquaintance only at this late stage are inclined to regard their latter-day antics as typical.

Mr David L. Smith has told the story of a James Stirling 4-4-0 stationed at Ayr in 1914. Originally built in 1873, she was one of a class having a splendid reputation as main line express engines, but due to the outbreak of war in 1914 she was allowed to go far beyond her normal span for overhaul, and as Smith wrote: 'so it was that about the middle of 1916 "205" had become something of a holy terror. We used to get her at Dalmellington when our 0-4-2s were washing out, and old Bob Porter, who had been driving trains since 1875, told me she was the wildest thing he had ever stood on. Between Waterside and Dalmellington, on the level stretch of the upper Doon Valley, they would hit up a healthy 50 of a night, and Willie Craig used to pull open 205's regulator at Waterside and say "Now for the Ride of Death!"'

In looking back to conditions of 50 or 60 years ago it is perhaps inevitable that the accidents and the incidents grave and gay have been preserved in memory, rather than the well-ordered working of everyday running. Then, the graceful, single-wheeler express engines required a driving technique all their own. In most cases potential tractive capacity, as represented by the size of the cylinder and the steam pressure in the boiler, was high; but with no more than a single pair of driving wheels the adhesion weight was limited, and any attempt to press such an engine to a rapid accleration would result in severe slipping. Old drivers have told me that the technique in starting was to open up as if you were going 'light engine', very gently, and give more throttle as the engine gradually took hold of the train. Some of the express drivers of the 'nineties did wonderful work with 'single' engines, especially with the Stirling types on the Great Northern; but with all 'singles' it was not only in starting that slipping troubles occurred. In bad weather they would often be slipping for miles at a time on wet rails, and this, of course, led to losses of time.

Ahrons relates an experience on the Great Western with the up Milford boat train, which in the late 'eighties was narrow gauge and left Swindon at 9.5 a.m. A tail of heavy milk vans was always added at Swindon, so that the load was quite an exceptional one for the period, of about 250 tons. It was worked by 2-2-2 engines, and had to run the 41¼ miles from Swindon to Reading in 50 minutes start to stop. The run was not all plain sailing either, for at that time a slack of 25 m.p.h. had to be made through Didcot. It was really hard work, and usually time could be kept only in the fairest of conditions. Then, as Ahrons relates: 'On one unfortunate occasion the engine was No. 1123 *Salisbury*, and the month being October, the leaves were falling rapidly. On running into one of the cuttings overshadowed by trees near Pangbourne (there were then only two, not, as now, four roads) we suddenly came to a long stretch of track the rails of which were literally covered with dead leaves. No. 1123 immediately started slipping, and nothing could stop it, while the regulator was open, so that our speed was reduced to a crawl. Only frequent visits with a bucket of sand to the buffer plank saved us from being pulled up altogether, and as it was we were 8 minutes to the bad at Reading.'

On the great majority of railways the mileages worked by individual engines were much less than those considered necessary on an economic basis today. One found engines and crews allocated to particular services, which they worked to the virtual exclusion of all others. On the Brighton railway each driver had his own engine, so much so that his name was painted in the cab, and he was held responsible for the maintenance of that engine in good order. Naturally he and his fireman did not do the day-to-day repair jobs needed, but it was their job before leaving the shed to see that any defects had been duly attended to by the fitters. As an example of the allocation of individual engines to a train, the 10.18 a.m. from Newport to Paddington can be taken. In 1897 this was the longest non-stop run in the world, and two of the Dean 7 ft. 8 in. 'singles' were stationed at Newport specially, engines 3006 *Courier* and 3042 *Frederick Saunders*. Each engine had its regular driver, and they worked the train on alternate days, a round trip of 286 miles. On the alternate days the duty was a semi-fast train to Swindon, by way of Gloucester. In this way the two men became absolute specialists on the job, and timekeeping was exemplary.

One of the most interesting of nineteenth-century engine workings was the Newhaven continental express on the Brighton line. This train was worked in both directions by contract, that is the driver undertook for a fixed sum to run the train at whatever time it was required. Departures were apt to be erratic in the early days of cross-channel packet service, and in any case depended on the state of the tide. The company provided an engine and fuel, and the driver paid the fireman and the shed cleaners. The engine on the job for many years was one of Mr Stroudley's famous 0-4-2 'Gladstone' class, No. 195 *Cardew*. She led a sheltered and clandestine existence, running only at night, and only 113 miles in the 24 hours. It was in the driver's interest to run the job as economically as possible, and old *Cardew* must have been one of the best kept engines to be found anywhere in the country at the time.

Mention once more of the 'Gladstone' engines and Mr Stroudley's theories that led to his adopting the front-coupled type of wheel arrangement leads me to an experience I had on the footplate of a front-coupled engine of Dugald Drummond's design. It was in the summer of 1945 when I was to ride on the modern express engines hauling an Ilfracombe to London express. I had stayed overnight on Barnstaple, and on going down to the shed in the morning found that a Drummond 0-4-4 tank was about to leave for Ilfracombe running light. The war was barely over, and there lay behind us six very lean years so far as locomotive maintenance had been concerned; yet that little engine ran like a Rolls-Royce. Quietly, effortlessly, we slipped out of Barnstaple; that one could understand with no train. But what I did not bargain for was a gradual acceleration to nearly 60 m.p.h., by which time the engine was taking curve after curve beside the broad estuary of the Taw, riding with superb ease, no jolting, practically no noise. Shades of Stroudley! I thought again of his classic exposition of the front-coupled theory. ' . . . The large leading wheels pass over the points, crossings etc., very easily; causing less disturbance than small ones. They pass round curves without shock or oscillation. . . .' Never could those words have rung more true than with that Drummond 0-4-4 tank, herself built in 1897, and showing her paces to me just sixty years after Stroudley's paper to the Institution of Civil Engineers.

The introduction of longer non-stop runs, and the desire to get more mileage per day from individual engines, began to break down the old principle of one driver, one engine. The later Webb compounds on the London and North Western were mostly double-manned, and the practice of enginemen lodging away from their home stations began to grow. In many ways the train services themselves were in course of change. On the Great Western, for example, Bristol had always been a divisional point; engines were changed there, and the men would work London to Bristol and back, or Bristol to Newton Abbot and back. But with the development of the train services to Cornwall non-stop running between Paddington and Exeter was introduced, to be followed later by the even more spectacular Plymouth non-stops; Exeter was the most important locomotive depot in the west, and the Exeter men immediately took a share in the working of the new trains. To do this they worked west to Plymouth, then took the non-stop to London. They then booked off, lodged the night, and returned with another train next day. On the London and North Western a typical duty from Crewe was: Crewe to London with an up early morning train; book off and lodge; London to Manchester with the evening dining-car train; Manchester to Crewe with the up 'midnight'.

These 'double-home' turns, as they are called, were regarded as tasks for the very *élite* among enginemen, and where two or more sheds were concerned in the working of a train or a group of trains there was usually intense rivalry as to who could do the most punctually, and most efficiently. There was a remarkable case of this on the Great Eastern Railway, when the fast Cromer expresses were put on in 1896. After a short time non-stop running was instituted between London and North Walsham, 130 miles in 160 minutes, and the working of the trains was shared between Norwich and Ipswich sheds, on alternative days. The Norwich men first took a slow morning train to Cromer, then went through to London with the fast up express. In London they turned, and worked back as far as Ipswich with another train. There they booked off and lodged. Next morning they took an express from Ipswich to London; then down with the fast Cromer, non-stop to North Walsham, and finally to their home station on a stopping train. The Ipswich men took the same trains one day earlier. There was a magnificent spirit of healthy rivalry between the two sheds, especially as engines lodged alternate nights at the rival shed! They were all watched and groomed like potential Derby winners, with the happy result that punctuality with the fast trains was almost perfect, and there was a negligible amount of trouble from mechanical failings. The daily mileage was 230— a high figure for those days. The engines first concerned were the Holden 4-2-2 singles of the No. 10 class, the first Great Eastern locomotives since Johnson's day *not* to have stove pipe chimneys.

Coming now to the more intimate details of the footplate at the end of the nineteenth century, a study of locomotives now preserved by the British Transport Commission, in the Railway Museum at York, and elsewhere, reveals an interesting cross-section, and some strong contrasts. Amenities such as seats, screen-wipers, side-windows, canopies were scarcely thought of; but the general finish of the interior showed some wide variations. On the Great Northern 'Stirlings' and the Webb engines of the L&NWR, things were truly spartan and the general impression rough. The North Eastern engines of Edward Fletcher had no more protection in their cabs, but the contrast, nevertheless, was extraordinary. The side sheets, the weather board and the atten-uated roof were all lined with timber; this lining was varnished, and kept beautifully polished, and with the gauges, cocks, and other brasswork kept in an immaculate condition, the effect as may well be imagined was delightful. The greatest contrast, however, was afforded by the later North Eastern cabs on the engines of Wilson Worsdell. The closed-in type, with two side windows, and a canopy extending to the front of the tender was very hand-somely designed; again the interior was wood-lined, though once inside there was not quite so much room as might be imagined. The splashers for the rear pair of coupled wheels were covered by large and wide tool boxes, which while providing seats for the driver and fireman were so wide that they cramped the space on the footplate. The cabs themselves were still built in the 'narrow' tradition, from which a driver could look out all the time without fear of striking his head on bridges, or other passing structures.

One of the locomotives preserved in the museum at York is Wilson Worsdell's 4-4-0 No. 1621, and mention of her brings me to the climax of nineteenth-century express running—the Race to Aberdeen of 1895. It is incredible to realize the improvement in booked running time that took place in a space of only 17 years. In 1878 the journey time from London to Perth was 11½ hours, and to Aberdeen 16 hours; after the Race the times were 8¾ hours and 10½ hours! One can hardly pause to trace every step by which the competition between the East Coast and West Coast routes was kindled and, after smouldering for some years, finally blazed out into the most thrilling out-and-out railway race the world has ever seen; but the final stages make a story that is ever worth the re-telling. By successive cuts in the timing the journey from London to Aberdeen was being done in about 10½ hours, from both King's Cross and Euston; the rival trains both left their respective London termini at 8 p.m., and excitement was mounting daily as faster and faster running was made. The Euston train ran via Crewe, through the Westmorland Hills to Carlisle; thence over the Caledonian—more than 1,000 ft. above sea level at Beattock summit—down to the crossing of the Forth at Stirling, on through Gleneagles, Perth and Forfar. The King's Cross train had easier gradients—York, Durham, Newcastle, over the Border beyond Berwick, then Edinburgh. The great bridge over the Firth of Forth was newly opened; a massive new Tay Bridge stood beside the ruins of Bouch's disastrous essay, and the East Coast route led on through Dundee, Arbroath, and Montrose. And at Kinnaber Junction, 485 miles from King's Cross and 501 miles from Euston, the two routes converged.

Just imagine it! Two express trains, starting from different London termini at the same time, and racing pell-mell through the night for the junction where their routes converged. And yet, withal, the race was not quite such an all-out affair as some would have had it. The West Coast managements, roused from their old dislike of speed, were now setting the pace, and they gradu-

Caledonian Railway: small wheeled 0-4-4 for Cathcart Circle service, built 1899.

The fabulous Great Eastern 'Decapod' 3-cylinder 0-10-0 of 1902; experimental for London suburban work.

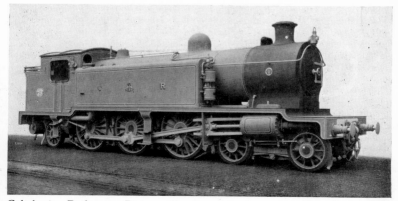

Caledonian Railway, a Pickersgill 4-6-2 tank of 1917, as originally built by North British Locomotive Company.

A Webb 18 inch 0-6-0 express goods of 1880, nicknamed 'Cauliflowers'.

The Whale 'Experiment' class of 1905: engine No. 2027 *Queen Empress*.

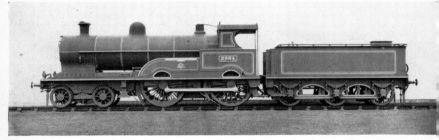

Bowen-Cooke's non-superheater 4-4-0 of 1910, No. 2664 *Queen Mary*, later rebuilt to conform to the 'George the Fifth' class.

The War Memorial engine of 1919: first of the post-war 'Claughtons', No. 191. *Patriot*.

ally worked up to some very fast running throughout from London to Aberdeen. Till the final week, till the 18th of August that was, there was some pretence of working to the published time-tables, though the West Coast regularly sent their train away from intermediate stations well ahead of time, and on one memorable occasion arrived in Aberdeen just 61 minutes early! Throughout the rush of traffic associated with the opening of the grouse shooting season the East Coast made no attempt to beat their rivals at their own game; but once that period was over they too decided to abandon timetables altogether, and get through as fast as they could. Even so this idea was not properly understood on the North British, and after the Great Northern and North Eastern had made fast time the train was detained at both Edinburgh and Dundee. But on the night of Tuesday August 20, both sides were for the first time really racing, and racing on level terms.

By this time the 'race' was being featured in the Press of the day as a popular sporting contest; partisanship began to run high, and the rival managements had their own prestige at stake. Yet at this extremely critical moment the Great Northern, hitherto indisputably the fastest line in the country, disappointed its most ardent supporters. The management was eager enough. The Superintendent of the Line, F. P. Cockshott, was the arch-priest of speed on the British railways, and one finds Patrick Stirling instructing his divisional officers: 'Put your men on their mettle.' But the men seemed reluctant to go really hard; there is evidence to suggest that they regarded the whole affair with some misgivings, and definitely held their engines in lest they should afterwards be compelled to run regularly at much faster scheduled speeds. Nevertheless the night of August 20-21 was, in retrospect, one of intense excitement. One writes 'in retrospect', for the news of the rival trains and their progress could not have come through other than slowly.

It is rather amusing to speculate as to how such an event would be 'covered' today: television cameras at King's Cross and Euston; BBC observers giving a running commentary from helicopters flying above the rival trains, while the *pièce de resistance* would have been another batch of television cameras in the lonely signal box at Kinnaber Junction. 'Viewers' would have seen the stately Webb compound *Adriatic* pull out of Euston to the cheers of her supporters, while at King's Cross a Stirling 8 ft. bogie single, No. 668, took out the rival train. Mile by mile the North Western was soon drawing steadily ahead, and the first 100 miles from Euston were covered in 95 minutes; but then came the unexpected. By a stroke of ill-luck the pick-up water scoop of the *Adriatic* sustained some slight damage; no water could be picked up at the troughs near Lichfield, and it became necessary to stop for water at Stafford. There they stood for $3\frac{1}{2}$ precious minutes, and then tore on to Crewe, where the *Adriatic* was relieved by the little 'Precedent' class engine *Hardwicke*. In the meantime the Great Northern had covered the $188\frac{1}{4}$ miles from King's Cross to York in 187 minutes, with an intermediate stop to change engines at Grantham. Throughout the night the West Coast were making the faster running; but the trains dashed on through Scotland and it became a question of whether the West Coast would be fast enough to overcome their $16\frac{1}{2}$-mile handicap in distance.

That night the Caledonian left Perth at 3.35 a.m., 450 miles from Euston in 455 minutes with 52 miles left to the winning-post at Kinnaber. At that moment the North British was storming up through Fife, with a stop to make at Dundee, engines to be changed, and a very difficult piece of line to cover between Arbroath and Montrose. She was nearer than the Caledonian, but her road here was far harder. But, by thunder, it was going to be a close finish! While the North British were in Dundee, the Caledonian were out on the level grades of Strathmore, going like the wind; but very soon the North British were going too, along the coast through Carnoustie, on to Arbroath, and then came that awkward stretch to Montrose. Attention now becomes riveted upon the lone signal box of Kinnaber, and one wonders how much the signalman there experienced the thrill of the race. Today television viewers would have heard his life story, and listened to his favourite gramophone record—but in actual fact, we do not even know his name. Then, earlier than ever before, at 4.20 a.m.

came a ring: Dubton Junction—the Caledonian were first! Road set; signals pulled off, but in less than a minute came a second ring. The North British were at Montrose, but they were too late; the Caley had the road and at 4.22 a.m. the flyer came past—501¾ miles from Euston in the amazing time, for the year 1895, of 502 minutes.

The next night the tables were turned. The East Coast pressed home their advantage in mileage, and passed Kinnaber, 485½ miles by their route, in 482½ minutes. One big factor in this most spectacular achievement was a marvellous run by the North Eastern over the 124½ miles from Newcastle to Edinburgh in 113 minutes. At Kinnaber they were 15½ minutes ahead of the West Coast, and Aberdeen was reached at the hitherto incredible hour of 4.40 a.m. From end to end now, the average speed was over 60 m.p.h., and on that night of August 21-22, the East Coast companies set up a world's record. As a railway wit remarked: 'The Aberdonians were now rubbing their eyes, and wondering if at this rate of acceleration their Granite City would soon become, in point of railway time, a northern suburb of London!' Well they might, for in one month a modest *three hours* had been knocked off the journey time. The East Coast people were evidently satisfied with their great run of August 21-22, and on the following night they reverted to normal running. But that very night the West Coast, with the train load cut to only three coaches, went their hardest yet, and made a run which stands as the British long-distance record, and which, so far as steam traction is concerned, seems likely to remain the record for all time. They reached Aberdeen in the utterly brilliant time of 8 hr. 32 min.—540 miles in 512 minutes!

That was the end of the racing, and perhaps as well too, for by that time some of the most fervid advocates of speed were beginning to grow apprehensive. It was safe enough out on the open road, with long spells at 65 to 70 m.p.h., but some of the drivers were running very fast through difficult junctions, and on the North Eastern, to judge from the personal experiences of certain shrewd observers, there were some really narrow escapes, particularly in the rounding of the Portobello S-curve in the early hours of August 21. The run from Newcastle to Edinburgh on the following night—124.4 miles in 113 minutes—was one of the finest performances of the whole race, and was in striking contrast to the unenterprising work done by the sister engine between York and Newcastle; for while this latter engine, No. 1621, over one of the most perfect racing stretches in the whole country achieved no better than level time from the start by Durham, 66.1 miles, No. 1620 over a harder road was through Berwick (66.9 miles) in the even hour. On the final night the Caledonian train covered more than 65 miles in the first hour northward from Perth, but perhaps the most brilliant performance of all was that of the North Western 2-4-0 *Hardwicke* — the smallest engine used by any of the companies concerned—in running the 141 miles from Crewe to Carlisle at an average speed from start to stop of 67 m.p.h. Of course, the load was light, but if one reckons the tender as part of the train the engine was pulling $3\frac{1}{2}$ times its own weight; this is almost exactly the same proportion as that of a modern 'King' class engine working the 7-coach 'Bristolian' express, on which the average speed scheduled between Paddington and Temple Meads is just over 67 m.p.h.

Those little Webb 2-4-0s were 'flyers', and used to romp away to 80 and even 85 m.p.h.; even so the pace round curves and through some of the junctions in Lancashire must have been pretty hot. Compared with modern engines, however, they had a fairly low centre of gravity, and would be less likely to turn over on that account. It may be no more than a coincidence, but a year later the same train carrying its normal load came to grief on the sharp curve north of Preston, through excessive speed. It was drawn by two of the Webb 2-4-0 engines and, although the coaches were flung in all directions and damage was severe, neither engine turned over. The leading one jumped the rails at the sharp curve, the second followed suit, and the two continued very nearly in a straight line, hurdling over tracks and obstructions till they came to rest completely upright, and relatively undamaged. Reverting to the race, however, speeds on level track ranged round 70 m.p.h.

not more, and the Great Northern 8 ft. bogie singles were generally slower than this. These speeds are important, and significant,
in view of developments that came early in the twentieth century.

Although one could hardly expect the speeds of August
20-21-22 to be sustained in ordinary service, the immediate legacy
from the race was the booking of some fast schedules by the rival
night Scotch expresses. The West Coast train, for example, was
required to average 56 m.p.h. from Wigan to Carlisle, and to run
the ensuing 117 miles to Stirling in 125 minutes. But the smash at
Preston in 1896 sounded a note of alarm and warning, and coming
at a time when there were pressing calls for increased amenities in
travel the companies competing for the Anglo-Scottish traffic,
faced with the prospect of considerably heavier loads, due to the
use of corridor coaches, dining and sleeping cars, were, generally
speaking, glad enough to ease the pace. In this respect they were
coming once more into line with all the rest of the country, which,
taken all round, was not famed for high speed running sixty years
ago. One must add, however, that save in the south and south-
east punctuality was taken very seriously and except at times of
the greatest holiday pressure the standard was high.

The race to the North had one unexpected consequence. Long-
suffering travellers reading of the nightly exploits of the Aberdeen expresses were moved to write to *The Times*, and in the
autumn of 1895 there was a long correspondence under the heading of 'The Crawl to the South' in which the speed achievements
of the London, Brighton and South Coast, and the South Eastern
Railways received some diverting publicity. There was a Hastings
express, booked to cover the 74 miles to Victoria in 200 minutes,
which without any delays contrived to be 53 min. late. There was
the comedy of the missing mailbag, which the guard of a late evening missed, and stopped his train forthwith; search parties were
sent in all directions, other trains were stopped, and kept waiting
far into the night; and above all there was that celebrated 'flyer',
the 10.31 p.m. train from Sutton to London Bridge. This train
seemed to have some mysterious objection to starting on the day
it was booked to start; all too frequently it left well after midnight,

until to support the rapidly growing snowball of correspondence in its columns *The Times* was moved to comment editorially:

'The Southern managers have no doubt been aware that it would be of very little use for them to attempt to rival the magnificent performances of the Great Northern and London and North Western companies. Their rolling-stock and the well-established traditions of their companies put it out of the question that they should try this with success. They have hit accordingly upon another method of distinguishing themselves more suited to their capacities. They have chosen frankly a very different form of distinction, and the struggle between them now is which of them can claim to have established the slowest, the most unpunctual, and the most inconvenient service of trains. The real rivals are the South Eastern and the London, Brighton and South Coast lines, and the performances of both are so singular, and their claims to the honour which they are seeking are so nearly balanced, that there are good grounds for a difference of opinion as to their respective merits. Very bad both are, this at least the most severe critic must admit, difficult as he would find it, on a review of the evidence, to say with certainty which of the two has the better right to call itself absolutely the worst line in the country.'

The engines of Stroudley and James Stirling got few chances to show what they could really do in the way of speed, and on the South Eastern the civil engineer had for many years imposed an overall limit of 60 m.p.h. By far the fastest running in the south was made on the Continental Mails of the London Chatham and Dover Railway. These did show some excellent speeds, and some runs made in June 1896 with special trains were certainly the equal of much performance during the 1895 race to the North. Outward bound there was a run from Victoria to Dover Pier, $78\frac{1}{2}$ miles in 82 minutes, start to stop, while on the return run two days later the time was only half a minute longer. The load in each case was 70 tons, the same as on the final West Coast racing run to Aberdeen.

One of the greatest handicaps to train running, affecting all trains alike, is fog. The history of signalling arrangements designed to cope with such conditions is a long and complicated one, and early suggestions included devices on locomotives that would flash a red light straight into the driver's face in cases of danger. In view of the prevalence of fog in the London area, reputedly on a worse scale sixty years ago than now, it is rather surprising that the first sustained attempt to provide a definite signal in the engine cab was made, not on any of the London railways but on the North Eastern. At the time of the race Wilson Worsdell had a very energetic assistant in the person of Vincent Raven, who was responsible for locomotive running and for the few electrical appliances then to be found on a railway. Now Raven, even at that early stage in his career, had a way of looking at things on a broad scale; he had a flair for administration rather than the finer points of detail, and he gradually acquired an enviable reputation for getting things done. Like F. W. Webb and Patrick Stirling he was the son of a clergyman, but one could hardly imagine a greater contrast than between Webb, who dictated down to the finest detail, and gave his subordinate little scope, and Vincent Raven.

It was with his assistant R. Baister that Raven developed the first system of cab signalling on the North Eastern Railway. It was extremely simple in theory. In the districts so equipped each signal along the line had working with it a small arm fixed in the middle of the track. If the signal arm was in the clear position the arm was lowered, but when the signal was at caution or danger the arm was raised. The locomotive had a pendulum lever suspended beneath the footplate, and when passing a signal at caution or danger the pendulum lever was struck and pushed upwards. This movement caused a steam whistle to sound in the cab, so warning the driver of the position of the signal he was passing. At first engineers of other railways were sceptical; it was thought that the blow imparted to the pendulum lever when passing—and 'distant' signals might be passed at almost full express speed—would lead to fractures, and fail to sound the whistle. In actual practice, however, the mechanism was so skilfully designed that no trouble was experienced on this account, and the engineman came to place full reliance in it—a very sure sign of its reliability.

Nevertheless the danger of a false clear remained. Damage to the arm might be caused in other circumstances, and if the head became broken away the conditions would be inherently dangerous. No whistle would be sounded, and a driver could be misled into believing the signal was clear. The system was used for many years on the North Eastern Railway, and there are no recorded instances of its failure in any way.

So we come to the turn of the century. The railway scene in Great Britain was undergoing many changes. The possibilities of electric traction had already been demonstrated and there were prophets foretelling the speedy obsolescence of all steam locomotives. Traffic was enormously on the increase; many railway directors and shareholders were appalled at the huge and rising coal bill, and in a spirit of economy, if not parsimony, there was tendency to 'make do' where schemes of capital expenditure were concerned. The use of automatic continuous brakes on passenger trains had been made compulsory by law, but many farsighted men urged the equipment of all goods trains as well. The example of America was hammered on many a public occasion. But there were arguments against such a move on operational grounds, quite apart from the cost of such a changeover, and the job remains largely untouched today.

And as the railways of this country entered upon the new century so too many of the older, familiar personalities were passing from the engineering scene. Patrick Stirling died in 1895, still in harness in his 76th year; Adams had retired, while Dean, Johnson and Webb were all nearing the end of their careers. The new men were already beginning to make their mark: Aspinall on the Lancashire and Yorkshire, H. A. Ivatt on the Great Northern, and McIntosh on the Caledonian had already produced outstanding locomotives while the Drummond brothers were approaching their zenith. Railways still attracted some of the greatest engineers of the day. Despite the steam turbine, despite electricity, despite the promise inherent in the new motor cars a tremendous field of research and development lay ahead in steam locomotion; but no one event gave a greater fillip to the improvement of train services, to the amenities of travel, or to the tightening up of punctuality than the momentous decision of the Manchester, Sheffield and Lincolnshire Railway to extend their line to London. This company had for many years had a reputation as a fighter, personified by the aggressively competitive character of its great chairman, Sir Edward Watkin. But the project of a London extension from the coalfields of Nottinghamshire surpassed all. There were already three trunk lines to the south; the MSL proposal was bitterly opposed by all established interests, but they won the day, and forthwith changed their name to Great Central Railway, with results to be told later.

This chapter may well be closed with a mention of the most spectacular of all Sir Edward Watkin's railway projects. He was at one and the same time Chairman not only of the MSL but of the South Eastern, and of the Metropolitan, and then, in 1894, he pioneered the railway up Snowdon. The lovers of mountain solitudes were aghast. Was there to be no escaping the onset of the age of steam? Yet when it came to be built the Snowdon Mountain Railway looked so puny a thing as to sink virtually into insignificance against the tremendous precipices and vast panorama of Snowdonia. Built on the model of several successful Swiss rack railways the first steam locomotive and coach ascended the mountain early in 1896; but the safety arrangements on the track to keep the pinion of the locomotive always in contact with the rack were not then perfect, and on the most exposed and thrilling piece of all, high on the Saddle, the locomotive overrode the rack, left the rails, and pitched 2,500 ft. down the mountainside into the Pass of Llanberis. It was not until more than a year later that the line was opened to the public. Despite the prophets of woe the venture was immediately successful, and today the line seems more popular than ever. All through the summer months the service is patronized to its fullest capacity, while to the locomotive enthusiast the sight of those little engines thundering away up the mountain, with a vertical column of smoke from their tall stacks rising sometimes 20 or 30 ft. into the air, is a vivid survival of Victorian railroading at its most picturesque.

CHAPTER SIX

THE HIGH NOON OF STEAM

FOR Great Britain the end of the nineteenth century was no mere milestone in the calendar. It marked, with a rather extraordinary precision, the end of an age—an age of evolution, of unrest, of expansion, of colonial wars; and over public affairs at home there brooded a vague, Puritanical kind of restraint that earned for the Victorians a reputation for stuffiness. But the accession of King Edward VII changed everything. The new sovereign, although passing beyond middle age himself, was intensely interested in all the mechanical and scientific developments of his time; and just as in court circles he restored all those many points of discipline, decorum and etiquette which had become slovenly or disused in the latter years of his mother's reign, so in public life his insistence on smartness and punctuality had a salutary effect all round. It was not enough for Britain to be the wealthiest nation on earth, and the memorable 'Wake up, England' speech of the Prince of Wales set a seal upon the leadership that was now coming from the Royal Family in general.

For the railways of this country the end of the century was also a milestone in their history. The art of locomotive engineering was rapidly approaching a vital system of cross roads, and viewing the events of the years 1900 to 1910 in retrospect it seems that some engineers—among them, too, some of the most eminent men of the day—were not sure which way to go. The Drummond 4-4-0, now seen in its full maturity on the London and South Western, and on the Highland, can be taken as a typical embodiment of all that was best in nineteenth-century practice: a robust chassis, simple cylinder and valve design, with ample passages for the flow of steam, and a good boiler, easily fired. The South Western earned the nickname of the 'Greyhounds', while of the Highland 'Small Bens', a Scottish driver once told Hamilton Ellis: 'Yer mither could driver her, ay, and get sixty oot o' her.' But certain of the basic features of the design that made it so simple and so successful precluded any enlargement. The slide valves were placed between the cylinders, and the cylinders were between the frames. Dugald Drummond had already used certain artifices in construction, at which some engineers looked askance, in order to obtain the port areas he needed for free running, and yet the increasing weight of trains clearly demanded larger and more powerful locomotives. The way in which various engineers tackled the problem of getting enhanced power forms an absorbing study. It was a time when locomotive superintendents still had a fairly free hand, and the lines they took in many cases reflected the personalities of the men themselves.

The direct successors of Dugald Drummond on the Scottish railways had an essentially sound basis on which to work; these successors were Matthew Holmes on the North British, and John Farqhuarson McIntosh on the Caledonian. There was actually a period of five years on the latter line between the Drummond and the McIntosh regimes, when John Lambie was locomotive superintendent; but the express locomotives he built were little more than repetitions of the Drummond type, with slightly altered boiler mountings. It has been suggested, too, that the influence of Hugh Smellie was also discerned in the Lambie engines. He was the chosen successor to Drummond, but died only a few months after his appointment. He had built for the Glasgow and South Western a class of very fine 4-4-0 locomotives, and some details of the valve setting of those engines may have been incorporated in future Caledonian designs. But it is with McIntosh that we are now concerned. One might broadly classify locomotive men of that day into those whose interests lay in engine design, in running, and in works matters. A blend of all three was necessary in order to hold down any job of major responsibility, but it is noticeable that many men naturally tended to lay emphasis upon the particular branch of the service in which the larger part of their earlier experience had been gained. McIntosh was essentially a running man. He had been a driver, and a locomotive inspector, and had lost an arm in a footplate accident; and immediately upon taking up the post of locomotive superintendent in 1895 he set himself the task of producing a real 'driver's engine'.

The Drummonds were excellent engines, but the Caledonian men had found that if they were thrashed up the banks they tended to run short of steam. This, of course, was exactly in accordance with Drummond's intentions—the engines were so proportioned that they couldn't be thrashed. Johnson did just the same on his Midland 4-4-0 engines. Although the process of thrashing extracts a thrilling performance out of a small engine it usually results in a disproportionately high consumption of fuel, and worse still causes heavy maintenance charges on the boiler. But McIntosh wanted more power, and he got it by building engines to the basic Drummond layout, but with much larger boilers. At first he was outstandingly successful. There were mighty few engines of 1895-1900 vintage, if any, that could have run trains of 170 to 200 tons over the 117·8 miles from Carlisle to Stirling in two hours, or less; the first engine of the new class, No. 721, was named *Dunalastair*, and very soon that name was a household word among locomotive men and enthusiasts alike. From the first series of 1896 McIntosh went on, and built bigger and bigger 'Dunalastairs', but on reaching the fourth series, although the total heating surface was 1,615 sq. ft., compared with the 1,208 sq. ft. of a Drummond, and boiler pressure had been increased from 150 to 180 lb. per sq. in., the cylinder diameter was only one inch larger—19 in. against 18 in. of the Drummond. In consequence one could not get true expansive working when running hard, and the McIntosh engines were accordingly extravagant on coal.

The climax so far as boiler design on the Caledonian was reached in 1903 when two huge 4-6-0 locomotives with no less than 2,523 sq. ft. of heating surface were built at St Rollox works. But by that time McIntosh and his Caledonian locomotives had already become something of a legend. They rejoiced in one of the most beautiful liveries that ever adorned a steam locomotive; they ran hard, kept excellent time, and looked massive and modern, while conforming to the best British traditions of simplicity and neatness in outline. Caledonian blue was a beautiful colour in itself, but in the high noon of steam the basic colour was not all. One realized that when the same colour, or something very near it, was adopted for a time on the largest express engines of the nationalized British Railways. When newly painted, and well-cleaned our modern 'Pacifics' of various designs looked well enough, but they lacked the magic of J. F. McIntosh's Caledonians; their underframes were black, and the wheels black too, whereas the Caledonians had the running-plate valences in a deep rich purple, and the wheels were painted blue. Mere ornamentation is of no account. For a time the Great Western 'Kings' also sported the blue, but their copper capped chimneys and polished brass safety valve columns that look so well with their own Brunswick green looked strangely out of keeping above a bright blue boiler!

The influence of McIntosh's work was profound. Following the race to the north in 1895 enthusiasts looked eagerly for any signs of the revival of the racing in the following year, and even if there was no racing, as such, those who travelled through the summer nights and clocked the running of the Tourist express between Carlisle and Stirling were usually well rewarded. With loads of 150 tons and more the 'Dunalastairs' were night after night making times nearly as fast as those of the race, but with nearly double the load. One of them starting from Carlisle—almost at sea level—passed Beattock summit, 1,015 ft. up, and 49¾ miles from the start in 52¾ minutes. Charles Rous-Marten, the leading railway journalist of the day, wrote enthusiastic articles in *The Engineer* and elsewhere, and the obvious success of the 'Dunalastairs' started a fashion among locomotive engineers for big boilers. Even before McIntosh himself had built his big 4-6-os of 1903, the Great Northern, throwing to the winds the small domeless boiler traditions of Patrick Stirling, had produced a locomotive that by the sheer girth of its boiler caused an out-and-out sensation in 1902. Until 1903, however, McIntosh himself had not felt it necessary to go beyond the old traditional bogie 4-coupled express engine of the 4-4-0 type for the heaviest passenger work.

In the last 25 years—1930 to 1955 that is—the 4-6-0 has become the most characteristically British type of all, and it is used in almost every type of main line service. Its first introduction took place on the Highland Railway in 1894. There Mr David Jones, who had succeeded Stroudley as locomotive superintendent, for many years remained faithful to the Allan style of front-end framing, and a Stroudleyesque cab. His outside-cylinder 4-4-0s were powerful so far as they went, but the Highland is a line of exceptional grading, and oftimes of exceptional weather, and there were no half measures about the advance in power made by Mr Jones with his 4-6-0 design of 1894. Compared with the largest existing 4-4-0s on the line the new engines, with larger cylinders, higher boiler pressure and smaller wheels had a nominal tractive effort of 75 per cent greater, and this potential capacity was backed up by a fine boiler. As we see later many engineers came to grief when they designed greatly enlarged boilers; the increased length of the barrel caused some difficulty. But David Jones struck almost ideal proportions in his pioneer 4-6-0 engines of 1894, and the fifteen locomotives of the class did excellent work from the outset. They had the distinctive louvred chimneys, and originally were decked in the later Highland version of the Stroudley style of painting, with all its gay lining out, but with a bright apple green for the basic colour instead of the Brighton yellow.

The next milestone to be recorded in the swing from small to large engines is the introduction of the 'Atlantic' type. By placing a pair of carrying wheels behind the drivers a longer boiler could be put on to the traditional British 4-4-0. By a coincidence the first English examples of the type came out within a few months of each other, both designed by engineers who had at one time been locomotive superintendents of the Great Southern and Western Railway, in Ireland: John A. F. Aspinall, who had left Inchicore in 1886 to go to the Lancashire and Yorkshire Railway, and Henry A. Ivatt, who succeeded him at Inchicore, and who became locomotive superintendent of the Great Northern Railway in 1896, after the death of Patrick Stirling. In 1896-1900 their problems were very different. On the Lancashire and Yorkshire an intensely complicated and interwoven network of train services and connections were being developed among the crowded industrial districts on either side of the Pennines; lengthy trains were not needed, it was speed and frequency of service that mattered. With such over-riding requirements a need to accelerate quickly went almost without saying. On the Great Northern and the East Coast route in general the competition in speed was over, and the competition in amenities had begun; with corridor coaches, more luxurious accommodation, dining cars, and so on, express train loads were rising from the 150 tons of Stirling's day to 250 and 300 tons.

Of the two 'Atlantic' designs Ivatt's was the first to appear, in 1898, from Doncaster works. At once it was seen that the practice of Patrick Stirling had been completely reversed; the cylinder volume was 20 per cent less than in the final batch of Stirling's 8 ft. bogie singles, though the Ivatt 'Atlantic' had a 40 per cent increase in total heating surface. The coupled wheels of the 'Atlantic' were naturally smaller, and the nominal tractive efforts of the two engines were almost exactly the same; but like McIntosh's engines on the Caledonian the larger boiler gave the 'Atlantic' a capacity for being thrashed, while the use of four coupled wheels with greater adhesion weight lessened the chances of slipping on a greasy rail. In practice the new 'Atlantics' were able to take much heavier loads than the Stirling engines had done. On the Lancashire and Yorkshire the whole problem of motive power was much more complicated, and the 'Atlantics' engines introduced in 1899 formed only one very small facet of the whole. Their designer, John Audley Frederick Aspinall, was rapidly becoming one of the really outstanding figures in the Railway world. Born of a well-known Lancashire family his father was a Q.C., and in his own approach to engineering and railway administration problems Aspinall himself brought something of the judicial cast of mind. He was trained at Crewe under those famous North Western engineers John Ramsbottom and F. W. Webb, and after his work in Ireland it was no coincidence that he came back to his native

Lancashire, in 1886. For John Ramsbottom after retiring from the L&NWR became a director of the Lancashire and Yorkshire, and was then Chairman of the Rolling Stock Committee.

In the thirteen years during which he was Chief Mechanical Engineer of the Lancashire and Yorkshire Railway he wrought a positive transformation. He built the fine new works at Horwich, to replace the cramped and inadequate depots previously used for engine repair at Miles Platting and Bury. Under his shrewd and sympathetic guidance a new town grew up round the works; he was prominent in founding the Mechanics' Institute, and simultaneously he designed and built a new range of powerful standard locomotives. In what might be termed 'the middle ages' of railways few men had such opportunities for building on the grand scale, and still fewer grasped their opportunities more brilliantly. John Aspinall was proving himself a man of very broad outlook and outstanding administrative ability, by no means confined to engineering work. In the intense traffic operated over some sections of the line he saw the possibilities of electrification, and in the early nineteen hundreds many shrewd observers felt it would not be long before the whole network of lines centred upon Liverpool and Manchester would be converted. In 1899 he had the distinction, unique among British locomotive engineers, of becoming General Manager of the railway he served, but while the range of his responsibilities widened immeasurably he remained first and foremost an engineer. In course of time he was President of the Institution of Mechanical Engineers, and he followed this by achieving the blue riband of the engineering profession, when he was elected President of the Institution of Civil Engineers in 1919.

The 'Atlantic' locomotives of 1899 remained a monument to his skill as an engine designer. Striking in appearance, if not entirely measuring up to the highest aesthetic standards, they soon gained a reputation for very fast running. At that time the Lancashire and Yorkshire was in hot competition with the North Western and the Cheshire Lines for the inter-City traffic between Liverpool and Manchester. A positive swarm of expresses covered

Cecil W. Paget, Midland Railway.

C. J. Bowen-Cooke, London and No Western Railway.

gald Drummond, London and South Western Railway.

R. E. L. Maunsell, South Eastern a Chatham, and later Southern Railway

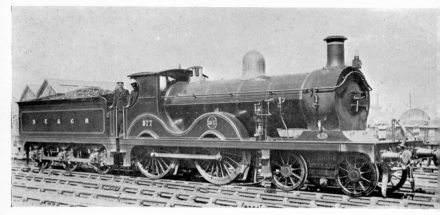

One of the beautiful Wainwright Class 'D' 4-4-0s of 1901, South Eastern and Chatham Railway.

A Drummond 4-cylinder 4-6-0 of Class T.14, London and South Western Railway

Drummond's last design, the LSWR large express 4-4-0 Class 'D.15' of 1912.

the distance in 40 minutes, and as the L&Y had the farthest to go —36 miles, as against 31½ miles over the North Western—they had to run the hardest. Many of the crack trains consisted of no more than coaches, and on these the Aspinall 'Atlantics' used regularly to run up to 85 and even 90 m.p.h. In their early days there were persistent stories of speeds of 100 m.p.h. and more, but these have never been authenticated. They ran the Manchester businessmen's 'Club' trains, to Southport and to Blackpool and took the longer distance trains to Leeds, York and Hull. In all 40 were built, and at a time when their designer himself was becoming very electrically minded they kept the flag of steam flying nobly, so long as the train loads remained relatively light.

On the Great Northern, however, Ivatt was not satisfied with his first 'Atlantics', for in 1902 he took the extraordinary step of building a further engine, identical with the 1898 class so far as machinery was concerned, but having an enormous boiler with a diameter of 5 ft. 6 in. In seven years Doncaster works had progressed in express passenger engine boilers from a total heating surface of 1,032 sq. ft. and a grate area of 20 sq. ft., to figures of 2,500 and 31 sq. ft. in Mr Ivatt's 'Atlantic' engine No. 251. The cylinders were small enough on the engines of 1898, but on No. 251 in relation to the size of the boiler they were tiny. I would not for one moment write deprecatingly of one who was at the same time a fine engineer, a great gentleman and a charming personality; but he does seem to have had a fetish in this one direction. On a railway occasion soon after he had succeeded Stirling he said to the men: 'I am following in the footsteps of a very great engineer, and whatever changes I have to make I will see to it that you have plenty of steam.' Again he laid down the oft-quoted principle, that the power of an engine is its capacity to boil water. True enough, but if the cylinders are not big enough to use the steam so generated the engine will be deficent in power. So it was with the '251' class. To get any speed on the level or uphill they had to be worked with a late cut-off; the back pressure was high, the blast terrific, and they could have put in a strong claim to being Britain's noisiest express engines.

And yet, while these engines would, in modern parlance, be called a 'near failure', Ivatt had incorporated in them most of the ingredients of a resounding triumph, and it was left to his successor to make those alterations that turned them into one of the locomotive phenomena of the twentieth century. Henry Ivatt never lived to see this triumph; he retired in 1911, and died in 1920. The changes to his 'Atlantics' were then being made, but the first World War had just put a temporary stop to all spectacular express running, and the prowess of the modified engines was yet to be demonstrated. A full 50 years after the building of No. 251, however, his son and his two daughters participated in a wonderful celebration, the Centenary of Doncaster Works, and travelled in a special train, The Plant Centenarian, hauled by two Ivatt 'Atlantics'—No. 990, the pioneer of 1898, and No. 251; the two engines, retired from active service and preserved as historical relics, were overhauled and rendered fit for express service, and on the southbound run from Leeds to King's Cross they reached at one point a speed of 80 m.p.h. On this trip my wife and I had the honour of meeting and travelling with the Misses Ivatt, and the vivacious interest of these two elderly ladies in every feature of the trip was most moving to see; they must climb on to the footplate of both engines, make themselves thoroughly and delightfully at home with drivers and firemen. Here indeed on this special occasion, both in locomotive power and in these passengers, was a link with the high noon of steam.

From the Great Northern we must now move to the Great Central. The building of the London extension, which was opened throughout to Marylebone in 1899, witnessed a striking repetition of earlier railway history. In 1850 the Great Northern had opened its line to London in face of terrific opposition from the established routes. The new railway had to fight tooth and nail for its traffic, and did so by offering accelerated service. But while the Great Northern had only one serious competitor for the north traffic, in the Euston route, the Great Central was up against three. Whereas she had previously been in partnership with the Great Northern in running a fast London-Manchester service via Sheffield, Retford and Grantham she now took on the North Western and the Midland single-handed, with the disadvantage of a longer and more severely graded route. There was only one way to attract business, and that was by speed. On the London extension the trains were light, and as soon as the track had fully consolidated a 55-60 m.p.h. standard of running was established for all the fast trains. Every express had a buffet car attached. The locomotive effort required to run these trains was small, but that did not matter.

At first the locomotives were of a neat though undistinguished design prepared by Mr Harry Pollitt; but in June 1900 he was suc-ceeded by Mr John G. Robinson, who, like Aspinall and Ivatt, came from an Irish railway, and this time the Waterford, Limerick and Western. But like Aspinall and Ivatt, J. G. Robinson was not an Irishman either by birth or training; his father, Matthew Robin-son, was locomotive engineer of the Bristol and Exeter section of the Great Western and 'J.G.' was trained at Swindon under Joseph Armstrong and William Dean. In the early nineteen hun-dreds the enterprise of the Great Central management in running attractive train services knew no bounds and Robinson matched the tremendous 'drive' of Sir Sam Fay with a series of locomotives that for sheer grace of outline have never been surpassed. Some engineers built handsome express engines; others built isolated examples that could be called real ornamental masterpieces, but Robinson produced a little gem every time. His six-coupled and eight-coupled goods engines were unsurpassed for grace of out-line, and when it came to express passenger types I need only re-call that his 'Atlantics' of 1903 were nicknamed the 'Jersey Lilies'.

At that time few of the expresses on the London extension loaded to more than five or six coaches, and one may well ask why 'Atlantic' engines were needed at all. For tractive purposes they certainly were not; Robinson's 4-4-0 engines could have done the job perfectly well. But for a line like the Great Central prestige was all-important, and they simply had to be in the fore-front of the 'big-engine' fashion of the day. The 'Jersey Lilies' may have been built for prestige, but they were beautifully proportioned, not only in their outward appearance but in their technical details.

Unlike the Great Northern 'Atlantics' their cylinder and boiler capacity was nicely balanced though it was not until many years later that their capacity for working heavy loads at high speed was seriously put to the test. Then they certainly emerged with flying colours, but in the colours of the London and North Eastern Railway—no longer the Great Central. In their early days they carried the rich dark green livery, with a restrained scheme of lining out, but with the side sheets of the splashers, and the underframes in crimson. The Great Central coat-of-arms, with its motto 'Forward', was displayed on both engine and tender. No opportunity was lost for showing off those beautiful engines, and on two occasions they worked special trains as far afield as Plymouth.

How utterly different was the locomotive situation that developed on the London and North Western Railway! Here was the richest and busiest of all the British railways; a line famed for smartness and service, for punctuality, and yet through the adventures in compounding indulged in by F. W. Webb this great company found itself desperately short of locomotives in the years 1901 and 1902. There were no featherweights trains here. While the Great Central was carrying 150-ton trains, and the Great Northern 250, many of the North Western expresses loaded to over 350 tons, and nearly every train of any importance had to be double-headed. In face of the new competition from the Great Central the Manchester service was accelerated; the Midland was speeded up too, and when Webb finally retired in 1903 his successor, George Whale, had a stupendous task. There was no question of winning prestige with large, highly embellished engines; the only prestige that mattered to the North Western was the punctual operation of the service, all over the line, without the absurdity of using two engines on every train of any weight.

George Whale was a 'running man'. He knew from the gruelling experience of operating the traffic during the Webb régime that by far the most reliable of the passenger engines were not any of the compounds, but the little 2-4-0 'Jumbos'. They could take the most merciless thrashing for hours on end; they steamed under almost any conditions, and they could run like stags. In 1903 there was no time for theory or experiments; the new engines were wanted quickly, and Whale at once set the Crewe drawing office to work on a modern 4-4-0. They worked swiftly, and so did the shops, and in May 1904, the new engine, the *Precursor*, took the road. Precursor indeed! It remains a classic example for all time; no frills, no gadgets, the work of a practical man who knew exactly what he wanted and produced the answer in record time. There were literally no teething troubles; they were put straight into heavy traffic, and by the summer of 1904 'Precursors' were coming out of Crewe works at the rate of one per week—an astonishing piece of productivity.

But no less astonishing was their work on the road. The men took to them at once. They needed no fussing, no nursing; the traffic department piled on the coaches, the firemen piled on the coal, and the drivers flailed them along with zest. Out of Euston went train after train: the Irish Mails, the Scotch expresses, the Liverpools, the Manchesters, loaded to 350 or 400 tons; one 'Precursor' to each, and no thoughts of double-heading now. Nothing like it had been seen in the country before, and the practical efficiency of the engines could be seen on the arrival side of the station where train after train of similar loading came in on time after long non-stop runs averaging 52 to 55 m.p.h. And behind it all was the retiring and unpublicized figure of the Chief Mechanical Engineer, an unsmiling bearded little man, who served nearly a lifetime as a subordinate, and who, in five momentous years, swept away the cherished and misguided precepts of Webb and gave the North Western a magnificent stud of new engines. The stature of Whale grows to gigantic proportions as his period is seen in retrospect: to use the Churchillian idiom, never in the history of locomotives had so much been achieved in so short a time; never had so much been owed by so many to the swift, decisive action of one man. At the age of 66, after no more than five years as chief, Whale retired. The strain had told heavily on him, and in little more than a year he died.

If there were all the elements of drama in the locomotive scene on the North Western in the years 1900-1910, on the North Eastern there was, as always, a complete contrast. Forty years earlier, while Ramsbottom was standardizing to the utmost degree at Crewe, Fletcher at Gateshead was doing just the reverse: Webb launched his ideas on an unwilling locomotive department and imposed them upon all with a rod of iron, while at Gateshead McDonnell tried innovations and was forced to resign by the hostility of the men; and now, in our present period, while George Whale worked himself to death, in putting the North Western locomotive position into order, the corresponding 'chair' on the North Eastern was occupied easily and gracefully by the jovial, sport-loving personality of Wilson Worsdell. But though he appeared to sit lightly upon his responsibilities Worsdell was no mere figurehead. He was, in fact, an extremely strong man. No one but a strong man could have held and controlled to such good effect two equally strong personalities as Walter Mackersie Smith and Vincent Litchfield Raven. Both were locomotive engineers of the highest class, Smith as Chief Draughtsman, Raven as principal assistant to Worsdell, but with special responsibilities for locomotive running and all electrical work. And despite his ruddy complexion, his loud checks, his love of fishing, and his shooting box in Norway, Worsdell himself was a first-rate mechanical engineer, and though delegating all the detail work kept a very close general watch on all that was going on.

Smith was of the most inventive turn of mind. He was one of the first to introduce piston valves for locomotive cylinders, instead of the old standard D-shaped slide valves; many North Eastern engines were so equipped, and for many years now they have been standard in the great majority of new locomotives built in this country. But Smith's greatest contribution to British practice was the first compound locomotive to be really successful on any railway in England and Scotland. The thermodynamic principle is sound enough, but in attempting to secure the two stages of expansion British engineers had so far failed to produce an engine of good working efficiency. Webb used two small high

pressure cylinders, and one large low pressure; by faulty proportioning the flow of steam was severely restricted and the engines
were sluggish in consequence. On the North Eastern Worsdell's
elder brother, who preceded him as locomotive superintendent,
had built compound locomotives with only two cylinders, one
high pressure and one low pressure, with the result that the engine had two unequal sized cylinders. They ran well enough, but
showed no advantage over a simple two-cylinder single expansion
engine.

Walter Smith designed a compound engine for the North
Eastern in which the cylinder layout was much more logical. While
the elder Worsdell used different sized cylinders, and Webb
expanded the steam from two small cylinders into one large one,
Smith expanded the steam from one high pressure into two low
pressure. While this arrangement avoided the need for having
individual cylinders of very large size, it also made possible a
much more reliable method of starting. The Webb 3-cylinder
engines were notoriously bad in this respect, but Smith invented
a valve which enabled his 3-cylinder compound engine to be
started as a 2-cylinder simple, by admitting the steam direct to
the low pressure cylinders. This North Eastern engine, No. 1619,
was beautifully proportioned in all her working parts, and was a
great success, though curiously enough the most striking result
of this success was seen not on the North Eastern Railway at all,
but on the Midland! At this period in railway history the locomotive departments of many railways were highly parochial in
their outlook; they took no apparent heed of what others were
doing, and where there was an exchange of views, as between
the Drummond brothers, it was inclined to be taken as a sign of
weakness. But just then there was a very friendly understanding
between Gateshead and Derby, and W. M. Smith's 3-cylinder
compound, completed in 1898, came at a critical point in Midland
history.

At Derby S. W. Johnson, like the majority of his contemporaries, was faced with the need for providing more powerful engines.
The loads of Midland express trains were leaping up as rapidly

as those of the Great Northern, and the beautiful, slender-looking engines of the nineteenth century were unequal to the job. Johnson had always had a special regard for efficiency in working, and his bogie singles had an enviable reputation for low coal consumption. The Smith compound system gave promise of an excellent performance, without going to the huge locomotives of the Great Northern, and Lancashire and Yorkshire, and Johnson built five 3-cylinder compound express engines on the Smith principle. As on the NER '1619' a multiplicity of controls was provided whereby the locomotive could be worked simple, full compound, or in what was termed 'reinforced compound'; in this latter state a certain amount of live steam was admitted direct to the low pressure cylinders and gave enhanced power when hill-climbing. As thus designed the original Midland compounds were extremely powerful and very fast engines; but they needed intelligent manipulation on the part of the driver if the best was to be got out of them. Smith would have undoubtedly have liked to build more for the North Eastern, but Worsdell favoured the 2-cylinder simple. The latter, with Smith's patent piston valves, were extraordinarily good engines, and of the 'R' class introduced in 1899 some still remain in service today. In the development of the compounds on the Midland, however, there lies a complex, and at times dramatic, tale that belongs to our next chapter.

Despite his serenity of outlook Wilson Worsdell fell momentarily as a victim to the extra-large boiler fashion of the early nineteen hundreds. It so happened that the North Eastern then had an intensely dynamic personality in its General Manager, George Stegmann Gibb. Unlike many of his contemporaries Gibb encouraged publicity, and following upon a tour of American railways in 1901-2 Worsdell was authorized to build a 'super' express locomotive. By a coincidence W. M. Smith was ill at the time, and with Worsdell directing the work of the drawing office himself, a huge 'Atlantic' engine gradually took shape; the boiler was as big as Ivatt's '251' on the Great Northern, but Gateshead had no inhibitions on cylinder size, and the tractive effort was some 50 per cent greater than that of Ivatt's engine. Though not having the superb grace of the Great Central 'Jersey Lilies' the new North Eastern engines were grandly impressive to look upon, but the story goes that W. M. Smith when he returned from illness was strongly critical. He was then reaching the end of his career, and possibly felt he could safely be outspoken in his views.

One looks back in some wistfulness to the days of that great triumvirate in the locomotive department—calm, spacious days, when the North Eastern was one of the busiest and most prosperous of all the British railways. Worsdell, a great gentleman in every sense of the word, led a very full life; he lived on the job, took a keen interest in the civic life of Gateshead, and was church warden of the parish church. W. M. Smith on the other hand was a Scot by birth, and lived north of the Tyne; he, too, was a devout churchman, and the Minister of Jesmond Presbyterian Church once said of him that his reports and engineering treatises were as good as a theological discourse for brilliance of reasoning! Raven, like Patrick Stirling and Webb before him, was a clergyman's son. And from Gateshead the North Eastern engines went out—north, west, south—glittering to the last split pin. Every engine had its regular crew, and no other; machines were not worked unduly hard, but there was intense pride in the job and in the railway, and failures on the road were almost unheard of.

Dugald Drummond was by that time the doyen of British locomotive superintendents. At the turn of the century he was sixty years of age, with a fine record of achievement behind him, and on the London and South Western Railway a status considerably higher than that of most of his contemporaries. In 1899 he built himself a private saloon and engine unit combined. It consisted of a single-driver tank engine, and a very small coach body; the whole outfit was only 35 ft. 9 in. long over buffers—little more than half the length of an ordinary bogie passenger coach. Drummond used this not only for inspections at distant parts of the line but to travel daily from his home station, Surbiton, to his office, first at Nine Elms and later at Eastleigh. He had his own driver and fireman, and it was just as though he had a private car, chauffeur-driven, to go anywhere he pleased on the line. It was often referred to as 'Mr Drummond's car', but much more often, I regret to say, as 'The Bug'!

On taking up the reins at Nine Elms he had immediately set to work to provide plenty of fast reliable engines to do the 'bread and butter' jobs on the line, and then he began to experiment. Age had not wearied his indomitable spirit, nor mellowed his temper; but as always, his staff and workmen were devoted to him, and in the big job of handling the locomotive department of the South Western he had of necessity to delegate much of the detail work. His earlier interests and friendships in Scotland remained, and J. F. McIntosh of the Caledonian used to tell with some glee of a visit he had from Dugald. It was in 1903, and the big 4-6-0 express locomotives 49 and 50 with their huge boilers were newly completed. In some justifiable pride McIntosh displayed them to his visitor, but Drummond was by no means impressed; in his usual blunt way, in fact, he criticized McIntosh for building 'such unnecessarily large engines'. Until then Drummond himself had built no larger engines for fast express work than the South Western version of his famous nineteenth-century 4-4-0; but in the following year competition blazed up with the Great Western over the Ocean Mail traffic from Plymouth, and with larger engines with larger boilers appearing on many of the leading railways Drummond began to move—very cautiously at first. In the summer of 1904 he turned out, at Nine Elms, a new batch of express passenger 4-4-0s with slightly larger cylinders, and a much larger boiler—a close parallel to McIntosh's policy on the Caledonian; but then in 1905, he who had chided McIntosh produced a colossal 4-6-0, with the largest boiler yet seen on a British locomotive. McIntosh was highly amused, and used to tell the story of Drummond's earlier visit to him, and its sequel, for many a day afterwards.

This step was all the more extraordinary for with South Western traffic as it was, duties for such enormous engines were indeed difficult to envisage. They had coupled wheels of the relative small size, for those days, of 6 ft. diameter, and may have been intended for the Salisbury-Exeter section; but on that line the alignment of the track and the quality of the permanent way was so good that the steepest gradients could be charged, by the simple process of piling on all speed on the preceding descent. The little 4-4-0 Greyhounds used to run up to 85 m.p.h. downhill, and with such impetus that they were half-way up the next bank before the gradient really began to tell. Drummond's colossal 4-6-0s of the '330' class spent most of their time in heavy goods service, and it was not until 1911 that a really fast express 4-6-0 appeared on the South Western. These latter engines had considerably smaller boilers than the '330' series, but the coupled wheels were larger, and the layout of the machinery was not so cramped. These engines were known as the 'Paddleboxes', the long, very deep splashers over the coupled wheels suggesting the paddlebox of a cross-channel or Isle of Wight packet steamer.

The 'Paddleboxes' were as fast as the 'Greyhounds', but round them, curiously enough, have grown up various stories that are frequently quoted as traditional. It is said that they suffered from insufficient bearing areas in the coupled wheel axle boxes, and were accordingly inclined to run hot; but a study of the drawings shows little evidence of this and I fancy that their erratic performance could be traced to a very different cause. Like a batch of similar locomotives with smaller wheels built in 1908 the firebox was very shallow; to get the area necessary for combustion of the coal the grate had to be made long, and to keep that grate adequately covered entailed really expert firing. With the 'Greyhounds' the box was deep, and the coal could be dumped in—not exactly 'anyhow', but with far less skilful placing than on the 'Paddleboxes'. In consequence the big 4-6-0s were occasionally short of steam, and showed that sluggishness in running that some contemporary observers were inclined to attribute to mechanical causes. I have questioned many of my friends among present-day enginemen on the Southern, drivers and inspectors who were firing in Drummond's day, and all have spoken of the difficulty of keeping an even fire, particularly with Welsh coal. Drummond himself was over 70 when these engines were built, and whereas in earlier days he was frequently out and about on the footplate one could hardly expect him to be so ubiquitous with advancing years. In all probability he was never fully aware of this trouble, for his long career came to an untimely end. In November 1912 while still in full harness, he suffered a severe scald on the leg, so severe that the limb had to be amputated. He never survived the shock, and he died the following day.

The hard running of relatively small but well designed 4-4-0 locomotives on the London and North Western Railway had a close counterpart on the Great Eastern, in the running of the famous summer holiday train, the Norfolk Coast Express. James Holden's big 4-2-2 'singles', to which reference was made in Chapter Five, were followed by the 'Claud Hamilton' class of 4-4-0, first introduced in 1900. Eventually there were more than a hundred of these fine engines, and in the height of the summer the work they did with the seaside holiday expresses was prodigious. The Norfolk Coast Express, running non-stop over the 131 miles between Liverpool Street and North Walsham, at an average speed of 51 m.p.h., was the show piece of the service; and at the height of their prowess the 'Claud Hamilton's' were taking anything up to 400 tons. Double-heading was never dreamt of, and the success and punctuality with which this hard work was invariably performed was due, as with the 'singles' that preceded them, to the most careful allocation and maintenance of the selected engines, and to a healthy rivalry between Ipswich and Norwich sheds.

Mention earlier in this chapter of Drummond's private railcar leads me to a very interesting phase of motive power development that belongs almost entirely to the high noon of steam. It was in the early nineteen hundreds, with the beginnings of road motor transport in evidence, and competition arising in suburban districts from electric trams, that increased attention came to be given to the means of operating the branch lines. There was a case in the Portsmouth district, where the branch from Fratton to East Southsea jointly operated by the Brighton and the South Western was suffering from a new tram route running parallel for almost the entire distance. For this line Drummond conceived the idea of a steam locomotive and passenger coach combined, which would be handier and cheaper to run than an engine and coaches. Several units were built in 1903 and the idea was hailed as an inspiration. Many similar ones were built by other railways, but while the new fashion was spreading far and wide Drummond himself was experiencing a difficulty; the indivisible nature of the combined unit was a nuisance, in that a defect on the coach portion would put the engine out of action, and vice versa. So in 1906 Drummond began building motor-train engines—tiny little 2-2-0s—capable of hauling two coaches at the most; they were pretty little engines, but with driving wheels of no more than 3 ft. in diameter they had no turn of speed. At that time a stopping train of any kind was a slow one, and no one seemed to consider it necessary to put on a spurt between stops. I used to travel daily, prior to 1914, in the Great Western rail-motor working the afternoon service from Reading to Basingstoke and I recall to this day what a painfully slow process it was!

In recalling the first decade of this century one is reminded of other happenings: the fabulous prosperity of the local railways in South Wales; the emergence of the Brighton as a first-class fast-running line, in contrast to its earlier confusion and sloth; the merging of the South Eastern and the London Chatham and Dover into a single operating unit under a Managing Committee; the prowess of Peter Drummond on the Highland, and the quiet, unobtrusive, little-noticed work of James Manson on the Glasgow and South Western. But by far and away the most significant developments were those in progress on the Midland, and on the Great Western—the one in administration and the other in engineering. Although both developments had swung well into their respective strides before 1910, the impact of them on the railways of this country was eventually so profound that they can be discussed at a later stage in this book. For while most of the work described in this chapter was leading its authors slowly but inexorably into a blind alley, the events of 1904-1910 on the Great Western and the Midland remain as vital predominant forces today, and will almost certainly survive until steam traction is virtually at an end on British railways.

There was a tendency in Edwardian days for some of the earlier embellishments of locomotives to be toned down. Peter Drummond changed the gay turnout of Highland engines into something that would have been drab in the extreme, but for the immaculate condition in which locomotives were kept; on the Great Western black replaced crimson as the colour for the underframes, and on the Midland much of the ornamental brasswork was suppressed. But after the merger, locomotives of the South Eastern and Chatham Railway, which combined the studs of two lines that were neither of them famed for beauty or colour of turnout, blossomed forth into some of the most highly embellished to be found anywhere in the country at the time. The Locomotive, Carriage and Wagon Superintendent was one H. S. Wainwright; he was a carriage man by training, and left all matters appertaining to locomotives to Robert Surtees, his chief draughtsman. Surtees, an old Chatham man, designed for express working two classes of 4-4-0, and the earlier of these, the 'Class D', as they were known, has now joined the ranks of the immortals of the locomotive world. They were built in 1900, and today, 56 years later, some remain precisely in their original condition—except, of course, for painting. They are by far the oldest passenger locomotives to claim this distinction, and as such form a lasting tribute to the sound design and excellent workmanship put into them. Their work over this long period has not savoured of the spectacular; high speed was discouraged on the South Eastern and Chatham, but these engines, designed by a subordinate, have got through an immense amount of unobtrusive, hard work and have amply survived the test of long service.

Our final picture here is of a minor railway, but of an intense, virile and efficient one—the London, Tilbury and Southend. With the shortest and quickest route from London to the group of holiday resorts and dormitory towns clustered around Southend the position of this small railway was the envy of others, notably the Great Eastern; but until the year 1912 the Board maintained a stout independence. It was a very busy line, prosperous and happy; the locomotive department, first under Thomas Whitelegg and

then under his son Robert H. Whitelegg, did its work with zest
and contentment. While I have no desire to bring politics into
this narrative I cannot forbear to mention that until 1912 there
was only one driver on the whole line who was a member of a
trade union. The passenger traffic was worked by a stud of seventy
4-4-2 tank engines, and the business trains involved some really
hard work; they were made up to the maximum length possible at
Fenchurch Street station, and as fourteen bogie coaches was just
too long they ran thirteen, and one six-wheeler. All the engines
were named, after the Stroudley style, after stations on the line,
and while such titles as *East Ham*, *Commercial Road*, and *Mark
Lane* may nowadays seem to us faintly ridiculous, the engines
themselves were so tastefully finished and beautifully kept that
one was not drawn instinctively to the names. They were painted
a rich medium green, with purple brown underframes, and a handsome lining of black, white and red. Much store was set upon a
smart turnout, and on occasions engines were taken out of traffic
for one or two days for the paintwork to be touched up. I can well
imagine what many present-day readers will think on seeing the
previous sentence in print!

While Thomas Whitelegg exercised the supreme authority
with kindliness, dignity, and a sound judgment borne of ripe
engineering experience, his son, as his assistant and eventual successor, brought all the fire and enthusiasm of a younger man to his
task. Endowed with a rich sense of humour Robert Whitelegg was
the life and soul of those occasions when the staff of the locomotive department travelled abroad *en fete*; he was no less a first-
class engineer, and on succeeding his father soon busied himself
with the design of a very much larger express tank engine, 4-6-4
type, for handling the heavier trains. Then to the surprise and dis-
may of all the staff on the line the management was at last induced
to accept the offer of a larger railway to purchase the London,
Tilbury and Southend outright, and in 1912 it became part of the
Midland Railway. Whitelegg, with his authority reduced to that
of a divisional man subservient to Derby, left the railway service
for a time; but his name recurs in the history of the steam locomo-

tive, and at the time of writing he is still living today, a hale old gentleman in whom the fount of good humour has not yet ceased to sparkle.

A Johnson 7-footer of the 1890-9 period.

A Deeley rebuild of a Johnson 6ft. 6in. 4-4-0, No 2585.

A Deeley rebuild of a Johnson 7ft. 4-4-0 No. 139 with new style of lettering.

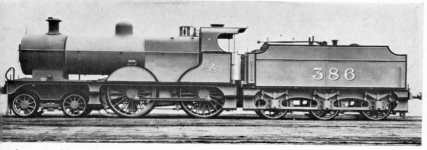

Fowler rebuild, with extended smokebox, and Belpaire firebox, also large tender.

GNR A Stirling 0-4-2 of 1875 for mixed traffic.

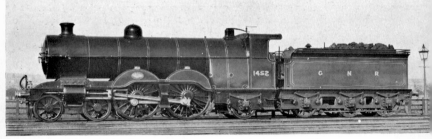

First of the Ivatt superheater Atlantics of 1910, No. 1452.

Wilson Worsdell's mixed traffic 4-6-0 of 1906.

One of W. M. Smith's four-cylinder compound Atlantic's of 1906.

CHAPTER SEVEN

MOMENTOUS YEARS

WHEN S. W. Johnson retired at the end of 1903, locomotive affairs on the Midland Railway seemed in the process of gradual evolution. The Smith compound 4-4-0s were dealing effectively enough with the problem of increased loads, though there were already signs of a change of policy in the general scheme of train services. In 1901, the Midland Railway had begun a special attempt to compete with the East and West Coast routes for the Anglo-Scottish traffic, and in the Midlands too they were faced with the unbounded enterprise of the Great Central. The Midland policy became one of running lighter trains and more of them, and although the need for larger engines as a matter of necessity grew less urgent, the increase in the number of trains to be run began to put something of a strain upon the locomotive department. But at this stage it is with personalities rather than engineering and operational details that we must first be concerned. Johnson was succeeded by Richard Mountford Deeley, a scientist and inventor, yet withal a very sound practical railwayman. A brilliant future seemed to be assured for the Midland Railway. Deeley had, as works manager at Derby, Cecil W. Paget, the dynamic son of Sir Ernest Paget, the Chairman of the Company, and with such an assistant the future prowess of the locomotive department seemed doubly assured. In 1905, too, continuity in the traditional style in operating seemed equally well set with the appointment of John Elliott as the new Superintendent of the Line; for Elliott was an out-and-out Midland man of 41 years' service, having risen from the very bottom of the ladder.

In 1905, however, the same year as that of Elliott's appointment, the Board selected Mr W. G. Granet to be Assistant General Manager. Granet, then in his thirty-eighth year, had not, up to that time, been a railwayman at all. After a distinguished academic career at Balliol College, Oxford, he was called to the Bar, and became Secretary to the Railway Companies' Association in 1900. While dealing mainly with legal and Parliamentary work he became acquainted with railway policy, but even so his appointment to so high an executive position on the Midland came as something of a surprise. Still more astonishing, in most quarters, was his further promotion a year later, when he succeeded Mr John Mathieson as General Manager. It was not long before the railway world, both inside and outside the Midland, realized that here was one of the toughest personalities and most forceful executive brains to be found anywhere at that time; and sure enough, within four years he had completely changed the top-level organization of the railway.

Transcending everything else was the creation of an entirely new post, that of General Superintendent in 1907. This might be regarded as making redundant the older historic office of Superintendent of the Line, and the appointment of so vigorous a character as C. W. Paget to the new post tended to thrust John Elliott in the background. It was probably intended to do so. Granet was the last man to be influenced by tradition, and in Paget rather than the more seasoned practitioners he found the man he needed. But from the locomotive point of view Paget's new command marked the beginning of a profound change in outlook. For the first time on a British railway the locomotive superintendent was relieved of the responsibility for running; the drivers, firemen, and shed staff came under the control of the General Superintendent, and Mr Deeley's title was changed more appropriately to that of Chief Mechanical Engineer. It is true that on some other railways, notably the North Eastern, the Lancashire and Yorkshire, and the London and North Western, the title had been changed some years earlier, while the officer concerned still retained control of the running; but on the Midland the change was logical enough. It was, of course, a demotion for Deeley—not in any case the kind of man to accept such a situation lightly; and this demotion came to him virtually at the hands of a man who had been his own assistant! Henceforth Deeley had to design, build, and repair locomotives, but Paget had to run them, as one part of his vast operating responsibilities. The seeds of discord were inherent in the person-alities concerned, quite apart from the awkwardness of a divided responsibility.

Already, however, Deeley had shown himself a shrewd judge of practical footplate work. The Smith-Johnson compounds were splendid engines, but they needed more than an average standard of intelligence from the drivers to get the best and most potent results. In contemplating a further batch of these engines Deeley felt sure that the controls were too complicated, and he decided to eliminate the change-valve altogether. He sacrificed the facility of 'reinforced compound' working to make the engines of better all-round utility, and the special regulator he designed, to give single expansion when getting under way and full compound in the ordinary running position, could hardly have been simpler to use. The Deeley compounds of 1905 were neither so fast, nor so power-ful as the Johnsons; but anyone could use them, and with the em-phasis shifting towards lighter rather than heavier trains the change, though retrograde, was justified. It seems, too, that Deeley was not entirely convinced of the need for compounding at all; for in 1907 he built a series of ten two-cylinder simple 4-4-os of roughly the same tractive power as the compounds. In connection with these latter he had taken out certain patents concerning the regulator and starting valve, and there is evidence to suggest that this action was not to the liking of the Midland management. It seems fairly clear that Deeley was of too strong and independent a nature for the 'New Deal', and aggravated by his resentment over Paget's appointment serious friction developed. In 1909 he resigned.

By this time it was obvious that with such a man as Granet at the head of affairs even the most senior of the departmental offi-cers had to 'toe the line', or else—! Paget, apart from being a man after Granet's own heart, was in a specially privileged position, for after all his father was still Chairman of the Company. The new Chief Mechanical Engineer was Mr Henry Fowler; he had already proved an able works administrator, and a metallurgist of distinction, but never throughout his long career could he be fairly described as a real locomotive man. From 1909 onwards design seemed to become a secondary consideration at Derby, and a state of stagnation gradually developed into a positive stranglehold that lasted as long as the Midland Railway itself. A system of centralized control was gradually extended from Derby to cover almost all activities of the Company. In traffic matters the judgment of individuals at divisional outposts was curtailed to the barest minimum; in the repair of locomotives rigid schedules of procedure were introduced, and they had to be followed whatever the needs and condition of individual engines. The result, of course, was an all-round lowering of the level of achievement; in a system of rigid standardization, that standardardization must inevitably be made at a level something below average, for in such circumstances it is too difficult to try to raise the level of achievement up to the standards of the few.

This unfortunate characteristic is nowhere more clearly shown than in the load limits fixed for the various classes of locomotive in express passenger service. The Deeley compounds were designated 'Class 4'; this was the most powerful category, and yet on trains averaging about 55 m.p.h. over runs of 100 to 120 miles non-stop they were limited to a maximum load of 230 tons. In later years, when the North Western 'Precursors' came within the Midland power classification, they were placed in Class 3, yet in 1910-14, when the Midland load limits were originally imposed, the 'Precursors' on similar schedules were taking loads of 350 to 400 tons! On the Midland, although the limits of load were fixed far below the known capabilities of the engines in all the four categories, the slightest excess led to the provision of a second engine on the train. Although this was unsatisfactory from the railway point of view it helped a great deal in the maintenance of punctuality; but on the other hand the policy of running more and lighter trains had given rise to an acute shortage of engines. Every effort was therefore made to keep train loads within the tonnages specified for one engine, and the frequent result was overcrowding. This was not a good feature on a line that was attempting to woo passengers from the faster routes by advertising the special charms of the scenery through which it passed.

And while travellers had to put up with degrees of discomfort at times, anything in the way of real enterprise on the part of the enginemen was ruled out by the strict loading regulations.

It is tempting to try to recapture something of the atmosphere that prevailed in those days. While one naturally thinks in terms of passenger trains the Midland had an enormous freight traffic, and with somewhat archaic methods of operation there was severe congestion before Paget became General Superintendent. He did a stupendous job in getting the freight fairly on the move, and in all probability he had little time in his earlier years to pay much personal attention to passenger working. As for Fowler, there is good reason to believe that strong restraint, if not a complete embargo, was placed upon anything of a 'new design' nature, with the result that no new passenger engines were built for the Midland express services after 1909. Authority was given for the complete rebuilding of many old Johnson 4-4-os; as rebuilt they were virtually new engines, but it was what might be termed 'an accountants rebuild', and the resulting engines were accordingly of limited capacity—Class 2 in fact. While the operating people would no doubt have welcomed a conversion to Class 4 it was more than the available funds would permit. These 'rebuilds', while excellent little things in themselves, were limited to a maximum load of 180 tons—a featherweight by the standards of 1910-14 elsewhere.

The relatively low figures at which maximum loads were fixed were very likely due, in part, to a new attitude towards fuel. On many railways specially selected grades of coal were used for the express trains, and particular care was taken in the loading up of the engine tenders. But in 1913 a very different state of affairs was revealed on the Midland. In that year bad coal on two night expresses was the primary cause of a serious collision near Aisgill summit; there were other contributory causes, including a fatal error by the driver of the second train. But it was bad coal that caused the first train to stall on the heavy gradient, and if the engine of the second train had not been short of steam, again due to bad coal, and in consequence giving its driver much anxiety, he might not have made the grievous mistake of missing the Mallerstang signals. In the subsequent inquiry many pertinent questions were asked about the coal used for Midland expresses southbound from Carlisle. On theoretical analysis the stuff was excellent, and the remote high authority at Derby thus had every reason to be satisfied; but more often than not it reached the engine tenders broken very small, and pulverized, and although conditions on the night of the Aisgill collision were perhaps exceptional, there were frequent difficulties of a similar kind. Here indeed was an example of that species of remote control that developed on the Midland Railway. Statistically all was well, but the man on the spot did not, in the prevailing circumstances, feel disposed to report the actual situation to headquarters. None of this makes very pleasant reading, and I would not have emphasized it, but for the unfortunate fact that Midland methods were perpetuated after grouping, and led eventually to muddle and deadlock on the London, Midland and Scottish Railway after 1923.

We must now turn to the Great Western Railway. In the previous chapter reference was made to the ways in which various prominent engineers reacted to the need for much larger and more powerful locomotives in the 1900-1910 period. Many imposing engines were built, but few gave a truly proportionate increase in tractive power for extra weight, and cost of construction, and some were very definitely retrograde on the grounds of overall efficiency. At the end of the nineteenth century the problem was not yet acute on the Great Western. That company was then getting back into its stride after the final abolition of the broad gauge, in 1892; in so doing the management was giving every indication of tremendous enterprises to be developed early in the new century, and although William Dean's handsome engines were fully masters of their work, they would not remain so for long if the various major projects turned out successfully. It is at this stage that George Jackson Churchward comes into the picture. In 1902 he succeeded Dean as Locomotive, Carriage and Wagon Superintendent of the Great Western Railway, but before he reached that eminent position his career had been one of great interest and significance.

Churchward was born in 1857, in the charming little village of Stoke Gabriel on a tidal creek of the River Dart. He inherited no engineering traditions. His family had been farmers in South Devon for centuries back; but there was something in this son of a typical old English yeoman that put him in the forefront of modern developments. In his boyhood the broad gauge South Devon Railway was still a novelty in the district, and in due course he commenced an apprenticeship in the shops at Newton Abbot. He was transferred to Swindon, and thenceforward his rise was rapid; but not the least of his qualities was a remarkable breadth of outlook. Although he was first and foremost a railway man, and then pre-eminently a locomotive man, he was one who foresaw, at a very early date, the possibilities of road transport for the private individual. A first-rate mechanic himself, he built with his own hands one of the earliest steam road motor cars. Even so he was no bigoted devotee of steam, and changed readily enough to a petrol driven car when such became reasonably practical propositions. But where Great Western locomotives were concerned he saw clearly—long before he succeeded Dean—that if the publicity campaign in favour of the Devon and Cornwall resorts succeeded there would be some heavy work for the locomotive department; and, again, before he succeeded to the chieftainship he obtained authority to begin the great development with which his name will ever be associated.

This development began with the boiler, just as McIntosh had done on the Caledonian; but whereas McIntosh merely began to enlarge the basic Drummond boiler, and came to a dead end with the *Cardean* in 1906, Churchward, in the late 'nineties, planned a boiler that was capable of enormous enlargement, the development of which has not, indeed, finished yet, nearly 60 years later! This is no place to go deeply into technical details, but some fundamentals may be mentioned. For a boiler to steam freely there must be facility for rapid circulation of the water, plenty of space above the water-line for the steam to form, and a firebox in which the correct form of the fire can be easily maintained by an average fireman. Somewhat naturally Churchward did not get the complete answer at once, and in outward appearance the so-called 'wagon-top' fireboxes, raised high above the line of the boiler, the absence of a dome, and a neat though purely 'functional' design of chimney flouted most of the canons, so far as aesthetics went. Such were the 'Atbara' class of 4-4-0s, built in 1899 while Dean was still in command. But they soon proved very fast and efficient engines, and the critics of appearance quickly switched to the 'handsome is as handsome does' theme. In 1903 Churchward developed his boiler theme into what was virtually its final form, by adopting a tapered barrel. This gave a much increased water space at the point where the barrel joins the firebox; it provided for better circulation of the water, and lessened the chances of hot spots developing on the firebox tube plates with consequent leaks in the joints between the flue tubes and the plate.

The taper barrel was tried out on one of the 'Atbara's' but the first new design to have it was the very celebrated 'City' class of 1903. They were like the 'Atbaras', but with the taper boiler they had a more compact look about them; to many eyes however they were still highly unorthodox, and on one occasion old James Stirling came out of his retirement to a meeting of the Institution of Mechanical Engineers to arraign Churchward for the ugliness of his engines. The locomotive world was soon to know what the 'Cities' could do, for on July 14, 1903, the first part of the 10.40 a.m. Cornishman, conveying special saloons for the Prince and Princess of Wales, and hauled by the engine *City of Bath*, covered the 193.6 miles to Exeter (via Bristol) in $172\frac{1}{2}$ minutes, passing through at slow speed; and despite the many handicaps of the curving and heavily graded South Devon line reached Plymouth, 245.6 miles, in 233 minutes 35 seconds from Paddington. Most significant, however, was that the cruising speed of the engine on level track seemed to be about 75 m.p.h.—first symptom of a new standard of express train running in this country. More important still was the spirit that animated these new developments on the Great Western, for Churchward, himself a great worker and enthusiast, carried every man-jack on the strength with him.

At Swindon the principle of the tapered boiler was applied to 4-6-0 locomotives, and with higher working pressures than ever before in this country. Many of his fellow superintendents on other railways were apprehensive, if not aghast at what Churchward was doing; many dire prophecies were abroad, but then, read the words of H. C. King, Locomotive Works Manager at Swindon, in 1906: 'He was not going to say that the measure of satisfaction had been produced without constant and unremitting care on the part of all those in the boiler shop and in charge of the construction; everyone was aware that boilers were being built from which great things were expected, and he could say truthfully that the difficulties had not been proportional to the increased pressure.' The keynote of the development is there: 'everyone was aware that . . . great things were expected . . .' And Churchward was no remote 'superman', confining himself to headquarters and his own office; the locomotive running was in his charge, and he was a familiar figure up and down the line. He seems to have enjoyed particularly sessions in the drawing office, when he would sit at a board and argue the points, not so much with the chief draughtsman or other seniors, but with the young men who were actually doing the job. It was the same with the running staff at the divisional stations. Of this latter point perhaps the classic instance is that of the ocean liner race with the London and South Western between Plymouth and London in 1904.

For some time certain Transatlantic steamship companies had been calling at Plymouth on their eastbound journeys to put off English passengers and mail. At first the Great Western had it to themselves, but late in 1903 the South Western decided to enter the business, and by common consent of the two companies the L&SWR took the passengers and the Great Western took the mails. What was perhaps entirely foreseen was that from each liner calling at Plymouth a friendly race to London would ensue. On the London and South Western side Dugald Drummond personally supervised the inauguration of this new fast working, but it is doubtful that if that gruff old Scotsman gave more unequivocal instructions than did Churchward. One of the Newton Abbot running inspectors, George Flewellyn, was put in charge of the Ocean Mail workings, and it was characteristic of Churchward on a special occasion to see the men concerned personally, and not to transmit instructions through the normal channels. At that interview Flewellyn received his orders, in terms that left no shadow of doubt as to what was wanted, and in the homely kind of phrasing that so endeared Churchward to his men: 'Withold any attempt at a maximum speed record till I give the word—then you can go and break your b—— neck!'

The climax of the race, and one of the most prominent milestones in the whole Age of Steam came on May 9, 1904, when the Ocean Mail off the German liner *Kronprinz Wilhelm* ran from Millbay Docks to Paddington in 3 hours 46 minutes, inclusive of a 2 min. stop in Bristol to change engines. From Plymouth the *City of Truro* was used, and in addition to reaching a maximum speed of at least 100 m.p.h. in the descent of Wellington bank she made an absolutely record time of $123\frac{1}{4}$ minutes for the 127.8 miles from Millbay Crossing to Pylle Hill Junction, Bristol, where engines were changed. For the completion of the run up to London one of the beautiful Dean 4-2-2 singles was used, the *Duke of Connaught*, and with four mail vans weighing about 120 tons (and as briefly mentioned in Chapter Four) the remaining $118\frac{3}{4}$ miles were covered in the magnificent time of $99\frac{3}{4}$ minutes. No finer run anywhere in Britain stands to the credit of the old single-driver type of express locomotive—all the more noteworthy because of some enforcedly slow running at the start, and through a slack to walking pace over a bridge under repair at Swindon. After that the *average* speed for the 70.3 miles from Shrivenham to Westbourne Park was *exactly eighty miles per hour*. In such manner did Inspector Flewellyn carry out Churchward's instructions. The *City of Truro* now stands as an historical relic in the Railway Museum at York. but no example of the Dean 'singles' has, alas, been preserved. It is fortunate enough, however, that so perfect a model as that of the *Majestic* is available for the eyes of the enthusiasts to feast upon.

The 'City' class engines, brilliant though they proved, were a mere stepping stone to Churchward's real development. He wanted power as well as high speed; he wanted speeds of 70 m.p.h. on the level, not with four and five-coach Ocean Mails weighing less than 150 tons, but with well-loaded holiday expresses of 350 to 400 tons, running non-stop from London to Exeter, or beyond. At that time the four-cylinder compound Atlantic engines designed by an Englishman, Mr Alfred de Glehn, were making a great reputation for their designer on the Northern Railway of France, and Churchward excited the British locomotive fraternity by receiving authority to purchase a similar engine for trials on the Great Western. From the standards of running put up in France it was fairly evident that the de Glehn compounds 'Atlantics' would give the power that was required; but like the Smith-Johnson compounds on the Midland they were relatively complicated machines to handle, and Churchward set out to design a single-expansion engine that would give the same performance. His tapered boilers gave all the steam that was required; it was then a case of using it efficiently in the cylinders. A range of expansion equal to that of a compound was necessary, and Churchward first designed cylinders in which the stroke was very long in relation to the bore, and then developed a valve gear which enabled the steam to be got in and out very easily. The free flow of steam was vital. Stroudley and Dugald Drummond appreciated this point, and Drummond in particular built engines that were very free-running. Churchward applied his ideas on three experimental 4-6-0 locomotives, the first actually built before Dean retired; but in the third, the epoch-making *Albion* of 1903, he produced an engine that was in every way the equal of the French compound, while having in addition the overwhelming advantage of being extremely simple to manage.

Albion was indeed a great triumph for Churchward; and all the Swindon staff concerned; but in her original form there was another big difference that might have contributed to her success over the Frenchman—she was a 4-6-0 and *La France* was an 'Atlantic'. So to carry the comparison still further *Albion* was converted to an 'Atlantic'. Still she triumphed, so much so that Churchward was temporarily diverted from his main line of development by building a series of new 'Atlantics', similar in nearly every respect to the converted *Albion*. In one respect the French compounds were superior to the large Great Western engines; the drive from the four cylinders was divided between the two coupled axles, and not only was it possible to have lighter working parts, and a division of the stresses, but the engines rode more smoothly. And so, in 1906, Churchward produced his final development, so far as the engine proper was concerned—the four-cylinder single expansion 'Atlantic', the *North Star*. Superiority over the larger French compounds purchased in 1905 was absolute, and as the 'Atlantic' wheel arrangement was adopted for no more than direct comparative working with the de Glehn engines, when authorization was received to proceed with four-cylinder express passenger locomotives on a production rather than an experimental basis they were built as 4-6-0s. With the *Dog Star*, and the nine sister engines that followed in 1907, Churchward had indeed produced his own masterpiece, and one of the greatest, if not *the* greatest masterpiece of the Age of Steam on railways.

It is true that there were still a few finishing touches to be applied, such as top feed on the boiler, a moderate degree of superheating of the steam, and an enlargement of the cylinders. 'Great things were expected . . .' and when an engine of the 1908 batch, the *Knight of St Patrick*, on a special test, ran the up Torquay luncheon car express, 390 tons, at 70 m.p.h. on level track with such ease and economy as to indicate a considerable amount of power in reserve, it was evident that the great expected had been successfully achieved. What loads were actually fixed for the Churchward 4-6-0s in their early days I do not know, but the drivers and firemen took trains of 450 and even 500 tons on the fastest trains, and double heading was never thought of. I myself have a much cherished record of a run behind *King Richard*, one of the 1909 batch, in which a load of 550 tons was worked to time between Taunton and Paddington. By comparison with the huge boilered Atlantics of the Great Northern and the North Eastern, and the 4-6-os of Dugald Drummond, and of McIntosh, the Churchward 'Stars', with their tapered boilers and relatively long chimneys, looked exceedingly slender machines; but a clue to their brilliant success could be seen in the size of the tenders. McIntosh and Drummond used large bogie affairs, for runs of 100 to 150 miles non-stop, while Churchward's relatively small six-wheelers sufficed for the 225-mile non-stop run from Paddington to Plymouth!

It would be wrong to attribute the success of the Churchward 4-6-0 locomotives entirely to the design and to the workmanship put into them at Swindon works. Co-ordination with the divisional stations at Newton Abbot, Plymouth, Cardiff, Wolverhampton, and Old Oak Common was very close, and through the whole-hearted and enthusiastic attention of the running inspectors the new locomotives were driven as they were intended to be driven. A magnificent tradition of enginemanship was gradually built up, so essentially sound that it served the Great Western until that railway passed into national ownership in 1948, and it still serves the Western Region today. The running inspector is regarded as guide and philosopher on the footplate, not an unwanted 'snooper', while the inspectors in their turn were encouraged to report back to headquarters difficulties and troubles experienced in the working of the locomotives. Many of the older drivers of today have vivid recollections of encounters with Churchward himself, and many are the tales—some no doubt apochryphal—told of his blunt good-humour, his readiness to listen, and of his shrewdness in diagnosing troubles. It is a great achievement to build efficient locomotives and to establish a tradition; but to establish a tradition that one's very able successors are proud to carry on for a quarter of a century after one's retirement—25 years of such change and such storm and stress as 1922 to 1947—is a symbol of undying fame.

In reading contemporary literature of the period it seems that the significant though widely dissimilar developments on the

Midland and the Great Western Railways were scarcely realized, still less apprehended at the time. Following the big-engine cult of 1900-1906 there was something of a recession in the ensuing years, out of proportion to the boom in traffic, and engineers were looking to ways and means of reducing running and maintenance charges on locomotives. To this end neither the new small-engine policy of the Midland, with its frequent recourse to double heading, nor the very high boiler pressures used by Churchward seemed to contribute much. It was the introduction of superheating that seemed to offer the most promising results. Until the period around 1908-1910 the great majority of locomotives running in this country had used steam taken direct from the space above the water-line in the boiler—'saturated steam' as it is termed. With superheating the steam is taken through a series of tubes inside the flues, and heated to a degree much above its normal temperature of formation. The great advantage of superheated steam is the increase in volume that takes place, so that when it reaches the cylinders it needs less weight of steam to do the same amount of work in thrusting on the pistons. It is, however, not entirely a case of 'something for nothing', as slightly more coal has to be used in the process of superheating, and there are added complications in that special attention has to be paid to the lubrication of pistons and valves. Moisture present in saturated steam acts as a natural lubricant, whereas the intensely dry and searing nature of superheated steam can cause a good deal of trouble with carbonization of the oil, and consequent blocking-up of valve ports, and so on.

But the advantages of superheating are such as to outweigh all these incidental troubles, and by 1912 the locomotive engineers of most British railways had some superheated engines running, if only of an experimental kind on some lines. In this phase major interest came to be focused on the London and North Western Railway. In 1909 Mr C. J. Bowen-Cooke was appointed to succeed Whale as Chief Mechanical Engineer. The new Chief, like his predecessor, was a running man, but thanks to the outstanding success of Whale's work the situation on the line was very different from that existing six years earlier. Bowen-Cooke was a man of wide outlook, and he had a little time in which to look around before embarking on his own programme of new engine building at Crewe. He began by examining the road performance of certain locomotives of other companies by means of interchange trials for a week or more. A 'Precursor' was tested against an Ivatt large-boilered 'Atlantic'; one of Whale's six-coupled express engines of the 'Experiment' class was tested against McIntosh's *Cardean*, while another 'Precursor' worked between Rugby and Brighton in competition with one of the new superheated 4-4-2 tank engines of the '13' class.

The Brighton line then had a locomotive superintendent of exceptional energy and drive in Mr Douglas Earle-Marsh. He came from Doncaster, and arrived in the south full of enthusiasm for the Ivatt 'Atlantics'; but his own record of engine designing is rather a patchy one. He had built some indifferent 4-4-2 tanks for branch line service; his passenger 'Atlantics' were an almost exact copy of Ivatt's, save that they had larger cylinders, and then in 1907 he tried a series of express passenger tank engines, 4-4-2 type, incorporating the boiler of the 'B4', his predecessor's 4-4-0 express design. Some of these engines were built to use saturated steam, but a series of ten were superheated; these latter were in themselves successful beyond measure, but their designer could hardly have foreseen the remarkable influence they were to exert on the locomotive policy of the London and North Western Railway. Engine No. 23 of this class was pitted against the 'Precursor' 4-4-0 *Titan*, which was then non-superheated. The task set to each was the haulage of the Sunny South Special express on alternate days between Rugby and Brighton. The load was about 250 tons, and this, of course, the 'Precursor' managed easily enough; but the Brighton superheater tank engine not only did the job, but did it on such an astonishingly low water consumption that Bowen-Cooke soon had the Crewe drawing office at work on a superheater version of the 'Precursor'. Marsh himself had little opportunity to develop the design that had scored so signal a triumph. The Brighton engines were numbered in hundreds, whereas Bowen-Cooke had charge of more than three thousand.

In the meantime other locomotive engineers were making their own applications of superheating. Ivatt on the Great Northern, and McIntosh on the Caledonian at first used the principle as an opportunity to obtain the same tractive power from these engines, but with lower boiler pressures, thus saving on boiler maintenance. Churchward used it as a means of avoiding condensation in the cylinders after a long range of expansion, giving just enough additional heat to the steam to secure this result, while Dugald Drummond adopted a kind of half-way house towards all-out superheating by use of a so-called 'steam dryer'. But Bowen-Cooke wanted more power. North Western train loads were still on the increase, and in the new 4-4-0 express engines turned out at Crewe in 1910 the boiler pressure was the same as in the 'Precursors', while the cylinder diameter went up from 19 inches to $20\frac{1}{2}$ inches. On the basis of nominal tractive effort the capacity of the new engines was increased by 12 per cent over that of the 'Precursors', but with improved design of valves and valve gear, and freer flow of steam, due to the increased fluidity and absence of moisture consequent upon a high degree of superheating, the new engines showed an improvement far greater than that suggested by the tractive effort formula. The first of the new class, completed at Crewe in July 1910, two months after the accession of the new sovereign, was named appropriately *George the Fifth*.

But Bowen-Cooke had barely got this engine on the road before there was thrust upon the London and North Western Railway, an event that attracted an unusually wide publicity for those days—another interchange trial, this time with the Great Western Railway. Some contemporary observers, and many subsequent writers, have regarded this test as a culmination of the series of trials initiated by Mr Bowen-Cooke in the previous summer; Crewe had examined the crack engines of several other companies, so why not those of Swindon? But the disparity of power between Churchward's 'super' four-cylinder 4-6-0s and George Whale's 'Experiment' class was so obvious to any well-informed observer that the result of the contast seemed a foregone conclusion before

Reproduction of a painting by Lance Calkin of H. A. Ivatt at his
desk at Doncaster, with a picture of an 'Atlantic' engine in rear.

The last Ivatt 'Atlantic' to run, in 1950, with H. G. Ivatt and the
driver standing on the buffer beam on arrival at Doncaster.

One of R. J. Billinton's 'Scotchmen' of 1896, No. 45, *Bessborough*
fitted temporarily with the Drummond system of cross water tubes
in the firebox.

One of the first Marsh Atlantic's non-superheated variety,
of 1905.

An L. B. Billinton 2-6-0 express goods engine of 1913, for the
Newhaven continental 'Grande Vitesse' trains.

it started. Indeed some commentators, with more glib verbosity than perception, deemed it astonishing that Crewe should have considered it possible for their engine to compete at all, and hinted that this was just another case of that parochial outlook that characterized many of the British railways at that time. Against some, to be sure, the charge of parochialism might with some justification have been made; but to no one less than Mr Bowen-Cooke. He was exceptionally well informed on current practice both at home and abroad. Although it might have seemed obvious to a superficial observer the trial was, in fact, not initiated by the North Western at all. It came about in a very different way.

There are one or two gaps in the chain of events that I have not been able to fill in from my inquiries into the affair, but it so happened that in that period two members of a very famous shipping family were respectively on the Boards of the Great Western and the London and North Western Railways; both men were deeply interested in locomotives, and it would have been very surprising if at some time they had not compared notes. Crewe engines were still being built very much 'on the cheap', and engine for engine it is not surprising that Churchward's big 4-6-0s were much more expensive in first cost. Certain Great Western directors, so it seems, became uneasy; the General Manager, Sir James Inglis, grew interested, and this undercurrent reached its climax when Churchward was asked to explain to the Board why the North Western could build three 4-6-0s for the price of two Great Western's. Churchward's reply was brief and to the point: 'Because one of mine could pull two of their b——— things backwards!' His claim was put to the test in the interchange trials of August 1910, when the loads of West of England expresses were at their very peak.

The element of drama present during the inception of the trials were continued in the actual running. In the exchanges of 1909 initiated by Mr Bowen-Cooke the engines had been evenly matched, so far as haulage capacity was concerned. The test trains were run comfortably to time, and for the most part the travelling public and the daily newspapers were not aware of what was going on. But in 1910, while the Great Western engine *Polar Star* had an easy enough task on the expresses between Euston and Crewe, the dice were loaded against the North Western *Worcestershire* from the outset. While Bowen-Cooke was glad to have an opportunity of running the *Polar Star*, he cannot have been other than apprehensive about his own engine's ability to run the West of England trains, and sure enough she came a 'cropper' of the first magnitude. On her first trip with the Cornish Riviera Express she was 33 minutes late at Plymouth; the daily newspapers got hold of the 'story', put two and two together and made the answer somewhere up in the 'teens, and so the world had a colourful account of *Worcestershire's* failure. She went from bad to worse, and finished the trials a day before the appointed end. For her size she was, of course, vastly overloaded, and from a technical viewpoint her crew did remarkably well; but her failure to run the crack Great Western expresses to time could not have been more public or ignominious. Not could the personal triumph of Churchward have been more complete. I need only add that engines of the 'Star' class are still running express passenger trains on the Western Region today, 46 years after the trials, whereas *Worcestershire* and her kind had all been demoted to secondary and slow train work by 1915-6.

The result of the trials must have been particularly galling to Mr Bowen-Cooke, who had, in the *George the Fifth*, produced a really brilliant engine. From the quality of its pristine work there is no doubt that it could have run any of the heavy Great Western expresses to time. Had such a trial been carried out, and a 64-ton 4-4-0 been shown the equal in haulage capacity of a 75-ton 4-6-0 —for such were the Great Western 'Stars'—the issue might indeed have been complicated for Swindon! When I write 'equal', however, I must not be misunderstood. Equality only applies in the loads offered to *Worcestershire* and her rival, *Lode Star*; Churchward's engines could do a great deal more than was asked of them in the 1910 trials. Furthermore, the old traditions of economy in construction still prevailed at Crewe, and although the workmanship into the *George the Fifth* was nothing other than first-class the lightness of the frame construction caused the engines to become very rough after a time. There were other features in the design that tended to cause deterioration in performance after several months running. While perhaps it would be unkind, in view of their sterling worth as dividend earners, to call the North Western's the 'Tin Lizzies' of the locomotive world, it would, on the other hand, be true enough to call Churchward's four-cylinder 4-6-os the 'Rolls-Royces' of the breed.

In 1908 Churchward had built his now almost legendary 'Pacific' engine *The Great Bear*—no more than a 'Star', so far as machinery was concerned, but fitted with an enormous boiler. This huge engine was intended to carry his boiler development a big stage further, but, through weight restrictions, it was not possible for 'The Bear' to take up the duties for which it was eventually intended, and by the time the 'pre-war' period came to an end the initiative so far as new design was concerned had passed to the London and North Western Railway. At the time of the 1910 challenge from the Great Western, Bowen-Cooke was planning a big new 4-6-0 of his own; from that point of view he was glad enough of the opportunity to try the 'Star', for it was the nearest English equivalent to his new project. Indeed, when this project eventually took shape in the famous *Sir Gilbert Claughton* 4-6-0 of 1913 some observers, not knowing what had been afoot in the higher councils of the L&NWR in 1910, saw in the new engine a direct result of the interchange trials, as it was a 4-cylinder 4-6-0 of roughly the same nominal tractive power. But in basic design and in details the 'Star' and the 'Claughton' were very different. Churchward reached his beautiful solution of the valve gear problem with a mechanism that was inside and rather inaccessible; but great things were expected of it, and special care was taken in maintenance at the sheds. A tradition was set up, and the Churchward layout of the valve gear still flourishes today, when extreme accessibility has become the watchword.

In the 'Claughtons', Bowen-Cooke used a simpler, more accessible arrangement, but one not so theoretically perfect; his boiler was more conventional, and much cheaper to construct than the tapered barrels of Swindon. In one vital respect, however, the two engines were the same: the firegrate was level over the rearward half of the box, and then sloped down toward the front. On the Great Western the technique of firing that grate with soft Welsh coal had been mastered by the running inspectors and assiduously practised by the top link firemen; it became another Great Western tradition, founded before 1910 and handed down through generations of enginemen to the present day. On the North Western, however, the 'Claughton' firebox was one by itself. The 'Precursors' and the 'George the Fifth' had the old deep, narrow boxes into which you dumped the coal thick and fast; and it has been said with some truth that they would steam under the efforts of a navvy. But many of the North Western men never really mastered the craft of firing a 'Claughton', and in consequence the performance of the class as a whole was inconsistent. This cannot be regarded as other than a black mark against the design; for a machine must be designed to suit the staff who have to use it. Nevertheless the 'Claughton' engines at their best put up some astounding performances, and whereas Churchward had not revealed the more intimate details of the working of the engines, Bowen-Cooke released to *The Engineer* the full technical results of two wonderful runs with engine No. 1159 *Ralph Brocklebank*, made in the late autumn of 1913.

On both runs the dynamometer car was used and details of drawbar, temperatures, and horsepower recorded throughout. The first run was with a 'special' from Euston to Crewe, carrying what was in those days a heavy load of 435 tons. The 158 miles were run in exactly 159 minutes, but this time included two bad slowings for permanent way work, and a dead stand for signals outside Crewe lasting two minutes. The power output was greater than anything that had been recorded with Great Western engines up to that time, and two days later Crewe went one better. This time the *Ralph Brocklebank* was put on to the morning Scotch Express—the train now known as the Royal Scot—to make the non-stop run from Crewe to Carlisle. The start was 7 minutes late, but so superb was the running that Shap Summit was passed 10 minutes early! Some of the horsepower figures recorded were tremendous for that period; there were many of over 1,500, and a truly record maximum of 1,669 at Tebay when they were working up impetus to 'charge' the Shap Incline. How exceptional this output of power was for the year 1913 will be realized when I add that even today our largest modern engines, with nominal tractive efforts of nearly double that of the 'Claughtons', rarely develop much over 2,000 horsepower in the cylinders.

Then, as now, the records of indicated horsepower were taken by men riding in the shelter erected round the front of the engine, and in North Western days there one would always find that great little man Tommy Sackfield. He was head of the locomotive section of the Crewe drawing office, and with draughtsmen taking the actual diagrams, and another of his kind recording on the footplate, Sackfield within the narrow confines of the shelter presided over all—a striking little figure with a shaggy grey beard, and a dreadful old bowler hat jammed down hard on his head. Bowlers were the fashion then, even within the indicator shelters; and though they still linger today among the older school of running inspectors, the majority of those whose work takes them on the footplate favour a cloth cap or, more comfortable still, a beret. Bowler hats or not, however, the runs of 1913 with the *Ralph Brocklebank* rank among the great classics; and when war came in August 1914, and the brilliant high noon of steam gave place to an afternoon of violent storm, Bowen-Cooke, Crewe, and the L&NWR had certainly had the last word, so far as engine performance was concerned.

CHAPTER EIGHT

IN THE BALANCE

WHEN the shadows closed in upon Britain in that terrible August of 1914 the whole structure of railway organization was thrown into the balance. On the outbreak of war all the independent companies were immediately taken over by the Government. For the duration of the emergency control was vested in the Railway Executive Committee, a body composed of the General Managers of the ten leading railways, under the chairmanship of Mr (as he was then) H. A. Walker of the London and South Western. The adaptability of the railway workshops was immediately shown by the speed with which coaches were converted to make up splendidly equipped ambulance trains, and in due course all the locomotive shops came to take a hand in the production of direct munitions of war. But a major effect of war was to break down many of the lingering survivals of parochialism between the companies, and before the conflict ended there was much talk of nationalization. Even before the war came upon us, however, the locomotive engineering scene was markedly changing, and many new personalities were coming to the fore.

In 1912, for example, the fabulous Drummond saga entered upon its final stage, with the death of Dugald Drummond, on one hand, and on the other the selection of Peter to succeed James Manson as locomotive superintendent of the Glasgow and South Western. On the Great Northern H. A. Ivatt retired, and was succeeded by an energetic and brilliant young man of 36 named Herbert Gresley; while on the Highland Railway an appointment that was to have a dramatic sequel was that of the former works manager, Mr F. G. Smith, to succeed Peter Drummond in 1912. But an appointment of perhaps the greatest moment was made in 1913 on the South Eastern and Chatham Railway. There the control of the locomotive department had drifted into a rather unsatisfactory state. The chief, H. S. Wainwright, was a carriage man; locomotive matters were left to Robert Surtees, the chief draughtsman, and the locomotive running department was ruled with a rod of iron, but on a totally non-technical basis, by J. S. McColl, the chief clerk, a dour indomitable Scot who had come to the South Eastern in the days of James Stirling. To succeed Wainwright the directors appointed Mr R. E. L. Maunsell, of the Great Southern and Western Railway of Ireland. Maunsell was the fourth head of Inchicore to be selected for high office on an English railway, thus following in the footsteps of the unlucky McDonnell, of Aspinall, and of H. A. Ivatt. With mention of Gresley and Maunsell we are now coming to very familiar names, but while Gresley was proud to continue in the Doncaster tradition, set up by Sturrock, and continued by Patrick Stirling and Ivatt, Maunsell took one look at the *status quo* in Ashford, and began to build up an organization wholly his own.

Maunsell will go down in history as the first British locomotive engineer to show practical appreciation of the remarkable work in progress at Swindon. In Ireland he had in E. A. Watson, his works manager, an ex-Great Western man, and showed not a little 'sales-resistance' to the exuberant advocacy of Churchward's practice; but in building up an almost entirely new staff at Ashford he chose a surprising number of Swindon men! There was certainly need for reorganization. The locomotive department had put forward certain proposals for an express passenger 4-6-0, but these had been turned down, on account of excessive weight, by the civil engineer; little else of a new-work character was in hand, and when Maunsell succeeded Wainwright he found a desperate shortage of engines for the work to be done. A design for an enlarged 4-4-0 was practically completed in the Ashford drawing office, but engines were needed immediately and arrangements were made to borrow some, from the Great Northern, and from the Hull and Barnsley. By a curious coincidence the engines loaned to the SE&CR were all designed by members of the Stirling family: Patrick's 2-4-0s from the GNR, and his son Matthew's 0-6-0s from the Hull and Barnsley. With James Stirling's locomotives much in evidence in the South Eastern corner of England this arrangement quite savoured of a family party! At one time Matthew Stirling was considered the most likely successor to Ivatt, at Doncaster; but when the time came for the appointment to be made the directors of the GNR favoured a younger man.

The locomotives borrowed from the two northern lines helped out the general motive power position on the South Eastern and Chatham, but with the prospect of a bumper season in the summer of 1914 more first-line express passenger power was needed. Although the possibilities of a major war in Europe had been long discussed in many circles the danger seemed to have receded by the opening of the year 1914. Things looked far more ugly in Ireland. And when it was announced in January that an order had been placed with A. Borsig, of Berlin, for the first ten of the new SE&CR 4-4-os, it was interest, rather than surprise and apprehension that was expressed. An extremely short delivery was specified, for June 1914, and with heavy commitments for overseas railways the British locomotive building industry was not able to meet such a demand. An order for a later batch of the same engines was, however, placed with Beyer-Peacock and Co. Borsig worked with speed, and parts for the first five engines were landed at Dover on the 24th and 26th of May; a squad of about 20 German fitters was sent over to do the assembly work at Ashford, and all concerned on the SE&CR were immediately impressed with the excellence of the workmanship put into these locomotives. Apart from some tram engines, and a few contractor's locomotives, they were the first main line German-built steam locomotives to be used in this country, and a fine finish was evidently a matter of prestige with the builders. The whole class is still in service today, 42 years later.

The Borsig fitters were working at Ashford to within a few weeks of the outbreak of war, and the engines went almost immediately into service, not on holiday expresses to the Continent, but on troop and ambulance trains. The impact of war upon the railways and the railwaymen of this country came to take many forms. Before the outbreak many men of all grades were serving in the Territorial Army, in line regiments, where nothing more technical was demanded of a soldier than an ability to take care of his rifle; the majority of these men were called up at once irrespective of their civilian duties. There was no schedule of reserved occupations in 1914. Almost at once tasks of a special kind fell upon the railway mechanical engineers at home. Maunsell was appointed as Chief Mechanical Engineer to the Railway Executive Committee—a high honour for one of the youngest superintendents in the country—and immediately he was faced with an unusual and urgent problem. A gratifying number of Belgian locomotives had been evacuated in the face of the rapid German advance, but then, though safely ensconced behind the Allied line, these engines were immobilized by lack of stores and spare parts. Ashford works had to fill the gap.

But as the exciting and anxious first months of the war gave place to the ghastly deadlock of the Western Front, and it was realized that in its principal theatre the war was developing into a colossal effort of attrition the services of technical men in their professional capacity, rather than as fighting infantrymen, became apparent. The Government arsenals were not large enough to supply all the munitions needed; the feeding of supplies to the front line was getting beyond the capacity of the Army Service Corps. At home the railway shops undertook much special works; two Chief Mechanical Engineers, Fowler of the Midland and Raven of the North Eastern, were seconded to the Ministry of Munitions, while the formation of the Railway Operating Division of the Royal Engineers gave many of the younger men an opportunity of serving in close proximity to the battle-line, in locomotive running, or traffic operating. In Cecil Paget of the Midland the ROD had a commander of rare capacity, and with him were many men who came to serve with great distinction on the home railways afterwards. Names that occur to mind on the operating side are Malcolm Speir, who became Chief Officer for Scotland, LMSR; R. M. T. Richards, later Operating Superintendent of the Southern, and particularly Sir Michael Barrington-Ward, as he afterwards became. Sir Michael won the DSO, for great gallantry, on the night the enemy succeeded in exploding the ammunition dump at Audruicq in July 1916, when some 27,000 tons of 'H.E.' went up. Among locomotive men with the forces may be mentioned particularly O. V. S. Bulleid, later to become Chief Mechanical Engineer of the Southern Railway.

At home the burden of work steadily and inexorably increased. Train services were cut down, schedules were decelerated, to save coal, to save engine mileage, and to defer the time at which individual engines would need repairs. With slower trains locomotives could take heavier loads than before, and this practice gradually reached its peak on the Great Northern and North Eastern Railways where 'Atlantic' engines were regularly called upon to take 500 to 550-ton trains without assistance. True, the schedule for the $105\frac{1}{2}$-mile run from King's Cross to Grantham was expanded at one time to as much as 148 minutes, compared with the pre-war figure of 117 minutes; but the main thing was to keep the traffic on the move with as few engines as possible. In conjunction with this a maximum speed limit of 60 m.p.h. was imposed on the great majority of lines, so as to lessen the need for permanent way maintenance and renewal. New engine construction had to be largely confined to types needed to sustain the war effort, and several cherished schemes had to be abandoned. Of these none was more interesting than Peter Drummond's proposed four-cylinder 4-6-0 for the Glasgow and South Western Railway. This great machine was designed in full detail at Kilmarnock, and from a study of the drawings there is no doubt that it would have been one of the most handsome engines ever to run in this country.

Mention of Peter Drummond leads me to his former Company, the Highland, of which it is safe to say that none was more seriously affected by the coming of war. The establishment of Scapa Flow as the principal base of the Grand Fleet meant that all supplies, munitions and personnel had to be conveyed by train to Thurso; and supplies then included coal. When it is recalled that on the day the Battle of Jutland was fought Sir John Jellicoe led out of Scapa Flow an armada of 22 battleships, to say nothing of smaller craft, something will be realized of what the running of the 'Jellicoe specials' on the railway entailed. Most of the coal necessary for the big battleships came from South Wales, and while the London and North Western and the Caledonian were able to cope with the extra traffic—not a great deal at first, in relation to the total volume of their freight business—to the Highland it nearly proved overwhelming. On the latter line by far the greatest pressure of business normally came in the summer tourist season. Maintenance work on the locomotive stock was so organized that the whole stud of 152 engines was available from June onwards, and repairs were done in the winter. But the autumn and winter of 1914-5 brought no relief, rather the reverse, and at the turn of the year an order was given to Messrs Hawthorn, Leslie and Co. of Newcastle for six new passenger engines of an improved type; delivery was expected in the late summer of 1915, but before this the motive power situation was becoming desperate. In August, no fewer than 50 locomotives were out of service for one reason or another, while another 50, while continuing in traffic, were so overdue for repair as to render them liable to failure at any moment. Many of the regular engine-fitters were serving in the Forces; in response to urgent appeals men of every estate came to in help man the shops at Inverness, and somehow the Highland Railway struggled on.

It was at this crisis in the locomotive affairs of the Company that the first of the new 4-6-0 engines arrived at Perth. The design had been prepared by Mr F. G. Smith who, prior to his appointment to succeed Peter Drummond, had been works manager at Inverness since 1903. Although he was not a Scotsman himself he had become thoroughly familiar with the conditions under which Highland engines had to work. He was an extremely able and far-sighted engineer, but unfortunately he did not seem to have the way of getting along happily with his colleagues. There had indeed been more than one clash with the Chief Engineer, Alexander Newlands, a man of the strongest character and ability, but a martinet where engineering practice and standard were concerned. The affair of the 'River' class engines has been wrapt in a certain amount of mystery, but some years ago I came to know 'Big Bill' Paterson, and after his retirement I visited him in his beautiful home at Beauly looking out to the Moray Firth. Now Paterson had been a junior draughtsman in the civil engineer's office at Inverness in 1915, and I heard from him the inside story of this extraordinary affair.

Smith received authority from the Board to obtain six new engines of greatly enlarged dimensions, and he was evidently so confident of their satisfaction in all respects that he did not submit the design to the civil engineer, to obtain his agreement so far as weight distribution was concerned. Smith knew the Highland line and its engineering restriction, and felt he could trust his own judgment. It is said that Newlands was not only not consulted, but was kept in ignorance of the fact that some large new engines were under construction at the Newcastle works of Hawthorn, Leslie and Company. This latter point I find hard to believe. The Highland headquarters was a small, closely-knit community at Inverness, and even if no official announcement had been made the news would surely have passed round and reached Newlands indirectly. One can well imagine how incensed a man of his methodical, punctilious mind would have been, at so being kept in official ignorance. With the feeling that already existed between Smith and himself the stage was certainly being set for a major 'show-down' between them. In the meantime the star driver at Perth shed, Will Tulloch, was warned to stand by to bring the *River Ness* up to headquarters as soon as she was delivered at Perth.

In the design of these engines Smith showed himself to be many years in advance of his time. He appreciated that it was not so much the dead weight on the axles that determined the effect a locomotive had on the track and the underline bridges, but the combined effect of dead weight and the unbalanced loads set up when the engine was running at speed. The 'River' class engines were very skilfully balanced, and although they were considerably heavier than any previous Highland engine their 'hammer-blow' effect at speed was no more than that of Peter Drummond's 'Castle' class. They could have been run with complete safety and success. Then the first two, *River Ness* and

River Spey, arrived at Perth. Newlands went at once to see them, and was horrified by their huge size, by previous Highland standards. A hurried gathering of senior officers, and some directors, took place, at which Newlands placed a complete embargo on the use of the two new engines until some calculations of stresses in bridges had been made. At Inverness every man in the civil engineer's department was put on to the job. They worked throughout a wartime week-end checking stresses that would be set up in the various bridges and long viaducts. It soon became evident that by the standards then existing in bridge design the 'Rivers' would have set up undesirably high stresses in many of the bridges. In the tense atmosphere that had arisen since the first dramatic appearance of the engines at Perth it was no use Smith arguing the finer points of balancing. Newlands forbade their use, and that was that.

The directors were furious. Smith was given a week to resign, or be sacked. He resigned, and the engines were sold to the Caledonian. The one element of comedy in the whole affair was that the Highland succeeded in selling them for £500 more per engine than they actually cost, and thus on the six engines they netted a profit of £3,000! The irony of the situation was emphasized subsequently in two ways. Smith's successor, Christopher Cumming, put some smaller and lighter 4-6-0s on the road in 1920, as will be mentioned later in this chapter. They were balanced in the old style, and though conforming to Newlands's requirements so far as dead weight was concerned had a total hammer-blow at speed that made them far more detrimental to the track and bridges than the 'Rivers' would have been. Then, in early grouping days, the work of the Bridge Stress Committee completely vindicated Smith's design, and the 'Rivers' went on the Highland line in 1928 to do excellent work. If only Smith had been as good a diplomatist as he was an engineer he might have risen to the very highest levels in the locomotive world. As it was, the 'Rivers', which were without much doubt the finest express passenger engines built for any Scottish railway in pre-grouping days, were largely wasted. The

Caledonian did not appreciate their quality, and used them mainly on express goods trains; while by the time they went back to the Highland the standardization programme of grouping days on the LMSR was getting into its stride, and officially they were regarded as just another non-standard 4-6-0. In actual fact they would have given the Stanier 'black-fives' a very close run for their money!

Behind the battle line in France and Flanders the traffic of the Railway Operating Division was worked by a great variety of locomotives, mostly on loan from the larger railways of this country. The Great Western, Midland, North Western, North Eastern, and Lancashire and Yorkshire sent out many freight engines, but as the struggle continued there were not enough, and the Government invited all the leading locomotive engineers of this country to submit a design for a heavy freight engine for service with the ROD. The type chosen was J. G. Robinson's standard 2-8-0, already doing yeoman work on the Great Central Railway. Simple in its details, massive, and reliable in service it proved ideal for the rough and tumble usage abroad, and a large number was built to Government order. In retrospect the 'o4', as it became in LNER days, seems likely to go down in history as the most famous of all British freight designs. After the war, the Government-owned locomotives were purchased by several of the home railways, and no finer tribute to the design could be found than the existence of 28 in 1957 on the strength of the Western Region, more than 35 years after their purchase. One might have imagined that on a line like the Great Western, so steeped in its own tradition, these engines would have been regarded as no more than stop-gaps, and scrapped when the engine-shortage of the post-war period was passed. But they did survive the Second World War, during which many of the 'o4' engines in LNER stock were sent abroad on war service for the second time. At one period some were working as far afield as Persia.

As wartime production became gradually geared up to the highest pitch, railway locomotive engineers, for the first time for several years, began to find a little time to think of the future. The co-ordinating authority possible through the Railway Executive Committee had demonstrated certain advantages, notably on one occasion in helping the Highland with a loan of some 40 locomotives of various types, from the London and South Western, the North Eastern, and other of the larger railways. Among them was one of the little North Western 'Precedent' class 2-4-0s, *The Auditor*. The senior locomotive engineers and their chief assistants, who in pre-war years had met together in the friendly and social atmosphere of the Association of Railway Locomotive Engineers, a rather exclusive 'club', were now brought closer together when there was a definite prospect of full nationalization after the war. Mr (later Sir) Winston Churchill, who was the Minister of Munitions, realized that when victory did come there would be widespread unemployment in the munition factories unless some alternative work was immediately available, and the ARLE was asked to consider the possibility of new designs that could be put into large-scale production at short notice. While all members of the association took a share in the discussions four engineers in particular came to play a leading part; these were Churchward, Fowler, Gresley and George Hughes, of the Lancashire and Yorkshire. As Chief Mechanical Engineer to the Railway Executive Committee it fell to R. E. L. Maunsell of the SE&CR to co-ordinate the work.

The detailed design work, so far as it progressed, was entrusted to James Clayton, chief locomotive draughtsman of the South Eastern and Chatham, an ex-Midland man who had served under Paget, and who came to Ashford at the time of Maunsell's big reorganization in the early months of 1914. During the first steps towards the new British standard designs he was in the unique position of working with several eminent engineers, quite apart from his own chief. Clayton told subsequently how, above all, it was his contact with Churchward that influenced his own design practice in later years, and as he came to be responsible to Maunsell for all Southern Railway work that influence was very great indeed. In 1917 Maunsell had built two prototype locomotives for the South Eastern and Chatham Railway—a 2-6-0 mixed traffic tender engine, and a 2-6-4 passenger tank. These bore the first fruits of the Swindon influence that had come to Ashford in 1914, including a tapered boiler barrel, and an arrangement of the valve gear based upon Churchward's successful practice. When the end of the war came the ARLE had not progressed sufficiently far for a standard engine to be ordered, and so Woolwich arsenal was set to build some of the Maunsell 2-6-os.

After the war the Government policy toward the railway turned to a grouping scheme under private ownership rather than nationalization, and the half-formed ARLE designs were allowed to lapse; but before leaving the war period it is interesting to reflect that the men most concerned were between them to influence the whole trend of British locomotive practice during the twenty years to the Second World War. The old order had begun to change even before the war, and it was changing still more rapidly by the time of the Armistice in 1918; but the spirit of the railway service notably survived. Many are the stories, grave and gay of the war years, but one which always delights me is that of a wounded soldier who in peace time had been a fireman on the London and North Western Railway. One day in hospital he was visited by a young lady in the uniform of an ambulance driver, and in the course of conversation she told him that her father also worked on the L&NWR:

'What kind of engines did you fire,' she asked.

'Well, I don't suppose it would mean much to you miss. We had lots.'

'Did you fire a "Claughton"?'

'Why, yes, miss,' stuttured the astonished soldier. 'What do you know about Claughtons?'

It was the young lady's turn now to be a little reticent: 'You see, my father designed them'—for she was none other than Miss Bowen-Cooke.

At home the great strain of the war years had told heavily upon the older men, though in the heat of the fray few realized it at the time. Early in 1919, for example, Bowen-Cooke, then 61 years of age, was keenly looking forward to plans for new locomotives,

One of the Ivatt 'Long Tom' 0-8-0s of 1901

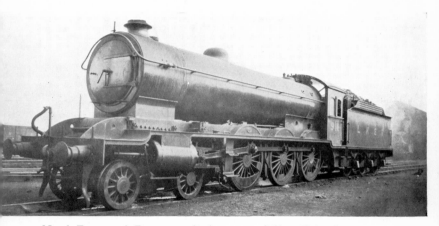

North Eastern: A Raven 3-cylinder 4-6-0 of Class 'S3', of 1919.

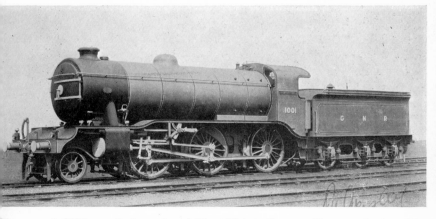

The second GNR 3-cylinder 2-6-0 of Class 'K3', built 1920. Photograph signed by Sir Nigel Gresley.

A Pickersgill 4-4-0 No. 14498 (in lined black).

A Pickersgill 4-6-0 No. 14637 (in Derby red).

A Pickersgill 3-cylinder 4-6-0 No. 14800 (in lined black).

McIntosh's epoch-making 4-6-0 No. 49, of 1903, as LMSR No. 14750, in plain black.

and at this stage in railway history one could write whole chapters upon the 'might-have-beens' Overshadowing all post-war plans, however, was the scheme for the grouping of the railways. This plan was no whim or catspaw of one or other political party in Parliament. The period of Government control had certainly shown certain advantages—though many hampering restrictions —but above all the wage structure had been established on a national, rather than an individual, or local basis, and in any reversion to their former independence many of the smaller, and indeed some of the larger companies would have found the greatest difficulty in footing the bill. This became evident when the grouping scheme was first formulated. It was at first intended to have a purely Scottish group; but in pre-war days even the largest of the Scottish lines had rates of pay very different from the most prosperous of the English railways, and it was necessary to incorporate the associated Scottish lines into the groups based on the former East and West Coast routes.

The effects and incidents of grouping, which took effect from January 1, 1923, will be discussed as long as there are railways. In some cases the new alliances were natural and not unwelcome; with some others, as with the various Welsh lines incorporated in the enlarged Great Western, it was a case of Hobson's choice, but with a few the whole business was extremely distasteful, and it was not long before there were clashes of personalities at almost all levels. Here we are concerned with locomotives, and locomotive engineers, and on three out of the four new groups the appointment of a Chief Mechanical Engineer was not only settled quickly, but in such a way as to ensure continuity of policy over a long period. On the Great Western, Churchward, who had retired in 1921, had been succeeded by his principal assistant, Mr C. B. Collett, and he naturally continued in office after 1923. In the Southern group, with the South Western and Brighton chiefs both at the point of retirement, R. E. L. Maunsell of the SE&CR was the obvious choice; but in the Eastern group the situation was at first not so clear cut. On the lines merged to form the London and North Eastern Railway there was, for example, the tremendous personality of Sir Vincent Raven who had returned to the old NER from his special war work with a knighthood and a KBE; there was A. J. Hill on the Great Eastern, and the relatively young H. N. Gresley on the Great Northern.

The most senior of all the Chief Mechanical Engineers in this group, and one who had held the highest office for more than 20 years, was J. G. Robinson of the Great Central Railway; early in that momentous January he was summoned to meet the Chairman and Vice Chairman of the new company, and he was duly offered the post. But Robinson was then 66 years of age, and felt strongly that the post of co-ordinating the locomotive and mechanical engineering work of seven large companies not only called for a younger man, but one who could remain in office for a number of years and give some continuity to the new practices that must necessarily be introduced. Robinson's interviewers thereupon invited him to name his own choice for the post, but good-naturedly he refused to be drawn. In stipulating a younger man, however, he had virtually named his candidate. A few days later he was at the Great Central Hotel, when Gresley came into the lounge, crossed to where he sat and shook him warmly by the hand. 'I've got the job, John,' he exclaimed. No one was more pleased than Robinson, and during Gresley's long career the former Great Central chief was able to look on with the approbation and interest of an older statesman of the locomotive world. Indeed, he outlived Gresley and died at the great age of 87 years. Many of his engines almost outlasted steam on British Railways.

Before turning to the tangled and stormy history of locomotive affairs on the London Midland and Scottish Railway in the early years of grouping, there are a few notable engines to be mentioned, built between the Armistice of 1918 and the end of 1922. It is one thing to design powerful and efficient locomotives when conditions are straightforward, but a change in the post-war traffic policy of the South Eastern and Chatham Railway set Maunsell and his staff a pretty little problem. Prior to the war the bulk of the Continental traffic via Dover and Folkestone had been run from Charing Cross terminus, and with certain mail dispatches from Cannon Street; but after the Armistice it was decided to concentrate all this traffic at Victoria. This involved use of the former London, Chatham and Dover line out to Bickley Junction, and on account of weight restrictions the most powerful SE&CR engines—the big 4-4-os of 1914—were barred. The largest engines permitted were the earlier non-superheated 4-4-os of the Wainwright era, and with these the maximum load the motive power people were prepared to take on the boat trains was 250 tons. The traffic department stipulated a load of 300 tons, and so Maunsell had the task of producing an engine no heavier than the existing ones, yet capable of a power output 20 per cent greater. It would have been easy enough to get the power by using superheated steam and larger cylinders; indeed in Wainwright's own time two of the beautiful 'E' class 4-4-os had been so modified. They were splendid engines, and would have easily have taken the 300-ton loads, but they were too heavy.

Maunsell therefore took another engine of the 'E' class, No. 179, and very thoroughly rebuilt it. The same sized cylinders were incorporated; the boiler barrel was used, though, of course, re-tubed, while structurally every scrap of surplus weight was removed. The elaborately curved splashers were cut to an austerity minimum; the heavy cast iron drag boxes were replaced by fabricated steel ones—and so on. But still on the basis of nominal tractive effort the power of the engine had not been increased. The front-end, however, was completely remodelled. Not for nothing had Maunsell and Clayton been associated with Church-ward in the war years. The rebuilt '179' had large diameter piston valves, and a valve gear on the Swindon pattern, giving very free flow of the steam into and out of the cylinders. The result was an extraordinarily good little engine, that took the 300-ton boat trains with ease. Many more were converted, and in 1957 they were still doing excellent work, after a busy life of 36 to 37 years. Naturally they had long been displaced from the boat trains, which often loaded up to over 500 tons then; but on the lighter trains to the Kent coast they romped along just as freely as they did on their first days on the crack Continental expresses. Their performance, then and now, stands as a classic example of what can be done with a really well designed valve gear.

Switching now from Ashford to Inverness, Mr C. Cumming had taken over Highland locomotive affairs at a very difficult time, upon F. G. Smith's resignation in 1915; but the deficiency left by the 'River' class *débâcle* was repaired by the ordering of six new engines of existing classes, and despite the extreme pressure of war-time traffic, and the continual anxiety over the repair of engines Mr Cumming found time to design, and have built by Hawthorn, Leslie and Company, two very handsome outside-cylinder 4-4-0 engines *Snaigow* and *Durn*. For many years they worked the Farther North mail trains, between Inverness and Wick, the two engines working down and up over the 161 mile journey on alter-nate days. Except when laid off for repairs *Snaigow* and *Durn* had a virtual monopoly of these two trains from the time of their construction, late in 1916, until ten years later. Mr Cumming will be mainly remembered, however, by his eight 4-6-0s of the 'Clan' class, introduced in 1920. For hard slogging service over heavy gradients these neat and compact engines have had few superiors, weight for weight. On the long toiling ascents, as from Blair Atholl to Dalnaspidal, and from Inverness to Daviot, no refinements of valve gear design can make up for shy steaming, or a tendency to slip. I have travelled with, and ridden on the High-land 'Clans' in all kinds of conditions, on their own line, and on the equally difficult route to Oban; and always the steaming has been rock-steady, and the drivers have been able to pound away to their heart's content. There was beauty in their plain, simple style, in the immaculate cleanliness of their sage green paint, un-adorned though it was by any lining. Their names were carried in large, bold letters on the valence over the driving wheel splashers, and alongside was the Highland coat of arms—that most striking of railway heraldic devices, with a giant eagle embracing in its wings the Lamb and Flag, of Perth, and the Crucifix, of Inverness. To see and hear *Clan Cameron*, *Clan Fraser*, *Clan Mackinnon*, one after another on the afternoon expresses to the south, come thundering up the last mile into the rock-strewn wilderness of the Slochd Mhuic pass was a railway experience ever to be remembered.

By contemporary standards on the railways of the south the 'Clans' were not large engines, and in the spring of 1922 a new era began with the completion at Doncaster works of the first Gresley 'Pacific'. This epoch-marking engine, No. 1470 *Great Northern*, punctuated an interesting stage in a locomotive development dating back to 1917. Two railways closely associated with the GNR in traffic matters, the Great Central, and the North Eastern, had built some interesting examples of 3-cylinder simple engines; J. G. Robinson adopted the principle for his huge 0-8-4 banking engines working in the Wath hump yard, and for one experimental express passenger 'Atlantic', but on the North Eastern Sir Vincent Raven had used it for all his large engines—passenger, mixed traffic, and mineral alike. In all these engines three separate sets of valve gear were used, but on the GNR Gresley designed an arrangement that eliminated one set of valve gear, and this promised to be simpler and cheaper to maintain. It was tried, first of all, on a 2-8-0 mineral engine, but in its original form the mechanism was so complicated as to outweigh the advantage of dispensing with the inside set of valve gear. The design came in for some severe criticism in the technical Press. Much of this criticism was of a general nature, but intense interest was aroused by a communication from Mr H. Holcroft, of the South Eastern and Chatham Railway, and formerly of the Great Western. He had been in the drawing office at Swindon when Churchward's new development programme was at its height, and had himself designed a conjugated valve gear for a three-cylinder engine. On Churchward's instructions a patent had been taken out, but no practical application of Holcroft's very simple and ingenious mechanism was then made.

Gresley's first three-cylinder engine was built in 1918; the war was still in progress, and at the time Holcroft had been seconded from his normal duties at Ashford, and was in charge of a Railway Executive Committee depot at Purfleet. At this time there took place one of those backstage manoeuvres that are so fascinating to read about in history, and which have occurred, no doubt, time and again during the Age of Steam; the great majority of them are lost to us, however, because of the principal actors, who have chosen to say nothing. In the 1918-9 episode, however, we do know the inside story. Holcroft, while still at Purfleet, was invited by Gresley to a private talk on the three-cylinder engine valve gear, and the designs of further Great Northern locomotives were discussed. One outcome of this meeting might have been Holcroft's transfer from the SE&CR to Doncaster; but instead Maundell recalled him from the REC depot at Purfleet, and gave him the task of designing a three-cylinder version of the 'N' class 2-6-0 mixed traffic engine. Meanwhile, on the Great Northern Holcroft's version of the conjugated valve gear was adopted as standard for all Gresley's future large mixed traffic and passenger engines. The engine proper—cylinders, motion, smoke-box saddle—was designed round the conjugate gear, and it featured prominently in the big 'Pacific' engines of 1922.

Those pioneer engines, Nos. 1470 and 1471 of the Great Northern Railway, were the forerunners of one of the most famous ranges of express passenger engines that have ever run in this country—the original 'A1' class, the 'Super-Pacifics', and finally the amazing streamlined 'A4' class of 1935. They have always been known generically as the Gresley Pacifics, and Gresley's they certainly were; but he owed a profound debt of gratitude to Holcroft for the very simple version of the valve gear. The pioneer engines 1470 and 1471 carried the Great Northern colours, but the third to be built, and perhaps the best-known of the earlier batch—1472 *Flying Scotsman*—came out just after grouping, and so carried the initials L&NER on her tender. The Pacific is a natural development of the Atlantic type in that it permits the use of a wide firebox extending over the trailing wheels. The technique of firing such a box was well known on the GNR from long experience with the Ivatt 'Atlantics', and by the autumn of 1922 the new engines 1470 and 1471 had fairly settled into their stride. Gresley claimed that they were designed to work trains of 600-tons unassisted, and on a special test run on September 3,

1922, a train of 20 corridor coaches was worked from King's Cross to Grantham at an average speed of 52 m.p.h.—105½ miles in 122 minutes start to stop. At the time this was considered a great run, but more recently we have come to regard it as no more than a very modest curtain-raiser to the story of Gresley Pacific achievement.

Returning now to the subject of grouping and its effect upon locomotive men, the situation on the newly-formed London, Midland and Scottish Railway was by far the most difficult of any. On January 1, 1923, five men of major seniority were still in office, but even before this the locomotive department of the greatest British railway of pre-grouping days, the London and North Western Railway, had received a great shock. Their former chief, that great gentleman C. J. Bowen-Cooke, had died in 1920, at the early age of 62. He had been succeeded by his principal assistant Capt H. P. M. Beames, another man to whom Crewe and the L&NWR made up his very life blood. But in January 1922 the grouping scheme was anticipated in one respect by an amalgamation between the North Western and the Lancashire and Yorkshire; so far as the Chief Mechanical Engineers' departments were concerned, although the North Western post would be considered the greater in status, the L&Y chief, George Hughes, was by far the senior in years. He had, indeed, held the post since 1904. So it came about that Crewe was made subservient to Horwich—a sad enough blow in itself. Hughes though not particularly successful as an engine designer was a delightful character, and the exchanges of views that took place between the two works were of the friendliest. Beames, though demoted, remained very much a power in the land.

But when grouping proper came it was a very different story. Behind all the administrative and financial negotiations prior to amalgamation was the tremendous personality of Sir Guy Granet, who became a Deputy Chairman of the new combine. The Midland and its methods came to overshadow all, and the organization of the vastly enlarged railway was based upon Granet's re-organization of the Midland in 1906. The effects upon the locomotive department were far reaching, and for many years unsettling in the extreme. George Hughes was appointed Chief Mechanical Engineer, and Fowler, who had returned from his war service with the Ministry of Munitions with a Knighthood and a KBE, became deputy. The others assumed the role of divisional chiefs—hardest of all for Beames, who was still a relatively young man. From the technical viewpoint the locomotive situation was not generally healthy. While Maunsell on the Southern and Gresley on the LNER each had a solid foundation on which to build, the LMSR had little that was generally acceptable.

On the Caledonian a marked recession had followed the great days of J. F. McIntosh, and the Glasgow and South Western was caught in a singularly unfortunate state at the time of grouping. Technically, the Midland had scarcely advanced beyond the 1907-8, and the Lancashire and Yorkshire had only just managed to pull some of its chestnuts out of the fire, before grouping took place. In 1908 Horwich works, under Hughes direction, had built a class of 20 very large four-cylinder 4-6-0s; in their original condition these engines could have put in a strong claim to be called 'the world's worst!' They were sluggish, they rode badly, they were inordinately heavy on coal, and as for the repair bill, the situation at Southport at the end of 1918 may be taken as typical. There were eight engines of the class stationed at that shed, and yet there were only three turns that could be booked to them; only three out of eight that could be relied upon! Some of them were burning more than 100 lb of coal a mile on very moderate duties, while on the Great Western the Churchward 'Stars' rarely exceeded 40 lb on the heaviest of their workings. In 1920 a start was made with the complete rebuilding of these L&Y engines, and all-in-all Horwich made a good job of it; but even so there were details that detracted from their performance, and the appetite for coal, though greatly reduced, was still pretty healthy.

At the time of grouping the whole attitude towards the job was different at the three main English centres, an attitude humorously but very truly summed up by Mr D. W. Sandford: 'At

Derby the nice little engines were made pets of. They were housed in nice clean sheds, and were very lightly loaded. There must have been a Royal Society for the Prevention of Cruelty to Engines in existence. At Horwich they had gone all scientific and talked in "thous", although apparently some of their work was to the nearest half-inch. At Crewe they just didn't care so long as their engines could roar and rattle along with a good paying load, which they usually did.' No one of these three policies could obviously be adopted for the future, but in the event, the situation that developed did not present the Chief Mechanical Engineer's department with the chance of making a clear cut decision on its own account. The imposing of the Midland organization meant the dividing of responsibility, with the locomotive running and footplate staff transferred to the department of the Chief General Superintendent. Engine loadings were revised, and the 'good paying loads' previously taken by North Western engines were very much whittled down—to the onlooker, without rhyme or reason. One could dilate for pages on the inconsistencies of the new regulations, and the result, of course, was a sudden epidemic of double-heading.

The trouble went a good deal further than that of revised regulations. The enginemen were bitterly resentful. North Western drivers and firemen had always prided themselves on what they could do, roar and rattle though their engines might; and to be compelled to take assistance when they didn't want it was worse than painting their black engines red! A wave of Midlandphobia swept over the whole line, and there were many cases of the new officials getting the rough side of North Western tongues. Of this there is no more amusing story than one told by Mr T. Lovatt Williams about a driver we will call 'Fred'. 'One morning,' Williams writes, 'his engine, a "George the Fifth", was standing at the head of a train in No. 15 platform, Euston, and Fred was leaning over the side of the cab, surveying the scene on the platform with a cynical eye. A few minutes before starting time a rather pompous Midland official walked up Platform 15 and counted the coaches as he went along. Thirteen coaches, two "diners"—loading equal to "23½". A bit staggered by this he walked up to Fred and said: "Good morning, driver, where's your pilot engine?" Fred looked him up and down, removed the dreadful old pipe from under his straggling moustache and remarked, "In the shed, where she ought to be. Who do you think we are, the b—— Midland?'"

While regulations were made limiting the loads to be taken by existing engines, for some years nothing was achieved towards providing enhanced power. Hughes retired in 1925, after which Sir Henry Fowler became Chief Mechanical Engineer. Already thoughts had turned towards a larger development of the Midland compound, but already, too, conflict had developed between the operating department and that of the CME as to the best type of locomotive for future work. The Midland policy in pre-grouping days had been to run a frequent service of light trains, requiring small engines; and a sustained attempt was made, in the planning stage, to remodel the North Western train services on similar lines. But the volume of traffic on the line weighed heavily against any such schemes, though the operating department proceeded to block any proposals that came from Derby for large new engines. Fowler had put forward a 4-6-0 version of the Midland three-cylinder compound, and followed this with a four-cylinder compound Pacific. In this respect the new operating authorities found a ready collection of allies in the older North Western traffic men. Derby might point to their own successful use of compounds and to the numerous varieties of de Glehn compound in France; but on the West Coast route the word 'compound' brought nothing but hectic memories of the old Webb compounds, and the sentiments were unanimous—'never again!'

In spite of misgivings, protests, and scepticism on the part of the operating people Fowler finally decided to go ahead with the compound 'Pacific', and in 1926, with the drawings complete, work was started in the shops. Then suddenly, like a flash of lightning on an oppressive day of uncertainty and gathering storm, there came the event that revealed the lack of cohesion, the cross-currents, the prejudices that bedevilled the LMS in its early years. In September 1926 there suddenly appeared in regular daily working between Euston and Crewe a Great Western 4-6-0 of the 'Castle' class; her trials were afterwards extended to the Crewe-Carlisle run. In mentioning the 'Castle' class I have drawn rather ahead of the general period, as the first of these engines was not built at Swindon until 1923, and I have not yet come to post-grouping history on the Great Western; but it is clear that one of the warring factions on the LMS had persuaded the management to arrange this loan of a modern and efficient 4-6-0 engine in direct opposition to the construction work in progress at Derby.

Sir Henry Fowler was at once placed in a very difficult position. The traffic people were intending to make a big show with the summer service of 1927. The historic 10 a.m. Anglo-Scottish express of the West Coast Route was to be named *The Royal Scot*, and run with no passenger stops between London and the Scottish cities of Edinburgh and Glasgow. The tare load of the new train was to be approximately 420 tons. On the very moderate schedule proposed, engines of the 'Claughton' class, if in their true form of LNWR days, could have managed the train south of Carnforth, if not through to Carlisle; but double-heading would in any case have been necessary with such a load in Scotland. Under the new order, however, 360 tons was the 'Claughton' limit, and thus new engines were necessary by July 1927. Virtually the ultimatum put to Fowler was of the 'heads I win, tails you lose' category. He was required to test the Great Western engine: if this 4-6-0 with roughly 30,000 lb. tractive effort was proved adequate the justification for the great compound 'Pacific' was thrown seriously into doubt; if the GWR engine was not powerful enough he had to press on in the teeth of opposition, with the plain certainty that the compound engines would be un-kindly received on the line. The outcome was harder still. The Great Western engine, ably handled by one of her own driv-ers, showed that she could very comfortably manage the schedule and loading planned for the Royal Scot express; in face of this demonstration Fowler was not merely instructed to stop work on the compound Pacific, but to have 4-6-0 engines of comparable power to the 'Castle' ready for the summer traffic of 1927. Thus while the design of the 'Pacific' was completed and had gone into production, the Derby drawing office had to start all over again, with a clean sheet of paper, and produce a new design of 4-6-0. The operating department made a strong plea for three, rather than four cylinders, since it was hoped that maintenance work would be reduced thereby.

The LMS story has been carried into the grouping era with the account of actual engine building, as it is most important to appreciate how the interplay of policies and personalities produced the stalemate of 1923-6, when the other groups were so notably forging ahead. It would perhaps be an exaggeration to say that in those first years the LMS was reaping the Midland whirlwind of 1906-7. But the division of responsibility for locomotive affairs is at its best a somewhat delicately poised piece of organization, and it speaks volumes for the conciliatory and co-operative nature of Sir Henry Fowler's character that he continued in office after his cherished project of the compound Pacifics had been so peremptorily vetoed. But he was not first and foremost an engine designer, as Churchward, Dugald Drummond and Patrick Stirling had been; he had an extraordinarily wide range of interests, and perhaps the *coup d'etat* by the operating people—for such it surely was!—did not strike so deeply at his feelings as one might imagine.

CHAPTER NINE

THE BIG FOUR

THE first years after the grouping witnessed a fascinating series of engine trials in many parts of the country. They were mostly unconnected. Some could be traced to individual appointments, others were part of a short-term policy to assess the capacity of existing locomotive stocks. These trials, made within the confines of the new LMSR and LNER systems, were apart from the great inter-railway trial of 1925 between the Great Western and the LNER. The more private trials were, of course, quite unpublicised, and it was only through the observations of interested travellers that railway enthusiasts as a whole learned of what was going on—usually too late to see anything of the trials themselves. Taking the LNER first, Mr W. G. P. Maclure of the Great Central was appointed Running Superintendent of the Southern Area, Western Section, and it was doubtless at his instigation that various express engines of J. G. Robinson's GCR designs were used for some years on the crack Great Northern Pullman trains between King's Cross, Leeds and Harrogate. These engines were 4-4-os of the 'Director' class, and 4-cylinder 4-6-os of the 'Lord Faringdon' class. The Chief Mechanical Engineer seems to have had a particular regard for Great Central designs, as he built 24 further engines of the 'Director' class for service in Scotland, and a batch of Robinson's 4-6-2 suburban tank design for the Tees-side service.

Use of Great Central engines on the King's Cross route was not preceded by any set trials with the dynamometer car, but in the summer of 1923 a Gresley Pacific was tested between King's Cross and Doncaster against one of Sir Vincent Raven's even larger Pacifics, the first two of which had been completed at Darlington works just early enough to have the inscription 'North Eastern' on their tenders. Another trial, of which little or nothing was known until recently, was a kind of 'triple bill', on the main line between Newcastle and Edinburgh, in which Great Northern, North Eastern, and North British 'Atlantics' were matched against each other. In this latter series the Great Northern representative had very much the worst of it, both in coal consumption and general performance. But curiously enough, by one of those snowball effects—rumour, more rumour, and still more rumour —it came to be understood in railway circles that the North British 'Atlantics' were very heavy on coal; the results of those trials of 1923, which were first published in 1955, gave the lie to any such rumours, and the good performance of both North British and North Eastern engines probably accounts for Gresley's policy of 'live and let live' towards locomotives of the constituent companies of the LNER, in contrast to the 'scrap and build' policy later adopted on the LMSR.

With the Pacific trials on the London-Doncaster road it was another matter. Here it was a case of deciding upon the future standard of heavy express locomotive power, and from all accounts the two designs were fairly evenly matched. The Gresley type then had its original valve gear, which was not a very good one; but with the performance of the two classes of Pacific locomotive as they were at that time it is not really surprising that Gresley should have favoured his own, rather than Sir Vincent Raven's. The decision to standardise on the Gresley type was naturally not popular on Tyneside. The North Eastern people, one-time servants of the richest and most prosperous of all the LNER constituents, felt that they had been given 'a raw deal', and for many years resentment showed itself among the locomotive men in poor running, particularly where the Gresley Pacific engines were concerned. Regular travellers have said that the difference in the work north and south of York was so extraordinarily marked that it was difficult to believe that the same class of locomotive was in use.

The principal LMSR trials were conducted between Leeds and Carlisle; there, Class 4 Midland express engines—compounds and '999' class simples—were matched against various London and North Western, and Caledonian engines. To say that the work done in some of these trials was phenomenal could almost be called an understatement. Whether the LMSR authorities ever foresaw that this series of scientific tests would develop to the pitch of excitement, partisanship, and 'all-out' human endeavour that it did is highly doubtful; if the actual running took them by surprise they had reckoned without the individual enginemen. In Chapter Seven I wrote of the strict limitation of Midland loads to 230 tons for a Class 4 engine on the heavy road from Carlisle southwards over Aisgill summit. How the test load came to be agreed, in the first place, at 300 tons I cannot imagine, unless perhaps the North Western people protested that anything less was not worth pulling! Anyway, 300 tons it was, and trials were first of all run between engines 998, the compound No. 1008 and a North Western 'Prince of Wales' class 4-6-0 No. 388. The Midland men rose to the occasion, whipped up their engines good and hard, and kept time easily with their 300 tons. Partisanship began to run high in Carlisle; the crew of the North Western '388' were near neighbours of the Midland men, and when their turn came the honour of the North Western was verily at stake! The trials were run in mid-winter, and the public knew nothing about it; but never before had engines been worked so hard over the Midland, and what 998 and 1008 had done the 'Prince' did likewise.

Such was the performance that the authorities took the extraordinary step of extending the trials, with the loads increased to 350 tons. This, of course, was nothing new to the North Western, but it was unheard of on the Midland. The blood of the men was really up. The 'Society for the Prevention of Cruelty to Engines' was completely forgotten, and day after day the Anglo-Scottish expresses were taken up to Aisgill in a style that for fire and fury bade fair to beat Crewe at its own game. The climax was reached when No. 1008, hauling a train of 370 tons, covered the 48¼ miles Carlisle up to Aisgill in 64½ minutes, climbing a clear 1100 ft. in that distance, and the North Western, 388, with an equally heavy load took 66¼ minutes. As the scheduled allowance was 68 minutes both trains were well ahead of time despite those enormous loads—by Midland standards at any rate. The LMSR authorities had every reason to be delighted with the performance of the Midland compound, and as its work was done more economically than that of the North Western 'Prince' the decision was taken to build many more compounds for general service all over the enlarged system. They came to do remarkably well on the Caledonian, and Glasgow and South Western lines, though they never became really popular on the North Western; the antipathy to the Midland, and everything to do with it, had gone very deep. While these trials served to underline the easy tasks that had been set to Midland engines in the ordinary daily round for a period of some twenty years it was hardly to be expected that work like that of No. 1008 could be relied on as a daily occurrence, even with the most expert of crews. While the newly-built compounds were set some very hard tasks in Scotland many more years were to pass before the loads limit on the Midland itself could be much increased above the old 230-240 tons standard. The old traditions were too deeply ingrained.

In 1923, in the matter of express engine power the Great Western had a substantial lead over all the other groups. It is true that so far as nominal tractive power was concerned the Gresley and Raven Pacifics were ahead of the Churchward 'Stars'; but while the latter was capable of considerable enlargement, just as it stood, the Gresley Pacific was at that time fairly hamstrung with an inefficient valve gear, and its best efforts of load haulage were achieved only at the expense of heavy coal consumption. Larger engines were certainly needed on the Great Western; in 1923 however the permanent way and underline bridge restrictions that had precluded the use of *The Great Bear* on the West of England road limited Swindon in the extent to which they could enlarge the 'Star', and the *Caerphilly Castle* of 1923, splendid engine though it was, fell some way below the full aspirations of Swindon at that time. The nominal tractive effort of 31,625 lb. was, however, some 12 per cent greater than that of the 'Star'; more significantly, it was higher than that of either class of LNER 'Pacific'. Here, indeed, was a challenge. The 'Castle' was a 4-6-0 weighing with its tender

One of Churchward's County class 4-4-0s, No. 3827 *County of Gloucester*.

A de Glehn compound of 1905 rebuilt with standard Swindon boiler: No. 103 *President*.

The Classic 'Castle': No. 5010 *Restormel Castle* in the painting style of the 1930s.

One of the '72XX' class 2-8-2 heavy main line tank engines.

W. Hawksworth, Great Western Railway.

O. V. S. Bulleid, Southern Railway.

Iward Thompson, London and North Eastern Railway.

H. G. Ivatt, London Midland and S Railway.

125 tons, while the Gresley Pacific scaled 148 tons. One might say that it is not entirely fair to include tenders in the total weight; but the engine and tender together form the complete, self-contained power plant, and if the one engine needed a very much larger tender than the other that in turn can be regarded as a measure of working efficiency—or lack of it. While with the Gresley 'Pacifics' through running between King's Cross and Newcastle was contemplated the Great Western 4-6-os were already running Wolverhampton to Paddington and back, and from Cardiff to Paddington and back on a single tenderful of coal —roughly the same mileage. In due course representatives of the two classes stood on adjacent stands at the British Empire Exhibition at Wembley in 1924. Some shrewd observers were convinced this was a portent of things to come.

Just how the locomotive interchange trial of 1925 did come about is not entirely clear, for those on whom the ultimate responsibility rested have now passed on, and they did not choose to disclose the whole story in their lifetime. One thing, however, seems quite certain; there was no question of a 'challenge' from Doncaster to Swindon, though looked at superficially the circumstances pointed to such a challenge. The Great Western had produced a much smaller engine, with a nominal tractive effort higher than that of the Gresley 'Pacific'; one could well imagine Doncaster flinging down the gauntlet and saying: 'Prove it! Prove that your much smaller boiler, and firebox, and your smaller coal and water capacity are equal to the job.' At that time, however, we know that Mr Gresley was not at all satisfied with the working of his 'Pacific' engines, and at the very time of the exchange Doncaster works was engaged on the manufacture of certain parts for an experimental modification to the valve gear. It is, therefore, not surprising that the idea of an exchange, at that particular time, was thoroughly distasteful to Gresley and his staff. But the Great Western then had in the late Sir Felix Pole a General Manager who was intensely proud of his railway, and all its achievements—not least the 'Castle' class engines—and one may be fairly sure that it was from him that the original suggestion came.

There was no secrecy about the interchange trials of 1925, no clandestine running in mid-winter over a remote stretch of line. The 'Castle' took the Leeds expresses from King's Cross, while the Gresley 'Pacific' essayed that most formidable of trains, the Cornish Riviera Express. Earlier in 1925 locomotive engineers had received a clue which, if it could really be believed, seemed to make the results of the interchange a foregone conclusion. Mr C. B. Collett had presented to the World Power Conference held in that year a paper in which the results of dynamometer car trials with the *Caldicot Castle* were published. That the new engines were capable of fine performance there was no doubt, but it was the economy of that performance on which attention was riveted. The actual coal burnt per mile on any particular journey has no more than a limited interest and value; it is the coal burnt in relation to the horsepower exerted in hauling the train that matters. In the years 1923-4 many British locomotives of excellent reputation were using 4 to $4\frac{1}{2}$ lb. of coal per hour for every horsepower exerted on the drawbar; on some the coal consumption was 5 or even 6 lb, while on very few, on especially favourable occasions, had given results just under 4 lb. The astonishment of engineers can therefore be well imagined when Mr Collett revealed that his new 'Castles' showed an average value of *less than three pounds*—2·83 to be precise. It is to be feared that the majority of locomotive men at that time just disbelieved the Great Western figures.

In contrast to this it was fairly obvious to any lineside observer that the Gresley 'Pacifics' were fairly heavy on coal; the continuous roar of their exhausts, and the apparent labour of their hardest efforts seemed to tell its own tale. But to the general public such technical considerations counted for little, if anything. With newspaper headlines, and a good deal of advance publicity the affair became a gigantic sporting contest, followed closely by thousands whose previous interest in railways was perfunctory, and in the eyes of that public the results indicated an almost runaway victory for the Great Western. The LNER had two engine failures on its own line, and while the Gresley Pacific kept good time with the Cornish Riviera Express, albeit with some very hard work, the GWR showed the margin they had in reserve by bringing in this crack train a quarter of an hour ahead of time twice within the test week, and each time on a lower coal consumption than the Gresley 'Pacific' had shown in working the normal schedule.

The immediate result, so far as the competing companies were concerned, was acrimony. Broadcasting was then in its infancy, but the event was of such widespread interest that Mr Cecil J. Allen was invited by the BBC to give a talk on the results. Now as all railway enthusiasts know, Mr Allen is one of the most fair-minded and impartial of commentators, and in fairness to the 'loser' he stressed some of the difficulties the Gresley 'Pacific' and her crew had been up against. But Mr Allen is one of the many men in modern life who have a dual professional capacity, and in addition to his well-known work as author and lecturer he was for many years in the civil engineer's department of the LNER. The substance of his broadcast soon became known at Paddington; it was taken by some as an official LNER version, and the next thing to appear was an extremely partisan account of the trials in the Great Western Railway Magazine. The heather was now fairly ablaze! Protests followed; there was a counter statement to the Press issued from King's Cross, and it was all very unpleasant. What was intended as a friendly and valuable interchange of ideas ended in a breach that took many years to heal. On the LNER side the technical lessons were well and truly absorbed, and after further experiments the 'Pacific' valve gear was re-designed, with such remarkable results indeed that the coal consumption was brought down to something very near to the Great Western figures. In any case it transformed the running of the engines and made them the greyhounds they proved in the thirties.

We must now turn to the Southern Railway, where the fine team of engineers built up by Mr Maunsell at Ashford, in South Eastern and Chatham days, was enlarged and strengthened to carry on the good work over the enlarged system. In the early days of grouping the Southern was unfortunate enough to become the butt of a group of daily newspapers. It is certainly true that at first things were far from well, but the campaign was of sufficient importance to require strenuous counter-propaganda from the publicity department at Waterloo, and in consequence various developments received more public attention, in advance, than had hitherto been customary in railway circles. The traffic department, for example, announced that the future standard in long distance passenger service would be 500-ton trains at average speeds of 55 m.p.h., and since there was, at the time of grouping, no motive power capable of such performance immediate consideration had to be given to new designs. But as often happens with advance announcements of such kind the detailed arrangements were not sufficiently ready for the plan to go ahead, and in the autumn of 1924 it became urgently necessary to build new engines of existing proportions to cope with the summer traffic of 1925, which was to include many additional trains and facilities. The London and South Western 'N15' class 4-6-0 was therefore taken as a basis.

The historic background of this class is worth recalling. The designer was Robert W. Urie, a charming old Scotsman who served for many years under Dugald Drummond, and who succeeded him as Chief Mechanical Engineer of the L&SWR in 1912. Urie perpetuated many of the Drummond precepts, particularly in the massive frame construction of his locomotives; but he anticipated the policy of the nationalized British Railways after 1948 in using only two cylinders for the largest express engines, when most railways were favouring three, or four. This suited Maunsell very well, because he had always stressed the point to his design staff: 'make everything get-at-able'; but in adopting the Urie 'N15' as a Southern standard he made important changes in design. On the South Eastern and Chatham Railway the GWR principle of valves with long travel had been adopted with excellent results, while the steaming capacity of the 'N15' was greatly improved by changes in the blast pipe and smokebox. When the construction of the new engines was well advanced the top management of the Southern Railway decided that for increased publicity value they should bear names. The choice of the 'King Arthur' legend, with engines named after Knights of the Round Table and other incidents of the stories, was a stroke of genius, though when the publicity officer went to Maunsell and put the suggestion, the CME replied drily: 'Tell Sir Herbert Walker I have no objection; but I warn you it won't make any difference to the performance of the engines!'

And so 'King Arthur class' the new 'N15's' became, with all the massive solidarity of an engine worked out by men brought up under Dugald Drummond, yet including some of the finer points of design that the Ashford school had learnt from Swindon. For the publicity people at Waterloo it was not enough that the new engines should be named, and while the Maunsell units carried the names of the Knights, *Sir Tristram*, *Sir Galahad*, *Sir Geraint*, *Sir Balin* and so on, the older Urie engines took other names associated with the Legend, such as *Iseult*, *Excalibur*, and *Morgan le Fay*. As sometimes happens when the search for suitable titles extends, there were curiosities; in the 'King Arthur' class two engines bearing different names actually refer to the same person, *Elaine* and the *Maid of Astolat*, and another one, while a very beautiful name in itself, *Melisande*, has no connection with the legend. When writing the first edition another of the Urie 'Arthur's', *Merlin*, achieved something akin to immortality as a television star, in the 'Saturday Night Out' programme of the BBC; but to appreciate the significance of what happened in that programme I must first tell a tale of 40 years ago. The traditions of massive construction practised on the London and South Western Railway were not to the liking of James Clayton, and when preparation were being made for the new 'super' express engine he tackled the old Scots chief draughtsman Jock Finlayson over the weight of the 'King Arthurs'. Why, he argued, must a Southern 4-6-0 of 25,000 lb. tractive effort weigh 81 tons without its tender, when a Great Western 'Castle' of 31,625 lb. weighs only 80 tons?

'Ah weel,' said old Jock, 'I suppose the spec-eefic gr-r-avity of steel is differ-r-rent at Swindon!'

Well, on the night of February 11, 1956, viewers were taken to

Longmoor Military Railway for a highly realistic example of train wrecking. The commentator's build-up of the situation was terrific! This was going to be no case of trick photography; no subterfuge with models. A real full-sized express engine was to be sent to her doom, and railway enthusiasts were saddened to see that the victim was old *Merlin*, then nearly 38 years old. The man at the 'mike' patted her a fond farewell; the driver and fireman started her, and then jumped off, and then we were taken down the line to the place where the 'sabotage' was to occur. The commentator may be forgiven for his excitement: 'You've seen nothing like it before', he exclaimed, and as the exhaust of the oncoming engine was seen above the trees, with his voice rising to the highest pitch he conjured up a vivid picture of the heap of twisted and ruined metal that was soon to lie at the foot of that embankment. One cannot blame him. He was not to know how British locomotives were built in the Age of Steam, especially those of the London and South Western. There was an explosion, and old *Merlin* left the rails all right; but then she ran down the embankment, remained bolt upright, and ploughed herself to a stand in the field at the bottom of the bank! The shades of Drummond, Urie, and Jock Finlayson must have chuckled. The engine whose doom was so deliberately and scientifically planned cheated her executioners, and stood there in the field, with steam blowing off, just as though she was ready to take the Atlantic Coast Express through to Exeter.

In their hey-day the 'King Arthurs' were grand engines. I have travelled thousands of miles behind them; I have ridden on their footplates at nearly 90 m.p.h.; on boat trains to and from Dover, on ordinary expresses to Southampton, to Exeter, to Ramsgate. But in 1925 they were not up to the 500-ton 55 m.p.h. standard demanded by the traffic, and once the new Maunsell 'Arthurs' were on order the attention of the design staff turned to thoughts of something considerably more powerful. Two contemporary British locomotive classes, working on other railways, seemed to Maunsell to meet the case so far as tractive power was concerned, and he anticipated the highly-publicized interchange trial of 1925 by carrying out a private and informal trial of the Great Western 'Castle' and the Gresley 'Pacific' in the late autumn of 1924. It was arranged for his personal assistant, James Clayton, to have foot-plate runs on both classes, and he returned to report strongly in favour of the 'Castle'. This was the first step towards the very famous Southern four-cylinder 4-6-0, the *Lord Nelson*. Much design work had yet to be done, and the arrangement of cylinders and boiler eventually proved different from Great Western prac-tice. But the inspiration was obviously there, When the *Lord Nelson* did appear, in the autumn of 1926, Southern enthusiasts learned to their delight that her tractive effort was higher than that of the 'Castle'; the much criticized Southern Railway now had the most powerful locomotive in the land! The publicity department at Waterloo made the utmost use of it, and the travelling public was duly impressed.

From this point onwards, to an onlooker it might have seemed that there was a race for the most powerful locomotive. With only four railway companies the issue now looked so clear cut that events that were really unconnected were apt to be regarded as sequels to one another. Thus the fact that the Great Western once more took the lead a year later has been quoted by men who were quite near to the heart of things, as the way Swindon rose to the Southern 'challenge'. Actually the new Great Western engine design of 1927 came about in quite a different way. In 1924 Church-ward's huge Pacific engine *The Great Bear* needed a new boiler; she had, however, been so restricted in her sphere of operations that renewal was scarcely an economic proposition, so Mr Collett scrapped the old boiler, cut down the frames at the rear-end, and renewed the engine as a 'Castle'—thus able to take her turn in the express working all over the system. This step, logical as it was from an engineering viewpoint, caused something of a stir at Paddington. To headquarters 'The Bear' had considerable publi-city value; it enhanced Great Western prestige to have the first British 'Pacific'. Her limited value as a motive power unit had not been fully appreciated, and vigorous inquiries were set on foot concerning the restrictions due to permanent way and underline bridges that precluded the use of larger and heavier engines. With the strengthening or renewal of certain structures it would be possible to use locomotives having an axle load of 22½ tons, compared with the existing 20, and so instructions were given to both the civil engineer and to Swindon to prepare for larger engines.

The 'King' class was the result. These extremely powerful engines were in the direct line of development from the Churchward 'Stars'; four-cylinder 4-6-0s with a big increase in tractive effort, due to larger cylinders and higher boiler pressure. Originally they were to have the standard driving wheels, with a diameter of 6 ft. 8½ in.; as such the tractive effort would have been 39,000 lb., at 85 per cent boiler pressure. But then Sir Felix Pole took a hand. Nothing if not a publicist himself Sir Felix suggested that if the driving wheels were made a little smaller the tractive effort could be pushed over the 40,000 mark. And so non-standard wheels of 6 ft. 6 in. diameter were adopted, and the tractive effort became 40,300 lb.—a tremendous feather in the publicity cap of the Great Western. In traffic the 'Kings' fulfilled all expectations; they were economical, they were fast, they took enormous loads in the holiday season. Half-day excursions at 5s. per head were run from Paddington to Swindon, to tour the works, to see 'Kings' under construction and repair; and these trips became so popular that the trains often loaded to sixteen coaches, despite which the 'King' class engines usually made the run at an average of over 60 m.p.h., start to stop. What great days those were on the GWR! But by the year 1927 the fourth of the great groups was seriously entering the field of railway publicity.

In the previous chapter I have told how the conflict of opinion between the various departments on the LMSR led to a virtual stalemate; how the operating department staged their *coup d'état*, in the borrowing of a Great Western 'Castle' class engine, and demonstrating that a well designed 4-6-0 without the complications of compounding could do all that was required for the haulage of the new Royal Scot express. *Launceston Castle* finished her dynamometer car tests between Crewe and Carlisle late in November 1926; the Royal Scot was to be introduced in June of the following year, and Sir Henry Fowler was instructed to have some three-cylinder 4-6-os ready for it. The chances were remote, but all concerned on the LMSR made a valiant try. There was no time for further trials and experiments; no opportunity for testing prototypes. A first order for fifty engines was to come straight from the drawing board. One cannot recall a single like case in the previous history of the steam locomotive in Great Britain, particularly in the case of an entirely new design—new in every respect—and for a first-line express passenger class too! By that time Sir Josiah Stamp had become President of the Executive on the LMSR, and the railway shops could not tackle the order in the time specified; the contract was therefore awarded to the North British Locomotive Company, and an arrangement made whereby engines should be built simultaneously at both Hyde Park and Queens Park Works, so as to secure more rapid delivery.

All this is enough to show us to what an extent the provision of new motive power on the LMSR had fallen into arrears. Even the detailed designing of the new engines was put out to contract, though this, of course, could not start until the basic design was settled. With everything now in such a shipwreck hurry, following the years of argument and deadlock, every possible means had to be sought to save time; there was no existing LMSR engine design that was acceptable for use as a guide, and in this crisis, although it was by a Swindon engine that the possibilities of a 4-6-o had been demonstrated, Derby sought the assistance of the Southern Railway in the earliest stages of the new design. Herbert Chambers, then chief locomotive draughtsman, was sent post-haste to Waterloo, and there he saw Clayton and Holcroft. As a result of that interview a full set of working drawings of the *Lord Nelson* was sent to the North British Locomotive Company, in Glasgow, and these were available for reference while the designing of the new LMSR 4-6-o was in progress. Chambers thereafter had the difficult task of supervising the design work, while carrying out his ordinary duties at Derby. That the 'Royal Scots' went straight into the service with practically nothing in the way of teething troubles is a monument to his work at this critical stage in LMSR history. But no mean share of the credit must also be given to Mr R. C. Bond, later Chief Mechanical Engineer to the British Transport Commission, who was resident inspector at the North British Locomotive Co.'s works during the time the 'Scots' were under construction.

The first engine of the class No. 6100, *Royal Scot*, was completed in September 1927, and at once created a favourable impression by her large boiler, and generally massive appearance. So far as tractive effort was concerned she ranked almost equal to the 'Nelson', and on the introduction of the winter service of 1927-8 the new engines were set to the task of running the Royal Scot express non-stop in each direction over the 299.1 miles between Euston and Carlisle. The average speed scheduled, namely 52 m.p.h. from start to stop, was not unduly fast, but with a regular load of about 440 to 450 tons all through the winter it set a severe task to both machines and men. Hitherto the record length of non-stop run had been held by the Cornish Riviera Express, with 225.7 miles from Paddington. Without any question the new engines were a great success; their work brought some badly needed prestige to the LMSR, and as more and more of them were completed they were drafted to duties over most of the old LNW and Caledonian lines. Dynamometer car trials showed that they were doing their work with good economy, and on more than one occasion Sir Henry Fowler expressed his particular delight at the interest shown by the general public, and in the little gatherings that assembled daily to witness the arrival and departure of the Royal Scot express at Euston. From the publicity point of view the LMSR had staged a remarkable entry into the field, particularly seeing that only a month before the debut of No. 6100 the Great Western had introduced the *King George V* to the public.

The year 1927 was indeed one of the most prominent milestones during the Age of Steam. In addition to the building of the 'Kings' and of the 'Royal Scots' it witnessed the perfecting of the modified valve gear on the Gresley 'Pacifics'. In connection with this change there is a story to be told. After the 1925 interchange trial with the Great Western certain of his assistants urged upon

Gresley the need for long travel valves; although himself dissatisfied with the performance of the gear as it was the chief was still reluctant to adopt a change that meant higher valve speeds and the possibilities of increased wear and tear. Moreover he was unconvinced of the advantages claimed. Grudgingly he gave permission for an engine to be altered on condition that as many as possible of the existing parts of the valve gear were utilized; No. 4477 *Gay Crusader* was the selected 'guinea pig', but the restrictions upon the conversions placed by Gresley rather cramped the style of the designer, and the engine was only partially successful. Again his assistants pressed Gresley for a more complete change, and eventually a second Pacific No. 2555 *Centenary* was altered. The results were so striking that at first Gresley was sceptical of the report brought to him; he was much involved at the time with his great project of a four-cylinder compound Pacific with a Yarrow water-tube boiler, and his closest associates feared that the long-travel valve conversion might well be pigeon-holed. Several weeks passed, and then one day he came into his office, rang for the assistant immediately concerned and said: 'I'm very pleased with that engine. Have the lot altered.' Without saying a word to any of his technical *entourage* he had sought out *Centenary* in traffic, ridden on her with a fast express, and formed his own conclusions.

The finishing touch in the development of the original non-streamlined Gresley 'Pacifics' came in that self-same eventful year of 1927, when engine No. 4480 *Enterprise* was fitted with a new boiler carrying a working pressure of 220 lb. per sq. in. Until the grouping of the railways only the Great Western had used to any extent pressures above 200 lb. per sq. in. Higher pressures, while affording greater power, are not attained without more than a proportionate increase in first costs and maintenance charges, and the locomotive engineers of other railways had mostly used 175 to 180 lb. But the need for increased power and for higher efficiencies was forcing their hand, and the LNER, from having the most powerful locomotives of all the Big Four at the time of grouping, would, with the completion of the *Royal Scot*, have dropped to the bottom of the table. But the alteration to the *Enterprise* was completed in July, so that in the tractive effort 'race' the positions in August were:

1.	GWR	*King George V*	40,300 lb.
2.	LNER	*Enterprise*	36,465 lb.
3.	SR	*Lord Nelson*	33,500 lb.
4.	LMSR	*Royal Scot*	33,150 lb.

Enterprise and the *Lord Nelson* each carried a boiler pressure of 220 lb. per sq. in., while the 'King' and the 'Scot' both had what was then the very high pressure of 250 lb. per sq. in.

Competition between the two groups had been carried into a different direction in the summer services of 1927—not one of speed, nor of locomotive power, but in length of non-stop run. In speed the Great Western had, by that time, a long start over their rivals, but in July 1927 the LNER began running an advance section of the Flying Scotsman non-stop from King's Cross to Newcastle, 268 miles, while the Royal Scot of the LMSR, which at first had to be run double-headed throughout, made a locomotive stop at Carnforth, 236¼ miles from Euston. The average speeds scheduled were not high, namely 48.7 m.p.h. to Newcastle, and 53.4 m.p.h. to Carnforth; it was, however, a beginning, and for that first summer the LMSR placed reliance on engines of the former L&NWR. There is no doubt that the 'Claughtons', unassisted, could, on their best form, have run that train,which loaded to just under 420 tons tare; but under the prevailing load limits, superheater 4-4-0s were provided as pilots every day. The inauguration of the winter service of 1927, with the Carlisle 'non-stop', put the LMSR well in the lead, but on May 1, 1928, the LNER again made history by running the Flying Scotsman non-stop between King's Cross and Edinburgh, 392.7 miles. In one way the East Coast *versus* West Coast rivalries of 1895 were being recalled. The new schedule of the Flying Scotsman, and the world record it would create, was somewhat naturally announced to the world with a considerable fanfare of trumpets; the LMSR were, therefore, tempted into the amusing step of breaking the new record before it had ever been made! The Royal Scot was then a 15-coach train—nine for Glasgow and six for Edinburgh; and on Friday, April 27, the train was divided, and both portions run non-stop from Euston to the Scottish cities: 401.4 miles to Glasgow, and 399.7 miles to Edinburgh. Both these runs were longer than that of the LNER Flying Scotsman, which was to begin on May 1. The 9-coach Glasgow non-stop was worked by a 'Royal Scot' engine No. 6113 *Cameronion*, while the Edinburgh train was run by a Midland compound, No. 1054.

The career of Mr Gresley was now beginning to move towards its most brilliant phase. Always a man of great enterprise, a driving force, and one with breadth and catholicity of outlook, he had, up to this time, moved with some caution in the wider sphere presented by the LNER since grouping. For he was above all a great railwayman. Whatever experiments he had in mind it was above all necessary that the trains must run. His innovations were at first confined to one or two locomotives; there was no flooding of the line with untried propositions, and of this his hesitancy to change the 'Pacific' valve gear was a case in point. But by the year 1927 he was becoming more assured of success, and when that assurance was combined with his innate qualities of enterprise and drive the other railways might well look to their laurels. And so it proved! To the running of the King's Cross–Edinburgh 'non-stop' of 1928, he brought one of those imaginative touches that came to immortalize him in the history of the steam locomotive—the corridor tender. The run of over eight hours was too long for one crew, and so Gresley provided a corridor through the tender by which one set of men could relieve the other, without stopping, at the approximate mid-point of the journey. As with the runs of 1927, the 'non-stop' Scotsman was easily timed, at an average of 47.6 m.p.h. throughout; but in the working of such a train many features of engine performance other than speed have to be considered: lubrication, coal supply, firing technique, and so on, and it is always wise to begin such a performance with plenty in hand.

Despite the greatly improved work of the Gresley 'Pacifics', and the new standards of performance that were being set up on the LMSR by the 'Royal Scots', both companies were, in 1927-8, embarking upon isolated experiments to try to secure higher thermal efficiencies than were apparently possible with the conventional type of steam locomotive. As early as the year 1924 Gresley sought the advice of Mr Harold Yarrow, of the famous Glasgow shipbuilding firm, with a view to a high pressure boiler of the water-tube type. Much careful design work followed, and eventually in December 1929 the 'hush-hush' engine appeared from Darlington works, a four-cylinder compound 4-6-4, with a Yarrow boiler carrying a pressure of 450 lb. per sq. in. In the meantime Sir Henry Fowler was building an experimental 4-6-0 using the Henschel type of boiler, and using the very high pressure of 900 lb. per sq. in. Neither of these bold experiments were successful, however, and progress continued on the lines of convention.

By this time the first signs of a really profound change in British railway motive power was beginning to show. In past years there had been much talk of main line electrification. Aspinall, on the Lancashire and Yorkshire, and Raven, on the North Eastern, had been staunch advocates; indeed a short time before grouping the North Eastern board, on Raven's advice, had decided to electrify the main line between York and Newcastle. So far, however, it had only been a matter of talk; but towards the end of the nineteen-twenties it was evident that the Southern Railway was in deadly earnest. In this book we are concerned with steam, and it is only for us to see how the electrification to Brighton, to Eastbourne, to Hastings, and to Portsmouth affected the steam men of the Southern. Its actual effects in the day to day running of the trains was only gradual, but to those who became aware of the policy decided upon by the top management the outlook was depressing in the extreme. Not only was steam development brought virtually to a stop, but no further money was available for renewal or repair of service and maintenance facilities. The steam men had to carry on as best they could, and they looked rather enviously to the electric services, which were magnificently planned, and provided with modern sheds and equipment.

But before the curtain descended temporarily upon steam developments on the Southern there is an interesting and remarkable engine design to be given its share of honourable mention, the 'Schools' class of 1930. Locomotives of greater tractive capacity than the Borsig 4-4-0s of 1914 were needed for the Hastings line; the gradients through Tunbridge Wells and the high country immediately to the south are severe, but weight restrictions, in addition to structural clearances, precluded the use of 'King Arthurs' class 4-6-0s. Maunsell began therefore to scheme out a miniature version of the *Lord Nelson*—a 'three-quarter Nelson' as it were; using the same sized cylinders, and motion parts, but with three cylinders instead of four, and having the 4-4-0 wheel arrangement. Originally it was intended to use a boiler and Belpaire firebox like the 'Nelson', but this proposal resulted in a greater axle load than could be permitted, and so the boiler eventually fitted was a shortened version of the 'King Arthur' type. The new engines, named after famous public schools, proved to have the highest tractive effort of any 4-4-0 in the country, or, indeed, in Europe. While the weight of engine alone in working order was no more than 67 tons the nominal tractive effort was 25,130 lb.—practically equal to that of the 81-ton 'King Arthurs'. A fairly restricted field of operation was at first envisaged for the 'Schools'. Their high tractive effort was intended for short spells of hard running up the heavy banks of the Hastings line, where the downhill stretches and the stops would give time for the boiler to recover. While, however, there are many locomotive designs in this story that did not come fully up to expectations— the *Lord Nelson* among them!—the 'Schools' provide one of those rare examples of a design giving its creators a very pleasant surprise.

Some of the 'Schools' went at once to the Hastings line; but others were put on to the fast expresses to Folkestone, Dover and Deal, and immediately showed that their capacity for sustained hard steaming was equal to that of the 'King Arthurs'. With the lightest of reins they would take heavy trains of 350 to 400 tons at speeds of over 70 m.p.h. on the level, and so economical was their working that despite their 6-wheeled, 4,000-gallon tenders, against the double-bogie 5,000-gallon tenders of the 'King Arthurs' there was no difficulty in running the Dover-Charing Cross stretch just under 80 miles, on one tenderful. More 'Schools' were built, and drafted to the Portsmouth expresses at a time when the timing for the non-stop run over the 73.6 miles from Waterloo was to be accelerated to 90 minutes. This is another very heavy road, with speed restrictions galore, and hard climbing to Haslemere and to Buriton Tunnel. With trains loading up to a maximum of eleven corridor coaches, 380-390 tons, the 'Schools', worked by a really splendid link of drivers and firemen at Fratton (Portsmouth), gave a magnificent record of performance until the electrification of the line in 1938. But though the finest work of the 'Schools' was yet to come we are getting well ahead of our period, and steps must be retraced to 1929 when the Great Western came very prominently into the picture once again.

Prior to the decelerations occasioned by the First World War the Great Western, despite its high all-round standards of running, had no train making a start-to-stop average of more than 60 m.p.h. In this respect the company was behind both the North Eastern and the Great Central. At one time it was behind the Caledonian too. But in 1923 the 2.30 p.m. express from Cheltenham to Paddington was accelerated to run the 77.3 miles up from Swindon in 75 minutes. For a long time this was the fastest run in the country, and then in 1929 there was an acceleration to 70 minutes. The train was not heavy, usually well under 300 tons and with engines of the 'Castle' class the going was at times very fast indeed. But no difficulties arose on occasions when the Churchward 'Stars' were employed, and on one journey, with the engine *Tresco Abbey*, the overall time was $64\frac{1}{2}$ minutes with a load of 265 tons. Sustained speeds of over 80 m.p.h. on level track were everyday occurrences. Then in the autumn of 1931 a further acceleration was tabled, to 67 minutes, and the introduction of this timing was signalized by some of the fastest running that had ever been re-

'Patriot' class 4-6-0 No. 5538 *Giggleswick* (1930 design).

Beyer-Garratt 2-6-0 + 0-6-2, with self-trimming coal bunker: built 1930.

he 'Princess-Coronation' class streamlined Pacific of 1937, No. 6222 *Queen Mary*.

anier Standard '8F' 2-8-0, of which large numbers were built by all British railways
in World War II.

The *Cock o' the North*, pioneer 2-8-2 express engine of 1934.

The final variety of 'A3' Pacific; No. 2500 *Windsor Lad*, first of a batch built in 1936

The Gresley 'A4': one of the 1937 examples built specially for the Coronation service
No. 4489 *Dominion of Canada*, with presentation bell, and C.P.R. type whistle.

A post-war variety, the Peppercorn 'A2' engine No. 525 named after the designer.

corded in the world at that time. For the first week the *Launceston Castle* was put on to the job, and the engine that had done so much in 1926 to influence LMSR locomotive policy now earned for herself and the GWR a new world's record.

For the first three days of the new schedule, September 14, 15 and 16, 1931, the drivers were encouraged to 'have a go'. Different crews, all from Old Oak Common shed, were on the job each day, and 'have a go' they did! On the first day the complete run took no more than 59½ minutes, an average speed from start to stop of 78 m.p.h. Then, with an extra coach on the train making a load of 230 tons behind the tender the second crew did very slightly better, with a time of approximately 58½ minutes. I use the word 'approximately' because on the second run the times were recorded in no greater detail than in the guard's journal. But all the time the eyes of enthusiasts were upon the previous fully authenticated world's record for a start-to-stop run by train, the 78.3 m.p.h. run of the Atlantic City Flyer, on the Reading Railroad, USA, made as long ago as 1905. Would the Cheltenham Flyer surpass this? The run of September 14 might almost be considered a tie, but on the third day Driver H. Jones and Fireman C. E. Brown put the matter beyond any doubt, with a magnificent run up in 58 minutes 20 seconds, an average speed of 79.5 m.p.h. The world's record thus passed unquestionably to Britain, and the Great Western Railway, but still more interesting perhaps was the inclusion in this run of a maximum speed of 90 m.p.h. on a track very little easier than level. I may add that Charles Brown, who fired *Launceston Castle* on this historic occasion, later became an express driver himself, and as a counterpart to the 90 m.p.h. with 195 tons on September 16, 1931, he once gave me a run from Chippenham to Paddington with the *King George VI* on which speed was held absolutely at 78 m.p.h. on level track with a 12-coach train of 445 tons.

Even with the achievement of September 16, the Great Western had not finished with record breaking, and on June 5, 1932, they surpassed themselves. This time it was engine No. 5006 *Tregenna Castle*, again with a 6-coach train, and after a magnificent run the

77.3 miles from Swindon to Paddington were completed in 56 minutes 47 seconds—an average speed from start to stop of 81.7 m.p.h. This time the maximum speed was 92 m.p.h., and the average for 39 miles of the journey was exactly 90. It might perhaps be thought that this was about the limit of speed that could then be achieved, even with such relatively small loads, but five years later another of the 'Castle' class engines, in running the Cheltenham Flyer, attained the extraordinary maximum speed of 95 m.p.h. near Didcot, on almost dead level track. So fast was the going indeed, that by Southall the times were actually less than those of the great record of June 1932. But this was an ordinary service journey and the driver had, perforce, to ease right down to avoid approaching Paddington far ahead of time. Apart from this however, I may conclude this chapter by quoting the words of Mr Cecil J. Allen after the run of 1932. 'A record of this character,' he wrote, 'is not merely the private possession of one single railway and its staff; it is a national triumph and a national asset.'

CHAPTER TEN

THE END IS FORESHADOWED

IN the early spring of 1956, when I was completing the first edition of this book, the end of the Age of Steam on the railways of Britain was certainly foreshadowed. But he would be a rash man who would forecast the exact date at which we could write *finis*; and unpalatable though it may be to the neophytes, the steam locomotive still had some pretty hefty shots left in the locker. At the very moment of writing a virtually new express passenger 'Pacific' engine had been turned out at Eastleigh works, by the extensively rebuilding of one of the 'Merchant Navy' class, and there were portents showing that development is by no means finished in other directions.

Through most of this book I have been writing of events distant enough to be seen in perspective, without the distraction of immediate day-to-day problems, which however large they may loom in one's own particular world may not after all prove of such vital consequence. In the years 1947-57 I had been travelling constantly in Great Britain, and in my professional work as an engineer I had been closely connected with certain aspects of railway work. I then felt too close to post-war railway history and the controversial topic of nationalization to give a considered review. New policies were still being worked out; radical adjustments were being made to suit labour and industrial conditions in the country as a whole, and it was yet to be seen whether the acute difficulties that surrounded all those who were connected with the steam locomotive would prove no more than an ugly passing phase, or whether it would hasten the end, and give a most embarrassing start to the new era of non-steam propulsion on British Railways. Rather than leave the book in a tangle I resolved therefore to end at VE day, 1945, and to postpone an account of the rest to some possible future occasion, which is now included in some additional chapters.

Returning now to 1932, the spring of this latter year marked the opening of the second phase of the grouping era. Ever since the racing days of 1895, and the recession that followed them, there had been a gentleman's agreement between the East Coast and the West Coast companies to eschew anything in the way of acceleration. The fastest booked time between London and Edinburgh was 7¾ hours, by the East Coast night trains, and 8 hours from Euston to Glasgow, also by night. The day expresses took 8¼ hours by both routes. In retrospect it does, indeed, seem extraordinary that 1932 of all years should have witnessed such a resurgence in railway enterprise as that revealed in the May timetables of the LMSR, and the LNER. As a nation we had scarcely begun to recover from the worst trade depression in history; in the heavy industries unemployment was rife, and an important feature of the programme of the National Government for the relief of unemployment was the State-financing of large reconstruction and improvement works on the railways. These plans, however, had been no more than formulated, still less carried through, by the spring of 1932, though the enterprise of the LMSR and LNER managements of that time can be taken as symbolic of the national will to surmount the economic crisis.

In May 1932, the overall times of the Flying Scotsman on the one hand, and the Royal Scot on the other, were cut 25 and 20 minutes respectively below the previously agreed time of 8¼ hours. And this was only a beginning. The services between London and Leeds and London and Liverpool soon included some very fast timings, such as 100 minutes for the 105½ miles from Grantham to King's Cross, and 142 minutes for the 152¾ miles from Crewe to Willesden Junction. While the Great Western still held the lead for the highest start-to-stop average, with the 69¼ m.p.h. run up from Swindon with the Cheltenham Flyer, the LMSR and LNER averages for their fastest trains were 64½ and 63½ m.p.h. respectively. But before these accelerations came into force there had been some important changes in the Chief Mechanical Engineers' department of the LMSR. At the end of 1930 Sir Henry Fowler, who was then 60 years of age, relinquished the office to become Assistant to the Vice-President for Works; he was succeeded for a short time by Mr E. J. H. Lemon, but from January 1, 1932, there was a further re-organization in which Mr Lemon was himself appointed a Vice-President of the company. By this time Captain H. P. M. Beames, who was Chief Mechanical Engineer of the L&NWR prior to the amalgamation with the L&YR, might well have been considered the natural choice; he was then only a little over 50 years of age, and had carried out a notable reorganization of Crewe works to speed up the repair of locomotives. But the LMSR management went further afield, and to the surprise and intense interest of the whole locomotive world they appointed Mr W. A. Stanier, then Principal Assistant to the Chief Mechanical Engineer of the Great Western Railway.

The Churchward influence was now to extend directly to the fourth group of the Big Four, and one can perhaps imagine 'The Old Man', living in rather a lonely retirement at Swindon, recalling his own words some 27 years earlier when G. H. Pearson, then the Carriage Works Manager, was chosen by Maunsell to be Assistant Chief Mechanical Engineer of the South Eastern and Chatham Railway: 'When other railways wanted a good man they came to Swindon.' For running the accelerated trains of 1932, however, the LMSR had to rely on existing locomotives, and the brunt of the work fell upon the 'Royal Scots'. By that time there were, in addition, some further three-cylinder 4-6-0s of a lower tractive capacity; they were reconstructions, or more truly replacements of the L&NWR 'Claughtons', and bore a strong family likeness to the 'Royal Scots' but with a smaller boiler. Somewhat naturally they were nicknamed the 'Baby Scots', though the official designation was 'Three-cylinder converted Claughton'. The original North Western 'Claughtons' became Class 5 in the LMSR power classification, and with the 'Royal Scots' Class 6, the rebuilds were classed '5X'.

To those who delight in the logging of fast runs, and who use split-second stop watches to clock the maximum and minimum speeds, the late Spring and Summer of 1932 provided a feast of good things. The inauguration of the summer services, on July

18, was indeed accompanied by a burst of publicity the like of which had never previously been seen in connection with British express train running. The LMSR in particular permitted the correspondents of daily newspapers to ride on the locomotives of some of the fastest trains, and one cannot be surprised that a few ultra-purple patches appeared in the Press the following morning. One can imagine the horror of permanent way men in reading that the new Manchester Flyer 'jangled across the tangle of many lines at Crewe ... at a dawdling 57 an hour!' Although the correspondent was very far out in his reckoning the mere fact that such a speed had appeared in cold print was enough to send even colder shivers down the spine of Authority, and when two years later I came to make my first journeys on the footplate of LMSR locomotives I was solemnly bidden to submit all my writings for approval before they were published!

Two 'Royal Scots', *Hector* and *Cameron Highlander*, were allocated to the working of the Liverpool Flyer; they were magnificently tuned up and specially maintained, and before the first summer was out some splendid runs stood to their credit. The fast timing of 142 minutes for the 152.7 miles from Crewe to Willesden was on one occasion cut to 136¼ minutes, despite 3 minutes delay *en route*, but those who retained an affection for the old North Western locomotives were also gladdened by the grand showing made by 'Claughtons' at weekends in the height of the season, when the train had to be run in two portions, and the second part was usually run by an ex-North Western engine. On one such trip a 'Claughton' made the trip in 140½ minutes, despite three minutes loss in running time from an engineering slack. But on the LMSR the use of engines other than the 'Scots' was reserved for exceptional or emergency occasions. On the LNER, however, while Gresley Pacifics ran the Leeds expresses, and the heavier Anglo-Scottish services operating via York, the very popular Pullman trains running non-stop between King's Cross and Leeds were entrusted to the old Great Northern 'Atlantics'. The Edinburgh and Glasgow train, by that time named 'The Queen of Scots', was speeded up to run the 185¾ miles between

London and Leeds in 195 minutes, and the Ivatt 'Atlantics', then nearly 30 years old, were called upon for some of the hardest and fastest work of their lives.

It is, however, not quite true to refer to them as the 'Ivatt' Atlantics. Certainly they were built during H. A. Ivatt's time at Doncaster, but since his retirement Mr Gresley had carried out a notable development of the original design. While some engineers were inclined to write down, if not to write off locomotives of earlier vintage Gresley seems to have had a genuine affection for engines, as such, and most of those of the constituent companies of the LNER were maintained largely in their pre-grouping condition for many years afterwards. For the Ivatt 'Atlantics', mainstay of the Great Northern express services during the first eleven years of his own chieftainship at Doncaster, he seems to have had a special regard. There were six stages in the gradual development of these engines, summarised in the accompanying table:

Stage	Engineer	Cylinders Dia.xStroke (inches)	Valves	Boiler pressure lb. per sq. in.	Superheater heating surface (sq. ft.)
1	Ivatt	18¾ x 24	Slide	175	none*
2	Ivatt	20 x 24	Piston	150	427
3	Gresley	18¾ x 24	Slide	175	427
4	Gresley	20 x 24	Piston	175	427
5	Gresley	18¾ x 24	Slide	175	568
6	Gresley	20 x 24	Piston	175	568

*non-superheated. Original design of 1902.

In his first superheater Atlantics Ivatt dropped the boiler pressure to 150 lb. per sq. in. but when Gresley began to apply superheating to the original engines he used 175 lb. and stages 3 and 4 represented an interim period, in which some of the original engines (stage 4) had enlarged cylinders and piston valves, while others (stage 3) retained the original arrangement. It was the introduction of the extra large superheaters, with 32 elements, that put the finishing touch on the development, and the engines of stage 6 did some remarkable work from 1932 onwards. I shall never forget a sweltering afternoon in the early summer of 1935 when I rode up from Leeds on the footplate of No. 4456 working the 'Queen of Scots' Pullman express. We made the run of 185¾ miles in 189½ minutes, but this time included a major delay at Peterborough. Due to permanent way repairs we not only had to slow down at Werrington Junction, but we could not take water from the troughs there. A special stop at Peterborough was made, and this, together with the effect of some checks in the approach to King's Cross, cost us some 13½ minutes in running. Our times on this occasion were equivalent to an unchecked non-stop run of 176 minutes from Leeds, *seventeen* minutes under booked time.

The accelerated schedule of the ordinary Anglo-Scottish expresses gave the Gresley Pacifics a grand opportunity to show what they could do, and details of many fast runs were recorded in those years. From the observations of day-to-day running, in ordinary service, without any special incentive to run hard, it became apparent that the normal maximum speed on favourable stretches was about 92 or 93 m.p.h. This is not to say that they would not or could not have run faster had they been 'pushed', but this was their optimum rate when linked up to their usual running position, and then allowed to run. The 'Royal Scots' were not usually so fast, but on the Southern Railway I have found that the 'Lord Nelsons' would top 90 m.p.h. without much difficulty. On my footplate journey with the 'Queen of Scots' express, and the Atlantic No. 4456 we reached a maximum speed of 93 m.p.h.; this was exceptional with those engines, and the more usual 'ceiling' lay in the high eighties.

Turning from engines to enginemen, I have written earlier of the disappointment felt by men of the former North Eastern Railway at the turn of events after grouping, when locomotive development followed upon the practice of the Great Northern Railway, and not their own, and how resentment showed itself in much poor running. At the time of the 1932 acceleration, however, the engine working diagrams on the East Coast Route were rearranged so that the crack day expresses were hauled between London and Newcastle by ex-GNR and ex-NER crews on alternate days. King's Cross was thus put into direct competition, as it were, with the Tyneside sheds of Gateshead and Heaton. There are no better locomotive enginemen to be found anywhere in the country than the 'Geordies', and put on their mettle in this way the keenness and enthusiasm for which they had been famed returned with a rush, and the accelerated services were run with splendid dash and punctuality whether London or Tyneside men were on the job. The Gateshead 'Super-Pacifics' *Trigo*, *Manna*, *Gainsborough* and *Blenheim* became as well known to the 'spotters' of King's Cross as *Flying Scotsman*, *Royal Lancer*, and *Papyrus*, while the down Flying Scotsman itself on Tuesdays, Thursdays, and Saturdays was worked by one or other of the Heaton engines *Dick Turpin*, *Bayardo* or *Neil Gow*.

Those were great days on the East Coast Route! The big 'Pacifics' in their apple-green livery were all beautifully kept, and behind them were the great trains of varnished teak coaches—rarely less than fourteen of them, and more usually fifteen, sixteen, or seventeen. I was working near King's Cross station at the time, and I came to know many of the drivers, firemen, and inspectors. Business took me fairly frequently down the line; occasionally I was privileged to ride on the footplate, but even while the new order of speed was settling happily into its stride still greater things were brewing. It was in the year 1931 that the railway world in general heard of the French engineer, André Chapelon of the Paris-Orleans Railway. In that year he had rebuilt one of the de Glehn compound 'Pacifics' with such astonishing results that details of the modernization attracted world-wide interest among locomotive men. Over many years Gresley had enjoyed the friendship of M. Chapelon, and also of his fellow engineers, Lancrenon, of the Nord, and Duchatel, of the Est; and he became convinced of the advantages of still higher boiler pressure, and of internal streamlining of the steam passages, and the inlet and exhaust ports of the valves. The Chapelon rebuilds on the Orleans Railway remained four-cylinder compounds, but

Gresley applied the principle of internal streamlining to a new and very powerful 2-8-2 express engine, the *Cock o' the North*, designed for the hilly road between Edinburgh and Aberdeen. It was built at Doncaster in 1934 and before going into regular service in Scotland it was tested over the Great Northern main line to King's Cross.

The *Cock o' the North*, with a nominal tractive effort of 43,462 lb., was the most powerful express locomotive in the country; but with eight coupled wheels and a wheel diameter of 6 ft. 2 in. she was intended for hard slogging on the Scottish banks rather than high speed. Following various experimental applications in this country, and their adoption for the high pressure cylinders of Chapelon's Orleans Pacifics, Gresley used poppet valves, rather than piston valves, and the result astonished everybody, even those most intimately connected with the design. When a senior assistant returned from some of the first runs and reported that this eight-coupled engine had reached 85 m.p.h. with ease, Gresley let out an incredulous 'What?!' Yet, so it was. Never before had Doncaster built an engine that ran so freely as this giant 2-8-2, with a boiler so big as to be devoid of all top mountings, and a smokebox tapered down towards the front and fitted with screens at the side to deflect the exhaust steam clear of the cab windows. A second engine of the same general type was built, the *Earl Marischal*, but with a more conventional front end and piston valves. A series of comparative trials was thereafter commenced in Scotland; the *Cock o' the North* worked from Edinburgh, and the *Earl Marischal* from Dundee.

So we come to the year 1935, and the Silver Jubilee of His Majesty King George V. Until a time roughly marked by the year 1930 electric traction had been considered as the only serious rival to steam as a form of railway motive power, but in 1930 attention was drawn to certain experiments in Central Europe with diesel locomotives, and in 1932 the German firm of Maybach built a twin railcar unit for high speed service between Berlin and Hamburg. There were similar developments in America. In Germany, after prolonged trials, 'The Flying Hamburger', as it was known, went into regular service, and maintained an average speed of 77.4 m.p.h. between the two cities; Gresley paid a visit to Germany late in 1934, travelled on the Hamburger, and was much impressed by the smooth running of the twin railcar set at speeds sustained around 100 m.p.h. for long distances. He was so impressed by the possibilities of extra high speed travel that he approached the makers of the German train to investigate the possibilities of a high speed service between London and Newcastle. Due to gradients, curves, and speed restrictions on the LNER line Maybach could not offer a higher average speed than 63 m.p.h. making due recovery allowances for bad weather, permanent way checks, and so on. The train was to be a 3-coach diesel-electric set, providing seats for 140 passengers, but in accommodation much more cramped than the ordinary LNER 'thirds'. Despite the speed such a train would not have been popular with the business men regularly travelling, and at this stage Sir Ralph Wedgwood, Chief General Manager of the LNER, suggested that providing the load was not too heavy a far better service could be provided by an ordinary Gresley Pacific.

His suggestion was put to a practical test on March 5, 1935, and the result ranks with the last night of the 1895 race, and with May 9, 1904, as one of the great classics in the Age of Steam. Arrangements were made for a special train of six coaches to be worked from King's Cross to Newcastle and back in the day. This train would have provided nearly double the accommodation of the proposed German diesel train, in far greater comfort, and with full restaurant facilities. The LNER test train weighed 214 tons, and the engine selected was a standard Super-Pacific No. 2750 *Papyrus*. Leaving King's Cross at 9.8 a.m. a splendid run was made to Newcastle in three minutes under the even 4 hours—an average from start to stop of 68 m.p.h., and 18 minutes faster than Maybach could promise with a diesel train. Moreover the Gresley Pacific had a handsome margin in reserve; it was not necessary to exceed 88 m.p.h. at any point, and 7 minutes lost by incidental delays were recovered *en route*. On the return journey, with the same engine but a different driver and fireman, some considerably faster running was made, and in descending the Stoke bank, between Grantham and Peterborough, opportunity was taken to see what one of these engines might do in the way of maximum speed, if really pressed. The result was a maximum of 108 m.p.h., lowering at last the Great Western record of 1904. The possibility of a 4-hour service between London and Newcastle had been amply demonstrated; but in regular operation, in all weathers, Gresley felt it necessary to have still more in hand.

So, there was designed and built at Doncaster, in the very short space of five months, the very famous Silver Jubilee train. The engine, classified 'A4', was a modified version of the standard Super-Pacific, with higher boiler pressure, smaller cylinders, and internal streamlining in the Chapelon style. But it was the external appearance that took one's breath away! Finished in silver and grey, in a bizarre streamlined casing, the first 'A4' engine *Silver Link* created a tremendous sensation before she had turned a wheel on an express train. But if her static appearance caused a sensation, how can the inaugural run of September 27, 1935, be described? On that afternoon, a Friday, representatives of the Press were invited to a demonstration run from King's Cross to Grantham and back. It was originally intended to run at the service speed of the Silver Jubilee train, which was to go into service on the following Monday: but due to signalling restrictions north of York a speed limit of 70 m.p.h. had been imposed pending some alterations, and opportunity was taken of the Invitation Run on the Friday to see how much time was in hand on the service schedule south of Grantham. To pass Peterborough 76.4 miles from King's Cross, $63\frac{1}{2}$ minutes were allowed—an average from start to pass of 72 m.p.h.; but when that special duly set out from King's Cross few of those on board could in their wildest dreams have foreseen the speed at which they were to be taken along.

Potters Bar marks the summit of the long climb over the Northern Heights of London; there the Flying Scotsman, and other heavy trains, are usually doing about 45 m.p.h. *Papyrus* on the March trial was doing 64, but *Silver Link* went over the top at *seventy-five miles per hour*. A terrific standard had been set from the start, and onwards to Peterborough the comparison between *Papyrus* and *Silver Link* tells its own tale:

Location (near)	Speeds m.p.h. *Papyrus*	*Silver Link*
Hatfield	80	98
Knebworth	68	88
Hitchin	82½	107
Three Counties	88½	112½
Sandy	83¾	105
Tempsford	86	109½
St Neots	82½	104½
before Offord	70	109½
after Huntingdon	74½	83½
Holme	86½	93½
Average speed Potters Bar to Holme	79.0	96.5
Time: King's Cross to Peterborough	63¼ min.	55 min.

A great crowd of railwaymen and others had gathered on the platforms at Hitchin to watch the special pass; she was through like a flash, at 107 m.p.h.! In the train itself things were exciting beyond description. The track, though safe enough, was not super-elevated for comfort at such speeds; and while the Press representatives were thrilled to the marrow the experienced senior railwaymen on board were apprehensive to the last degree—all, that is, save Gresley himself! With a huge chronograph he thoroughly enjoyed it all, and at each lurch or sway jocularly directed the attention of the terrified civil engineer to the state of his permanent way. It was small comfort to those in the train to learn afterwards that during that spell of hurricane running the engine was riding perfectly. Those on the footplate had no conception of what was happening in the coaches behind them!

Spectacular though this run was, with the world's records that it brought to Gresley, the LNER and Britain herself, a still more solid achievement was the magnificent performance of *Silver Link* during the first fortnight of the new service. On September 30, only one streamlined engine was yet available, and a fortnight passed before *Quicksilver* was ready to take up her share. During those first two weeks *Silver Link* did the whole job; 268.3 miles each way, five days a week, at an average speed of 67 m.p.h., with almost perfect timekeeping, and not a hint of mechanical trouble. When she commenced this remarkable *début Silver Link* was only three weeks old. In the King's Birthday Honours of 1936 Gresley was created a Knight Bachelor, the first British railwayman to receive such an honour specially on account of his locomotive work. In years gone by Gooch, Aspinall, Raven and Fowler were each knighted, but for other achievements. Sir Nigel Gresley, as he became, was honoured for his services—*The Times* happily expressing it—as 'engineer and speeder-up to the LNER'.

In the meantime things had not been standing still on the LMSR, where Stanier had faced a very different task in 1932. At the time of grouping that railway owned 10,316 locomotives, made up of 393 different types. The elimination of obsolete and ineffective types had from the first been taken seriously in hand, and by the end of 1931 the numbers were down to 9,032, made up of 261 types. At the Annual General Meeting of the company in 1932 Sir Josiah Stamp looked forward to the time when the number of types might be as low as 20: 'for obviously,' he added, 'the fewer the number, adequate to the task to be performed, the more steady, uniform and economic the flow for repairs'. The policy that John Ramsbottom had inaugurated on the London and North Western seventy years earlier, and that Churchward had applied on the Great Western in 1903 was now in process of application over the whole LMSR system, and to Stanier more than any of his predecessors fell the task to designing the new standard engines. While the locomotive position was, for the moment, sound at the highest level, with a total of 70 'Royal Scots' on the road in 1932, it was in respect of second-line motive power that the LMSR weakness lay. A stud of 190 new Midland compounds had been built since grouping but on a long term basis they were limited to the lighter classes of passenger traffic. If the number of engine types on the system was to be drastically reduced, in accordance with the policy laid down by the Chairman, the greatest need was for a general utility locomotive of Class 5 capacity, that could take passenger and goods trains with equal facility, that would be economic in light service, could run over all main and subsidiary lines on the system, and which could, in emergency, take the heaviest express trains.

The basic design for such an engine was already well known at Swindon. Among the standard classes Churchward had proposed in 1901 was a large 4-6-0, with coupled wheels, 5 ft. 8½ in. diameter. No such engine was built during his own chieftainship, as his 2-6-0s did all that was then necessary in the way of mixed traffic working. But in 1924 Mr Collett had altered one of the two-cylinder express engines, the *Saint Martin*, substituting 6 ft. for the original 6 ft. 8½ in. coupled wheels, and in 1928 he built the first batch of the now well-known 'Hall' class, generally the same as the conversion of 1924. These engines proved a great success, and Stanier took the design as a basis for his LMSR general utility class. Although not the first, nor the most spectacular of his locomotives, the 'Black Fives', or the 'Black Staniers' as they are variously called, can be considered the most important engines he put on the road. In general proportions and in maximum power output they are very similar to the Great Western 'Halls'; but on the LMSR a much higher degree of superheat was found desirable, and against the traditional use of inside Stephenson's link motion, on the GWR two-cylinder types, Stanier used Walschaerts radial valve gear, outside, with all parts readily 'get-at-able'.

I think it would be fair to say that never in the history of steam traction has there been a locomotive design more widely popular, with the footplate men, in the works, and with shed staff alike, than the 'Black Staniers'. In LMSR days they worked over the entire system, and beyond: from Euston to Wick; from Holyhead to Hull; from York to Bournemouth. Since nationalization they have penetrated still further afield, to meet an equally enthusiastic reception. They are capable of heavy and fast work on the road, they are light in repair costs, and are no trouble in the sheds,—what more could any locomotive designer produce! To the LMSR policy of standardization they were indeed 'the answer to a maiden's—or perhaps I ought to say a Chairman's (!)—prayer'. By the middle of 1945, a total of 574 had been built, and construction of them continued until after nationalization in 1948. I have ridden on them in all kinds of service: through a Highland blizzard at nearly 70 m.p.h.; over the Furness line; slogging nearly 'all-out', at under 20 m.p.h. over the 1 in 50 gradients of the Somerset and Dorset, and tearing down towards Nottingham at 88 m.p.h. with a Midland Scotch express. Nothing of the 'Rolls-Royce' about them, to be sure; they were designed for hard, knock-about service, and not infrequently they give their crews and their occasional visitors a rough ride. But they are not the first British locomotive to do this. The race of locomotive men born and bred in the Age of Steam did not seek a feather-bed existence, and to them engines like the 'Black Staniers' were the breath of life.

Apart from the prime necessity for providing engines of medium capacity for general service over almost the entire system, something considerably larger than the 'Royal Scots' was necessary if the development and acceleration of the heaviest main line express service was to continue. It was not merely a question of weight haulage and speed, nor yet a low consumption in relation to the work done. If the policy of reducing the total number of locomotives in service was to continue a higher daily mileage would have to be obtained from each individual engine, and one way to do so was to institute longer through runs. Supposing the turn-round time at a running shed was three hours, providing suitable services were available a greater daily mileage could be secured if the length of engine run was 300 miles, instead of 200; and so on. On the Anglo-Scottish services through engine working over the 400 miles between Euston and Glasgow was now envisaged; more-

lliam Stanier, a portrait taken around 1939.

R. A. Riddles. Formerly Member of Railway Executive, for Mechanical and E trical Engineering.

ond, General Manager, British Railways ops: formerly Chief Mechanical Engineer, British Railways Board.

E. S. Cox, Formerly Deputy Chief Mechanical Engineer, British Railways Board.

A fine action shot of a 'Britannia', No. 70029 *Shooting Star* near Wootton Bassett.

One of the Class '6' Pacifics, No. 72009 *Clan Stewart*.

The Class '5' mixed traffic 4-6-0.

One of the '9F' 2-10-0 fitted with the Franco-Crosti boiler.

over, instead of the 'up one day, and down the next' principle hitherto worked with the London-Carlisle non-stops, it was hoped for example that the engine of the down midnight sleeping car express, due in Glasgow at 9.35 a.m., would be ready to return with the up Midday Scot at 1.30 p.m. It was an ambitious project, and to Stanier fell the task of designing appropriate engines. He took up this challenge immediately upon his arrival from Swindon, and in a little more than a year he had built the largest and heaviest express locomotive then seen in this country. It preceeded by just over a year Sir Nigel Gresley's 2-8-2 *Cock o' the North*.

The development of the Stanier 'Pacific' design is one of great interest. The pioneer engine, No. 6200 *The Princess Royal*, was in many respects based upon Great Western practice; the nominal tractive effort was exactly the same as that of the 'Kings', and in the huge boiler and firebox no more than a moderate degree of superheat was intended. As originally designed, however, the area available for free-gas flow through the small superheater was found to be inadequate; the steaming was not always reliable, especially on the long runs between London and Glasgow, and within two years the boiler design had been considerably modified. While tests were in progress only two 'Pacifics' had been built; but on June 27, 1935, engine No. 6200 gave a magnificent display of her enhanced capacity on a test run with the up Liverpool 'flyer'. With a load of 15 coaches, 475 tons total behind the tender the 152.7 miles from Crewe to Willesden were covered in 129½ minutes start to stop. To maintain an average speed of nearly 71 m.p.h. from start to stop with a load of 475 tons was indeed a wonderful performance, and by that time construction of a further batch of 'Pacifics' engines was well in hand at Crewe. Heavy load-haulage was to be the keynote of their work; as yet there was no LMSR counterpart of the Silver Jubilee.

The hardest task ever set to the 'Princess Royal' class engines came with the summer service of 1936, when the 'Midday Scot' was further accelerated and included in its schedule the run of 51.2 miles from Lancaster to Penrith, over Shap Summit, in the

very sharp time of 59 min. start to stop. This also was no featherweight of a train—never less than 14 coaches, and sometimes rising to 16; yet in the climb to Shap Summit, from practically sea
level at Carnforth, a rise of nearly 900 ft. had to be surmounted
in 31.4 miles, at an average speed of 51 m.p.h. It was no isolated
effort, for on this duty the 'Princess Royal' class engines were
working through from London to Glasgow; 230 miles of hard
work had already been done, and even after Shap was climbed
there remained the 1,015 ft. altitude of Beattock summit, 50 miles
north of Carlisle. The grandest run on record with this train
stands to the credit of engine No. 6208 *Princess Helena Victoria*,
when, with a 16-coach train of 515 tons, the stretch from Lancaster
to Penrith was covered in 56 minutes, and the average speed
between Carnforth and Shap Summit was nearly 53 m.p.h.

By the late autumn of 1936 it was an open secret that special
preparations were in hand on both East Coast and West Coast
routes for further accelerated services to mark the Coronation
year of His Majesty King George VI. In August the LNER had
run dynamometer car trials with the Silver Jubilee express, and
fractionally increased their own speed record from 112½ to 113
m.p.h.; in November it was the turn of the LMSR. Hitherto the
latter company had concentrated its finest feats of locomotive performance into the working of heavy trains. The 5.25 p.m. from
Liverpool to Euston and the accelerated Midday Scot are outstanding examples. But with the LNER already running to Newcastle in the level four hours it would be an easy matter for them,
by extending the Silver Jubilee standard of performance, to cover
the remaining 124 miles to Edinburgh in a little under two hours,
and so make a 6-hour service from London possible; and already
there were rumours that the LMSR would attempt the same
between Euston and Glasgow. Obviously such speed could not
be expected with loads like that of the Midday Scot, and on November 16, a trial run was made with a train of almost exactly the
same weight as the Silver Jubilee, 230 tons. This special test
train was not only taken non-stop from Euston to Glasgow, but
was taken through in the unprecented time of 353½ minutes—an

average speed of 68 m.p.h. One of the 'Princess Royal' class engines was used, No. 6201, *Princess Elizabeth*, and the running was indeed magnificent throughout. Between Crewe and Carlisle at long last the great record of the 1895 race was lowered, though the Pacific engine's time over this 141-mile stretch—122½ minutes against *Hardwicke's* 126 minutes in 1895—was favoured by passing through Crewe and Carlisle stations at 20 m.p.h., whereas the little 2-4-os record was from a dead start to a dead stop. On the following day the *Princess Elizabeth*, with a heavier load of 260 tons, made the return trip to London in nine minutes less time—a wonderful run of 344¼ minutes for the 401.4 miles.

It now seemed as though there was no limit to the speed or tractive capacity of modern British locomotives, and from the opening of that gracious year of the Coronation until the fatal autumn of 1939 records of one kind or another followed in rapid succession. In speed of service offered to the public the Coronation Scot of the LMSR fell considerably below expectations, with a time no faster than 6½ hours between Euston and Glasgow. But before the train went into regular service two more records had been broken: the British speed record had been wrested from the LNER by the narrow margin of 1 m.p.h., and thus now stood at 114; and the fastest-ever run from Crewe to Euston had been made—158 miles in 119 minutes, that is 79.7 m.p.h. average. On the East Coast the LNER were sufficiently confident of the capacity of the Gresley streamlined Pacifics to load the six-hour London-Edinburgh express up to 312 tons against the 220 tons of the Silver Jubilee, and some of the hardest daily work ever set to British locomotives was involved in the running of that train. In the meantime the Great Western, which had done so much in earlier years to raise the standard of speed in this country, was rather eclipsed by the brilliance of the limelight drawn upon themselves by the LMSR and the LNER. In 1935, to celebrate the Centenary of the company, the Great Western had put on the Bristolian express running the 118 miles between Paddington and Temple Meads in 105 minutes each way; but this average of 67½ m.p.h. with a train of about 240 tons looked relatively 'small beer', compared with the 72 m.p.h. average of the LNER Coronation, with 312 tons, between King's Cross and York.

For the Coronation Scot, and for general heavy express service on the LMSR, the second class of Stanier Pacific engine was built. Magnificent though the work of the 'Princess Royals' had been it was felt that still greater steaming capacity was desirable. Already, however, the weight was up to the maximum permitted by the civil engineer but, in the later engines, by use of alloy-steel plates it was possible to provide a boiler having a total heating surface some 22 per cent greater than in the 'Princess Royals' with practically no increase in the total engine weight. The nominal tractive effort in both classes was almost exactly the same, but with a complete redesign of the front end, providing very large direct and internally streamlined passages, the freedom of running at high speed was considerably increased. The first engines of this class, built specially for the Coronation Scot, were fully streamlined. In later years further batches were turned out from Crewe, some streamlined and some not, but the streamlined casing has now been removed from all of them. Whether streamlined or not, the 'Coronation', or 'Duchess' class, as they are variously known, were among the finest express engines ever built in this country.

It has been my privilege to make many runs on their footplates, and at different times I have been over the entire 450 miles between Euston and Perth with them. One of the most interesting accessories that they carry is the steam-operated coal pusher in the tender. On a long non-stop run, such as Euston to Carlisle, Crewe to Motherwell and so on, things can become most laborious for the fireman towards the end of the run due to the difficulty of getting coal forward; no matter how carefully the coal space in the tender is designed there are times when the coal has to be got forward by hand. The tenders of the 'Duchess' class engines had a steam operated coal pusher. When more was required from the back of the tender the fireman turned the handle of a steam valve, and a further supply of coal from the back of the tender was rammed towards the shovelling plate. On a train like the night Inverness sleeper, which made only one brief stop in its 290-mile run from Crewe to Perth, one can imagine how welcome the coal pusher was to a fireman who had to shovel his way over Shap, Beattock and Gleneagles, in succession—all in a single night's work.

The speed record of 114 m.p.h. did not remain with the LMSR for very long. In June 1938 the LNER took the advantage of some special trials to make an all-out attempt upon the record on that finest of all British racing stretches, from Stoke tunnel down towards Peterborough. With the possible exception of the 108 m.p.h. with the non-streamlined Pacific *Papyrus* in 1935 the previous records of speeds in excess of 100 m.p.h. had been made in conditions more or less normal from the engine working point of view; the locomotives had been given their heads, but not unduly pressed. But on that ever-memorable Sunday in June 1938 the 'A4' engine *Mallard* was driven to her utmost limit; indeed, as events turned out she was pushed beyond it. In normal express train running the admission period for steam entry to the cylinders is shortened as the speed rises, so that while steam may be cut off after the pistons have travelled 30 per cent of their stroke at 30 m.p.h., the point of cut-off is usually not more than 15 per cent at 60 m.p.h. But on *Mallard* the point of cut-off was *increased* as the speed rose, until the driver had advanced to the extraordinary figure of 40 per cent at speeds of over 100 m.p.h. Thus they reached the very spectacular maximum of 126 m.p.h.—still the world's record with steam. This run is in some ways comparable to the greatest feats of motor car and speed boat racing, in that the speeds and the conditions under which they were attained were far beyond the realms of practical everyday operating. With *Mallard* the tremendous pounding at speeds of more than 100 m.p.h. led to heating of the centre big-end, and this particular test run had to be completed at Peterborough.

But the year 1938 witnessed not only the great record of *Mallard*, but the Munich crisis, in September, and thenceforward all events, railway and otherwise, were overshadowed by the growing realization that a second world war was almost inevitable. When war did come, a year later, its impact upon the railways was altogether more sudden and complete than in 1914. Then, more than two years were to pass before express train services were seriously decelerated and such amenities as dining-cars withdrawn, but in 1939, the black-out was immediate, literally and otherwise. In the ensuing six years the burden shouldered by the railways of this country was colossal. But it was not a normal burden. In normal circumstances an industry that is entrusted with vast additional contracts can equip itself with new factories and tools, and can take vigorous steps to recruit additional staff; but from 1939 onwards the railways were faced with an extraordinary situation. They were required to carry a great increase in freight train traffic; they faced a gradual diminution of staff, due to the call-up of many men, and the transfer of specialists to Government work elsewhere; they were asked to undertake much direct munition work of a special kind in the locomotive shops, and all the time the veto upon capital expenditure was almost complete. Locomotives had to run for longer periods between successive visits to the works for overhaul, yet the work demanded of them was greater than ever. The black-out and the ever-present danger of air-raids increased the nervous tension. Yet the response, whether in the technical quality of the war effort from the workshops, or in the devoted services given by the operating and footplate men, was well-nigh sublime.

When, for example, representatives of the ministries concerned visited Swindon to see if any precision work on certain highly specialized items could be done there, they were astonished at the capacity revealed; they left, not with ideas as to what might be done there, but with the impression that there was practically nothing that *couldn't* be done there. So it was also in other large railway works. Locomotive construction for home service was reduced to a mere trickle, but among railway men the situation was appreciated, and the industry toiled on. The public was exhorted not to travel. By posters we were told: 'Give your seat to a shell'; 'Is your journey really necessary?'; 'There is not even half an engine to spare', and so on. Main routes were occasionally blocked by air-raid damage, drivers and firemen often worked incredibly long hours without relief, and somehow the trains went through. Speeds were low, passenger trains had from the outset been deprived from their old priority, and the dinginess of war gradually descended upon all—stations, carriages and engines alike.

The Chief Mechanical Engineers and their staffs had many urgent problems, apart from any thoughts they might have had towards new engine designs, and by the year 1942 there had been a complete change of command. On the Southern, Mr R. E. L. Maunsell had been succeeded by Mr O. V. S. Bulleid, in 1938; Sir Nigel Gresley died, in harness, in April 1941, and in July of that same year Mr Collett retired. The change was completed in the summer of 1942 when Mr Stanier was seconded to the Ministry of Production for special duties. In addition to Mr Bulleid, the other new Chief Mechanical Engineers were Mr Edward Thompson, LNER, Mr F. W. Hawkesworth, Great Western, and Mr C. E. Fairburn, LMSR, acting in Mr Stanier's absence. Before the war was over the work of all four showed signs of forward-looking—not to any 'Land for heroes', but to a grim prospect, of austerity, of bad coal, of diluted labour in the sheds, and of a continuing embargo upon all schemes of heavy capital expenditure. And in America, even in the height of the war, the changeover from steam to diesel traction was gaining momentum.

The four British Chief Mechanical Engineers, while each seeing something of the prospects ahead, had different problems to face on their own railways. On the Southern the emphasis was upon electrification, yet in the post-war years capital for further large schemes would be slow in coming forth. Steam would have to carry on for some time, and the existing locomotives were ageing. While working out a mechanical design on principles new to British steam locomotive practice Mr Bulleid seems to have realized, more clearly than anyone else, the need to have something with a 'new look' about it. His new three-cylinder 'Pacific' engines were intended for mixed traffic working, and authority of the wartime Railway Executive Committee was therefore given for a limited number of them to be built during the war. The outcome was the *Channel Packet*, first of the well-known 'Merchant Navy' class. In these engines Bulleid attempted to reduce wear, and shed maintenance by putting the valve gear and the inside connecting rod in a totally enclosed chamber containing an oil bath. It was hoped that this gear would need no attention from one major overhaul to the next. The 'new look' was provided by the queer, air-smoothed outer casing.

On the LNER Mr Edward Thompson was also faced with the problem of an ageing stud of locomotives in the intermediate power class. Sir Nigel Gresley had been fortunate in the engines the LNER had inherited from the constituent companies at the time of grouping, and while he was building the big 'Pacifics', 'Green Arrows' and 2-8-2s for the heaviest main line duties, the pre-grouping engines did the lesser work admirably. But this could not continue indefinitely, and the war, with the longer periods inevitable between successive overhauls, affected the older engines most seriously. By the year 1940 many of the 'Atlantics' were over 30 years old, and were subject to all those troubles of cracked frames, and so on, that come to affect the very best of engines with advancing years. During the war it was a case of 'make do and mend', but Thompson, looking to the future, worked out a design of general utility engine that could be built as a replacement unit for use all over the system. In broad principle he was following the example of the Collett 'Halls' on the Great Western and of the 'Black Staniers' on the LMSR; but he produced a design that was a synthesis of existing standard LNER parts, avoiding the need for new patterns and new tools at a time when pressure on the railway shops was at its heaviest. The result was the neat, and workmanlike 'B1' 4-6-0, essentially a general utility job, which, like the 'Halls' and the 'Black Staniers', was at its best capable of an astounding quality of express passenger work.

The 'B1' was part of a great scheme of locomotive standardization on the LNER initiated by Edward Thompson. In correspondence, and in conversations I enjoyed with him at Doncaster he made no secret of the fact that the general scheme was based upon the Churchward model, though in detail, as in the use of a parallel boiler and outside Walschaerts valve gear, it differed considerably. On the Great Western itself Mr Hawksworth was faced with an ageing problem of a different character—nothing less than that of his 'super' top-line express passenger service engines, the 'Kings'. By the end of the war most of these famous locomotives were nearly eighteen years old, and replacement would have to be considered. With the worsening fuel situation in view thoughts turned to the possibility of larger boilers and fireboxes; Hawksworth in his younger days had worked on the drawings of Churchward's own Pacific, *The Great Bear*, and in the later war years the design of a new Pacific was prepared in outline at Swindon. But the restrictions of wartime precluded the possibility of this engine being built, and far from being replaced it seemed likely that the veteran 'Kings', now nearly 30 years old, would have to carry on for some time longer.

On the LMSR the portends were against any appreciable development. In the King's Birthday honours list of 1943 a knighthood was conferred upon Mr Stanier, and in the following year he retired from the railway in order to devote himself to certain industrial projects of great national importance. Mr Fairburn, who had been Acting Chief Mechanical and Electrical Engineer since 1942, was confirmed in the appointment; he was primarily an electrical man, and had been actively connected with the introduction and development of diesel shunting locomotives. His sudden death in the autumn of 1945 did not materially alter the line of development. His successor was Mr H. G. Ivatt, son of the Ivatt of Great Northern 'Atlantic' fame, and it was under his direction that the LMSR put into service the first British main line diesel-electric locomotive. As a steam man Ivatt had, in Mr Fairburn's time, been particularly associated with the modernization of the 'Royal Scots', giving them a new front end on the lines of a Stanier 'Pacific', and a taper boiler. The 'Converted Scots', as they became known, were among the finest engines for their size that have ever run in this country.

In the meantime preparations were in hand, on a colossal scale, for the Allied re-entry to the continent of Europe. After the naval and military assault the invading armies needed the support of heavy transport, and preparations included the provision of large numbers of locomotives suitable for military traffic. Experience in World War I and in recent campaigns farther afield had shown that the 2-8-0 type was ideal for this purpose. At the beginning of World War II it was proposed to use the Stanier '8F' of the LMSR, modified only to the extent of having certain continental fittings and the Westinghouse air brake. A number of these engines was built, but because of the sudden adverse turn of the war in 1940, construction was stopped, and when the Government was ready to place orders for further locomotives specially for war service the circumstances had very markedly changed. R. A. Riddles, formerly principal assistant to Sir William Stanier on the LMSR had been seconded from railway duties to take the very important post of Deputy Director General of Royal Engineer equipment, and on him fell the responsibility for laying down the specification, and much of the detail design of the Austerity 2-8-0s, and of the subsequent 2-10-0s.

Although the design was originally intended for use overseas no fewer than 732 of the 2-8-0 engines and many of the 2-10-0s were subsequently purchased by the Government and allocated to the various regions of British Railways. As such the 2-8-0 in particular became virtually a British standard type and performed a vast amount of excellent service in most parts of the country. The design itself was an extremely interesting one. It was prepared for mass production at a time when engineering materials of all kinds were in short supply; when pattern-making, castings, and drop forgings could at most be regarded as luxury processes, and not to be used for such run-of-the-mill jobs as building locomotives! The utmost use was made of welding; fittings and accessories were cut to the barest essentials, and yet withal a locomotive of very pleasing external appearance was produced. Riddles and his collaborators showed there was no need to go to the surrealist extremes in order to produce a good, cheap, reliable locomotive in an age of austerity. In time many

British manufacturers participated in the building of these engines; but the detail design and the first production runs were done by the North British Locomotive Company, under the general direction of Riddles himself.

Week-end after week-end, after a full week's work in London he travelled to Glasgow by night to spend Saturday and Sunday at Hyde Park, with that most able and co-operative of Scottish locomotive engineers A. Black. Thus the details of the design, and features of production were thrashed out, stage by stage, and a locomotive singularly free of teething troubles resulted. The 2-8-0 was followed by the 2-10-0 and the two types were built in such quantities that by the spring of 1945 no fewer than 1,000 had been ferried across the sea for service with the British Liberation Army, and elsewhere. The 1,000th engine was a 2-10-0 and was named *Longmoor* and fitted with a special commemorative plaque. In war service on the Continent both 2-8-os and 2-10-os quickly won golden opinions, in fact Major-General D. J. McMullen, Director of Transportation at the War Office, considered the 2-10-0 the finest freight locomotive ever built in Great Britain. But to my mind one of the greatest tributes, this time to the 2-8-0, came some years after the war. Locomotive men of the North Eastern, whether it was the old North Eastern Railway, the corresponding Area of the LNER, or the Region, knew what it was to handle freight, and right down from Fletcher's day they had always had first class heavy freight engines. One thinks instinctively of Wilson Worsdell's 'T' class 0-8-os, Raven's superheated 'T2s' and his 'S3' 4-6-os. In LNER days they had the Gresley 'V2s'. Yet at York one day, a very high officer who had the greatest affection for all North Eastern types confided to me that the 'WDs', as they were always known, were *by far* the best they had ever had.

To revert however to conditions on the home railways, it was ironical indeed that the end of the war came with the railways of this country lower in popular esteem than at any time in their history. The general public knew little of the difficulties that had been faced and surmounted, and it was not in the nature of things that they should seek to find out. The vast majority of men and women in the Forces travelled further afield by rail than ever before in their lives; the restrictions on private motoring forced many middle-class families to travel by train, and there were children rising into their 'teens who had never previously been in a train in their lives. From whatever reasons they went the experiences of those wartime travellers were not conducive to enthusiasm about railways. The trains were overcrowded; the times of travel were inconvenient, and often sorely delayed. These travellers know nothing of the spaciousness, speed and comfort of a pre-war express train, and I have heard it expressed more than once by serious-minded men and women that 'the railways had made such a mess of it, that it was high time they were put under new management'—with variations on the actual words, but the same theme every time. The railways were judged by the public transport they were able to provide, and just then it was not very good. The extent to which they were restricted by Government order is perhaps not realized, even by their staunchest supporters.

So, at the completion of the greatest task in their history the railways reaped, to use John Buchan's memorable phrase, a sour-apple harvest. The efforts of those concerned with the building, repair, and running of steam locomotives had been unceasing; much had been tried, much had been achieved in trying to keep motive power equal to the demands of the day, with less resources, less labour, and with shed facilities that deteriorated in the war, and which were untouched since.

CHAPTER ELEVEN

NATIONALIZATION

DURING the grim, glacial winter of 1946-7 the Labour Government of Mr Attlee, backed by a huge majority in the House of Commons, steam-rollered through the epoch-marking Bill to nationalize the railways of Britain. To a large number of railwaymen this was the moment to which they had been looking forward for many years, and they backed the Government's hastily-drafted and hastily-debated measure with enthusiasm. There were others, outside the railway service, who backed it no less enthusiastically, but purely on ideological grounds, and finally there were some, less discerning, whose experience of railway travel was mainly confined to the war years, and who felt that anything was better than a management that had allowed things to get into the state they had experienced. One need not dwell upon the conditions of the war years, nor of the circumstances of Government control that had prevailed for the past four or five years. The fact was that in the winter of 1946-7 the prospect of nationalization was not generally unwelcome.

Among senior railway officers there was much difference of opinion. The war years, under the overall direction of the Railway Executive Committee, had brought the old companies more nearly to unity than ever before, and many would have welcomed unification, though not necessarily under national ownership. The Great Western men however, with only the slightest exceptions, stood solidly against any such sentiments, and when nationalization did come and certain very high offices were offered to 'Paddington' they were firmly declined. In this book I am concerned with locomotive men, and the close of the year 1947 found the mechanical engineering departments of the 'Big Four' in a strange diversity of circumstances. That diversity had a profound effect upon future policy. The older ones amongst us railway enthusiasts looked sympathetically, yet critically, at the

personalities and records of the four chief mechanical engineers—
Bulleid, Hawksworth, Ivatt, and Peppercorn—and there was sad-
ness among us that, to all appearances, of four men who held high
and distinguished office one must be chosen and the others become
subordinates, or retire.

And what of their policies? The Great Western was still firmly
steeped in the traditions of Churchward. Unfortunately the early
years of Collett's regime had been so outstandingly successful
that design practice had virtually stood still since the production
of the 'Kings' in 1927. It is true that there had been important
developments in constructional practice at Swindon but the war
years found the Great Western still wedded to low-degree superheat, deep narrow fireboxes for its largest engines, and footplate
practice built up on the pre-war basis of first-class picked coal.
By 1947 Hawksworth had initiated some considerable departures
from tradition; but in the days of deep austerity, a tight purse-
string, and tenders of express engines sometimes loaded with a
mixture of ovoids and kitchen nuts he could not do very much.
The locomotive department of 1947 was still that of Churchward. By the rest of the British locomotive world it was regarded
largely as a closed shop, and a rather reactionary and retrograde
one at that!

The London and North Eastern was in far worse shape.
Whereas the most telling criticism of the Great Western was that
the Churchward tradition had gone on too long, the LNER was
suffering from a studied attempt to destroy utterly the traditions
established under Sir Nigel Gresley. I find myself in some difficulty in writing of the work of Edward Thompson. I enjoyed
many personal kindnesses from him, and am convinced of the
deep sincerity of the policy he developed towards the Gresley
locomotives. I shall always remember an evening at his own fire-
side, when he said: 'You know, Sir Nigel Gresley was one of the
greatest engine designers who have ever lived, and yet he made
one big mistake.' Step by step he went through the practical disadvantages of the conjugated valve gear, and then he outlined the
steps he was taking to obviate its use. It was the reasoned argu-

ment of an engineer faced with many failures in circumstances of unparalleled difficulty. It was an honest attempt to improve things, and not, as an outraged member of Gresley's former staff once expressed it to me: 'pure b——— spite'!

Make no mistake about it, Thompson's policy split the LNER locomotive department from top to bottom. I remember going to Scotland in the late summer of 1945, and a very senior officer in course of conversation said: 'I'm an out-and-out Gresley man.' It was the running men in particular who were up in arms: district officers, inspectors, drivers and firemen alike. I was riding north from Newcastle one day; we had an 'A4' Pacific, and the Gates-head inspector suddenly said, with a glow of enthusiasm: 'We're steaming to the memory of Sir Nigel Gresley!' Thompson's greatest success was undoubtedly the 'B1' 4-6-0. There was nothing of a new design about it, just a commonsense synthesis of existing standard parts: the 'Sandringham' boiler; cylinders from the 'K2' Moguls, and the 6 ft. 2 in. coupled wheels from the *Cock o' the North*. There will be more to be said about the 'B1' when we come to the Locomotive Interchange Trials of 1948.

Although I once or twice saw glimpses of a harsher side to his nature, Thompson, then a childless widower, was a very sensitive man. His work got a bad press, particularly in the 'enthusiast' journals, and it distressed him a good deal, and at mid-summer 1946 he retired. He was succeeded by Arthur H. Peppercorn, a genial soul who had spent a considerable part of his long railway career on the Great Northern and the LNER, in the running department. As assistant to Thompson, throughout the latter's five troubled years he was well enough aware of the resentment that had been caused, but as a running man he was equally well aware of the troubles that centred upon the conjugated valve gear. The LNER management was ready to place orders for many new 'Pacifics', and he put the Doncaster drawing office on to a modified design that was a blend of Gresley and Thompson practice. The new engines were scarcely ready to take the road by the winter of 1947-8, and with the design thus untried, and the department barely recovering from the upheavals of 1941-6, the practice of the LNER could not be expected to carry a great deal of weight in the early years of nationalization.

The situation on the Southern was extraordinary to a degree. During the time that Sir Herbert Walker had been General Manager the motive power policy of the Southern had been gradually geared towards complete electrification. Stage by stage steam traction was being eliminated, and no money was being spent on the modernizing of running sheds or manufacturing facilities. In Maunsell's time the construction of new locomotives, and particularly those for express passenger service, gradually dwindled. The 54 'King Arthurs' were built in 1925-6, together with the prototype *Lord Nelson*; 15 'Nelsons' followed in 1928-9, and then the 40 'Schools' were built in relatively small batches from 1930 to 1935. Thus only 96 new first-line express passenger engines were added to the stock in the fifteen years between the time of grouping and Maunsell's retirement. There were also the 15 4-4-0s of Class 'L1' built almost as a stop-gap measure in 1926, but even so if they are also included 111 new engines in fifteen years was significant of the declining status of steam on the Southern.

Then crash into this arena came O. V. S. Bulleid! Sir Herbert Walker was on the point of retirement, and on the outbreak of war Gilbert Szlumper took up vital Government duties. Missenden followed, and Bulleid so won his support that not only was authority obtained for the building of the first 'Merchant Navy' 4-6-2s in the middle of the war, but as soon as peace returned—austerity or no austerity—he obtained authority to build many more of them, and no fewer than 110 of the lighter version. Just think of it: one hundred and forty new 'Pacifics' in the space of seven years! The first order for the lightweight 'West Country's' was for 70!! As is known only too well so many novelties were packed into these queer-looking air-smoothed engines that troubles were inevitable, particularly with the valve gear; and with the line positively flooded with them, failures were at times embarrassingly frequent. At their best, backed by an enormous boiler, the Bulleid 'Pacifics' seemed capable of an almost un-

R. E. L. Maunsell 'Nelson' class 4-6-0 No. 856 *Lord St. Vincent.*

3-cylinder 4-4-0 No. 934 *St. Lawrence* 'Schools' class.

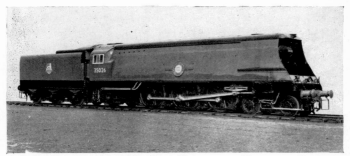

A Bulleid air-smoothed Merchant Navy 4-6-2, No. 35026 *Lamport & Holt Line.*

One of the West Country 4-6-2s as rebuilt with conventional valve gear, and air-smoothed casing dispensed with, No. 34052 *Lord Dowding.*

G. J. Churchward, 1902–1921.

C. B. Collett, 1921–1941.

Cook, 1950–1 and then Chief Mechanical
Electrical Engineer, Eastern and North
Eastern Regions.

R. A. Smeddle, Chief Mechanical and Ele
Engineer, Western Region, 1951–196

limited power output; at their worst they could be really shocking.

While Riddles in his 'WD' 2-8-os and 2-10-os had followed Maunsell's old *dictum* 'make every thing get-at-able', but carried much more completely into practice than ever Maunsell did himself, Bulleid had gone to the opposite extreme. In working out the design of the 'WD' engines with the men of the North British Locomotive Company Riddles had insisted that all fittings, all lubricating points and everything that would need attention should be accessible from outside. There should be no need to get underneath, or get the engine over a pit. Bulleid, on the other hand, not only encased the motion and the inside connecting rod and big end, but hid everything else behind his air-smoothed casing! Furthermore he was personally a great individualist. He was no architect of a team spirit; the drawing office and the works followed him in an attitude of 'do or die'. As one of his most faithful assistants remarked: 'If he'd asked for square wheels we'd have given them to him!' They no doubt knew there would be no point in arguing. Bulleid's words were a command. Clearly the Southern, no more than the Great Western nor the LNER, was not the place to seek the future mechanical engineering leadership of British Railways.

On the LMSR it so happened that Bulleid's own brother-in-law, George Ivatt, was in the chair at Derby, and there, following the great leadership of Sir William Stanier, who had all Churchward's genius for picking his men and building a strong organization, the house was most happily in order. Apart from those then immediately concerned with locomotives and rolling stock one figure stood out from all the rest. R. A. Riddles on returning to the LMSR after his conspicuously successful wartime duties quickly passed from the level of a top executive to become a Vice-President. He was nevertheless an engineer of very wide experience, intensely practical, and a true lover of locomotives. Tough years at Crewe, Derby and St Rollox, together with the priceless experience of serving as Principal Assistant to Sir William Stanier lay behind him, and the choice of him to be the member of the new Railway Executive for mechanical and electrical engineering, while leaving Ivatt as Chief Mechanical Engineer of the newly formed London Midland Region, solved the delicate problem that would otherwise have existed, of choosing one of the four reigning Chief Mechanical Engineers. That Riddles was an out-and-out LMSR man did not please everybody, and when very wisely he chose his principal lieutenants almost entirely from the LMSR it did not soften the original blow. But for the reasons already discussed in this chapter it was, as things were in 1948, the obvious and only answer.

Great and proud locomotive building centres like Doncaster, Eastleigh and Swindon were deeply resentful. The Great Western Chief Mechanical Engineer, for example, whose office had enjoyed almost complete autonomy from the days of Daniel Gooch, was summoned not to the boardroom at Paddington, but to meetings at which he and his fellow CMEs listened to the first proposals for the unification of design and constructional practice. Some of the second-line LNER engineers talked of throwing their hands in at once; but Peppercorn counselled patience, and one at least of those who found things so distasteful in those early months was later to do some great things for the British steam locomotive. However much the former chief mechanical engineers and their immediate assistants bristled, Riddles, by a single though rather expensive stroke, gave those a little further down the respective 'family trees' a tremendous fillip, by initiating the celebrated series of interchange trials of 1948. In earlier chapters of this book I have told of various locomotive exchanges, when engines have run on 'foreign' metals, in competition with the home types. The trials initiated by C. J. Bowen-Cooke of the LNWR in 1909, and the famous 'Castle' *versus* Gresley 'Pacific' running of 1925 aroused much interest. Imagine then the impact of a series in 1948, when engines of all four groups were to be matched against each other on four different routes, and when the contestants were to be drawn from the express passenger, mixed traffic, and heavy freight categories.

Young engineers, testing staff, engine crews warmed thoroughly to the prospect. Men from five out of the six regions of British Railways were thrown together, and immediately slipped into whole-hearted co-operation. Railway enthusiasts—photographers, stop-watch fans, and those who were just lovers of trains—flocked to the stations and the lineside. The conditions imposed, however, were such that the former CMEs and their immediate entourages were inclined to view the whole affair with indifference. Hawksworth, for example, was required to apply to the Railway Executive for permission to travel in his own dynamometer car, and the story goes that on one occasion, when trials were in progress between Waterloo and Exeter, Bulleid presented himself at the car without any central authority, and was forthrightly refused admission! So, for one reason or another, the most senior of the regional engineers were inclined to look upon the whole thing as rather a waste of time and money. They felt that the results eventually obtained could have been secured by much simpler and quicker means. They were rather inconclusive, and the testing methods employed were not those of the latest techniques being developed before nationalization either on the LMSR or on the Great Western.

Nevertheless, Riddles and his newly assembled staff had a principle of some importance to establish and demonstrate. On two out of the four private companies there was a generally held opinion that engines had to be designed to suit the road. Sir Nigel Gresley was a staunch upholder of this principle, having built engines specially for the local conditions in East Anglia, on the Edinburgh–Aberdeen line, and on the West Highland. Equally Great Western methods were particularly suited to the use of good quality soft Welsh coal. On the LMSR under Stanier entirely the opposite view had taken root, and the Black Five mixed traffic 4-6-os were used on all parts of the line, from Wick in the north to Bournemouth in the south and Swansea in Wales. Riddles was anxious to standardize as much as possible, largely on LMSR lines, though not necessarily using LMS designs, and the results of the interchange trials completely upheld the LMSR view. The Bulleid 'Pacifics', for example, far from being suitable only for Southern routes did some of their finest work between Perth and Inverness, while the Thompson 'B1' 4-6-0 representing the Eastern Region put up some outstanding performances between Bristol and Plymouth.

Taken all round, however, no existing engine design established a clear superiority over the others in its power class, and while providing ample evidence that there was really no need to design special engines for special jobs, the elaborate series of tests provided the Railway Executive with something of a dilemma, when it came to settling a policy for new construction. Riddles was most anxious to dispel any suggestion that, because he and his central staff were nearly all ex-LMSR men, there was a bias towards LMSR designs; and he therefore discarded one solution that would have been easy to have carried out, and which would to some extent have satisfied regional loyalties and pride. That solution would have been to choose certain regional designs for future standardization, and a possible apportionment of designs to power classes might have been:

Class '7' express and mixed traffic:
  The Bulleid 'West Country' 4-6-2
Class '5' mixed traffic 4-6-0:
  The Thompson 'B1' (ex-LNER)
Class '4' fast passenger tank:
  The Stanier 2-6-4 (ex-LMSR)
Class '6' Heavy mineral:
  The GWR '28XX' class 2-8-0

By such a procedure all the four private companies would be represented in the new standard locomotive stud, and the 4-6-2, 4-6-0 and 2-8-0 designs quoted had all done well in the interchange trials. There would, however, have been little or no standardization of fittings or design practice between the various types, and this alone would have been contrary to the very principles of railway unification.

Discussing his problems with me, many years after the event, Riddles confessed that by far the easiest, cheapest and most satisfactory solution, engineering wise, would have been to take the LMSR designs *in toto*, and adopt them as a national standard. They were well proved, and had a record of reliability and hard service that was probably unmatched at the time. At this stage I can imagine what has been called 'the lunatic fringe' of Great Western supporters demanding my head on a charger, for daring to make such an assertion. But it was true enough. As a policy, however, it was one that Riddles just could not adopt. The interchange trials themselves had fanned all the fires of regional partisanship, and to have chosen one group for standardization, particularly as it was the one for which Riddles, Bond and Cox had previously been responsible, would have caused resentment in every grade of the locomotive department. So the most difficult, and most interesting of all courses had to be taken, namely to design an entirely new range that would include all the best features of the previous railway practices. At the very outset it was realized that it would be a lengthy and expensive task. Inter-regional committees were set up, and while R. C. Bond, as Chief Officer, Locomotive Works and Maintenance set about the job of standardizing workshop practice, E. S. Cox, as Executive Officer, Design, presided over a committee of the Regional chief draughtsmen charged with the tasks of recommending the best regional practice to be followed in the new standard designs.

Designing by committee can be the most tedious and frustrating business, as I know only too well from certain experiences of my own; and in this case regional views (and prejudices!) had to be put forward, and carefully considered before recommendations on boiler design, frames, axle-boxes, valve gear and other vital features could be taken. Riddles was most anxious that the regions should be drawn together in this corporate task, and he personally examined the recommendations made before agreeing upon the adoption of each and every feature as a national standard. Having laid down the main features of the range of new standard designs there was next the question of how the detail designing and actual constructions should be dispersed among the major locomotive works, and their respective drawing offices. Prior to nationalization design work had been done at Brighton for the Southern, Derby for the LMSR, Doncaster for the LNER, and, of course, Swindon for the Great Western. But in addition to these centres where there were well-equipped drawing offices with staffs of long experience, there were also major works at Ashford, Crewe, Darlington and St Rollox.

In trying to make the production of the new standard loco-motive a corporate effort of the combined strength of all available talent and experience, a somewhat complicated procedure was laid down. It was decided that certain drawing offices would act as the 'parent' of a few selected designs, and as such make the general arrangement drawings; and in addition each major draw-ing office would specialize in a particular feature of the new standard locomotives as a whole. The allocation of detail design-ing was thus:

Brighton: Brakes and sanding gear.
Derby: Bogies and trucks, tenders, wheels, tyres, axles and spring gear.
Doncaster: Coupling and connecting rods, valve gear and cylinder details.
Swindon: Boiler and smokebox details, steam fittings.

Derby was selected as the parent office for the Class '7' mixed-traffic 'Pacific', later well-known as the 'Britannia' class; but whereas in the old days everything in connection with a new design would be done at one centre, the general layout of the '7MT' was prepared at Derby; important features of the design were worked out in detail at Brighton, Derby, Doncaster, and Swindon, and the engines themselves were built at Crewe. One can pause for a moment to wonder how the autocrats of the past like Webb, Patrick Stirling, Stroudley, or the twentieth-century giants like Churchward and Gresley would have viewed such a procedure. It was one of the results of unification, and that it worked, despite the inherent disadvantages from the co-ordina-tion point of view, is an everlasting tribute to the leadership of Riddles, who despite the manifold duties of his high office continued to hold the reins of design during this remarkable period.

The locomotives that resulted from it were sturdy and efficient, but for the most part an undistinguished lot. The smaller members of the new family fulfilled their purpose well enough, but one must be pardoned for doubting if there were not plenty of existing regional types that would have done almost as well, without the necessity of going through all the process of new design. Principal interest, both historically and in performance, centres upon the big engines and with the 'Britannias' there were enough teething troubles to make them controversial to a degree. Unless the Bulleid lightweight 'Pacific' had been accepted as a future standard there was no existing regional type that exactly filled the rôle cast for the 'Britannias', namely 'Pacifics' with wide firebox that would do work previously undertaken by LNER 'V2s', Great Western 'Castles', LMSR 'Converted Scots' and Southern 'Lord Nelsons'. The wide firebox was considered an absolute essential, to burn the indifferent coal so often supplied in those years for the first class duties.

At their best the 'Britannias' were extraordinarily strong and willing engines. The large boilers steamed magnificently and the frame construction was so robust that any amount of hard pounding could be sustained almost indefinitely. But they were hard, noisy things to ride on, and like the little schoolgirl, when they were off-form they could be 'horrid'. They were addicted to slipping, and they had a way of becoming unmanageable from this cause in the most inconvenient places. More than one case occurred of the engines of South Wales expresses slipping themselves to a stand in the middle of the Severn Tunnel, and I remember seeing an up Bristol express arrive in Chippenham one afternoon with a GWR pannier tank 0-6-0 piloting a 'Britannia'. The big engine had stuck in Box Tunnel, and the tank engine had been sent to help get the train on the move again. Incidents like this could, of course, be put down to faults in handling, and the 'Britannias' were never very popular on the Western Region. The 'Britannias' in general did very well on the Great Eastern, but I had one extraordinary experience coming up from Ipswich on the footplate of *Sir Christopher Wren*, when having gone in a violent slip at 80 m.p.h., she continued slipping at intervals all the way to Liverpool Street, sometimes with the regulator *closed*.

In relating these troubles, however, one must be careful to regard the British standard locomotives in true perspective, and not to forget that they were an entirely new range. In the old company days the well-established dynasties founded by Church-ward, Gresley and Stanier all had their troubles in early days. They were not put right in weeks, or even months; but the great difference was that troubles could be nursed behind closed doors, and not aired beyond, perhaps, the Locomotive Committees of the respective Boards. Riddles and his staff from the mere fact of national ownership of the railways, worked in the full glare of publicity, exposed immediately if anything went wrong to the hostile comment of those who opposed nationalization itself, on political grounds, or who had other axes to grind. Furthermore, *Britannia* and the smaller engines of the new family were not intended to be the ultimate in British locomotive design. They were envisaged as the first phase of standardization on a national basis just as the first 'Saints' and 'Stars' formed no more than the prelude to Churchward's great development on the GWR. Similarly, on the LNER Gresley did not attain to the brilliance of 'A4' performance in his first essays in three-cylinder propulsion. Nearly ten years of hard endeavour were to pass between the production of the 2-8-0 No. 461, in 1918, and the fitting of the 'A1' Pacific No. 2555 *Centenary* with long-lap, long-travel valves in a design that paved the way for such engines as *Papyrus*, *Earl Marischal* and *Silver Link*. That Riddles and his men achieved the success they did in the very first wave of development was a triumph in itself.

Riddles, looking at the problem of British railway motive power against the economic position of the country as a whole, envisaged a considerable life for steam, until finance should be made available for electrification. Purely on the dual grounds of high capital cost and the need to import fuel, he rejected the intermediate stage of diesel traction for long distance main line work. More than once he emphasized that he was backing the form of motive power that gave 'the most tractive effort per pound sterling'—steam. But for a multiplicity of reasons, few having much to do with engineering, he was eventually over-ruled, with the result that British Railways were plunged into a break-neck programme of dieselization. In the realm of steam locomotive standardization *Britannia* and her smaller sisters thereupon became the *omega* as well as the *alpha* of the pro-gramme. A space of three years elapsed, nevertheless, between the appearance of *Britannia* and the introduction of the last of the standard types. This latter was the 'BR9' 2-10-0 freight engine—unquestionably the most remarkable of the whole stud. The inter-vening years had been well spent, and the 'BR9s' were virtually right, from the word go. This was a particular feather in the cap of the Brighton drawing office, which played a large part in the design.

They were intended as heavy freight engines, and in such duty they have done an immense amount of hard work; but with coupled wheels as large as 5 ft. diameter, and a most efficient layout of the Walschaerts valve gear they proved so free and easy in running that it was not long before someone put a 'BR9' on to an express train in emergency. Two fully authenticated examples were recorded of speeds of 90 m.p.h., and successful runs were made on South Wales expresses between Cardiff and Paddington, and on the Flying Scotsman, between Grantham and King's Cross. Authority frowned at such exploits, particularly in the attainment of such high speeds, but at a later period engines of this class were used in regular passenger service on the Somer-set and Dorset line, and but for the rapid onset of dieselization they would also have been used on the Highland line between Perth and Inverness. The 'BR9' was the last new class to be introduced on the railways of this country, and engines of this class were the last steam to be built at both Crewe and Swindon. Engine No. 92220 was indeed the very last steam locomotive to be built in Britain for service on home railways. Swindon works had this rather melancholy honour, and in respect to the great traditions of that works the engine was painted in Great Western green, instead of unlined black, given a copper-capped chimney, and named *Evening Star*. At the time this engine was completed, in 1960, and named with appropriate ceremony, it was indeed the evening of the steam locomotive, and the shades were closing in.

CHAPTER TWELVE

ST MARTIN'S SUMMER

WHATEVER future was intended for the new standard locomotive
types the impact of the 'Britannias' upon the express passenger
motive power position in the country as a whole was virtually
negligible numerically, beside the many hundreds of relatively
modern express passenger engines of Class '7' capacity and
upwards, that British Railways had inherited from all members
of the previous 'Big Four' From the year 1950 the country in
general and the railways in particular were beginning the long
climb out of the period of austerity; faster and more enterprising
services were being planned, and it was evident that for the working of these trains reliance would have to be placed, for some
years at any rate, upon locomotives of pre-nationalization design.
On the Southern the Bulleid 'Pacifics' were relatively new, and
despite their frequent vicissitudes could be expected to cope.
The LMSR stud, with its 70 rebuilt 'Scots', and many 'Pacifics'
built during the war years was also well placed. Things were not
so certain on the East Coast route, and on the Great Western.

It was fortunate beyond measure, however, that in those years
between 1930 and 1940, when the locomotive department at
Swindon was popularly thought to be doing nothing but bask in
a late afternoon sunshine of the Churchward era, that some quite
advanced thinking on testing methods had led to the formulation
of some new and extremely simple techniques. These were being
worked out in detail at the time of nationalization, and were
capable of working most comprehensively with the existing tools
available, namely the Churchward stationary testing plant, and
the old Swindon dynamometer car. It is important to appreciate
the simplicity of the equipment involved, because in 1948 the
research people on the former LMSR had produced a very
elaborate mobile-testing plant with highly ingenious electrical
controls, which on its introduction was at first thought likely to

supersede all existing testing plants. During test runs on a stationary plant a locomotive had, of necessity, to be kept running at a constant speed. There was considered to be some merit in this from the viewpoint of obtaining scientific results and in the last years of the LMSR the new mobile plant and dynamometer car were designed to keep a locomotive running at constant speed regardless of whether a gradient was being climbed, or whether running downhill.

The testing philosophy developed on the Great Western Railway was quite different. At Swindon it was argued that a locomotive should be tested against a natural load, and a 'natural load' was that of a service train being hauled at variable speed over a road of varying gradients. Constant speed testing, on a stationary plant, was all very well, but there should be some means of relating the results to the performance of a locomotive in revenue-earning service. Examination of many past results indicated that when locomotives were being steamed hard over lengthy periods expert drivers would work in such a way that the steam consumption was roughly constant, at speeds varying *en route* between 40 and 80 m.p.h. S. O. Ell, the engineer in charge of testing at Swindon in 1947 and subsequently, therefore, began to use a constant steam rate, rather than constant speed as the basis of all future tests. Comparing tests made with the same engine, first at constant steam rate and roughly constant speed on the stationary plant with a constant steam rate *at variable speeds* on the road gave identical results: coal and water consumption, and general performance. Moreover, by such a method the basic thermodynamic performance of the locomotive was thereby linked to the working of a natural load, rather than artificial conditions set up by constraining a locomotive to run at constant speed on the open road—a circumstance *never* remotely likely in ordinary revenue-earning service.

Thus at the outset of the nationalization era Riddles and his staff had to weigh up the merits of two diametrically opposed philosophies of engine testing: constant speed, as developed on the LMSR, and constant steam rate as practised on the Great Western.

They decided in favour of Swindon, and in the years following 1951 a variety of locomotives was tested by what became known as the controlled road system by teams based on both Swindon and Derby. One of the new 'Britannias', a 'B1' 4-6-0 from the Eastern Region and a 'Merchant Navy' were among the engines put through their paces on the new stationary testing plant at Rugby, while Swindon dealt with one of their own 'Halls', an ex-LMSR 2-6-0 and then a Gresley 'V2' 2-6-2. Having established the basic characteristics of performance the engines first tested at Rugby went to that most famous of test routes, the Settle and Carlisle for verification of results by the controlled road system, while the similar tests on the Western Region were carried out between Reading and Stoke Gifford. In each case the testing was worked to the maximum steaming rates of which each engine was found capable, with the result that some very heavy trains were conveyed in the controlled road tests.

The testing of the ex-LNER 'V2' engine provided an extremely interesting case of how a design of pre-war vintage was adjusted to suit post-war running conditions. To reduce day-to-day work at the sheds to a minimum self-cleaning apparatus was being fitted in the smokeboxes of many engines. The LMSR had been a pioneer in this particular movement, and it found that the engines so fitted could run from one boiler washout day to the next without any need to open the smokebox door and remove ash. The apparatus consisted of a series of wire-mesh screens which broke up the larger particles and enabled them to be ejected, instead of accumulating in a heap at the bottom of the smokebox. The draughting arrangements of new locomotives fitted with self-cleaning smokeboxes were designed to suit the particular layouts; but when it was hoped to add the benefits of the arrangement to older engines, and the necessary deflector plates and mesh screens were fitted, the desired results were achieved so far as self-cleaning was concerned but the performance of the locomotives was sometimes affected in other ways. The 'V2', or 'Green Arrow', class of 2-6-2s was one of Sir Nigel Gresley's greatest successes. They were hard-working, free steaming engines that under the strain of wartime conditions were operated turn and turn about with 'Pacifics' on the heaviest East Coast duties. Lack of maintenance sometimes led to failures of the conjugated valve gear; but in relation to the loads hauled and the mileages covered those failures were not discreditable to the design.

Then in post-war conditions a start was made with the fitting of self-cleaning plates and screens. The interposing of these slight obstructions to exhaust gas flow had a considerable effect on the steaming, and it was evident that the draughting arrangements needed some attention. One of the engines concerned was sent to Swindon, and in a series of very careful tests on the stationary plant data was obtained that enabled the necessary alterations to · the position and diameter of the blast pipe orifice and to the chimney itself to be made. As modified the engine was capable of very fine work, and on one of the subsequent controlled road tests I have vivid recollections of seeing her come thundering up the 1 in 300 bank towards Badminton with a *twenty-coach train*. That immense rake was, however, no more than the shape of things to come, when the Swindon testing staff really got into their stride. With the Great Western engines the problem was to enable them to perform their pre-war feats of load haulage with the poorer qualities of coal generally available in the 1950s. The management was actively preparing for the restoration of some of the most spectacular pre-war services, such as the 1¾-hour 'Bristolian', with its average speed of 67¾ m.p.h. between Paddington and Temple Meads, and while many engines of the stud could have run that train the general average of the power available could not.

Sam Ell and his men took the 'King' design, and set about the draughting, which, as with the LNER 'V2', seemed the key to the problem. I have mentioned Ell in particular, because he did all the actual detail; but by that time there was a stranger in the famous chair at Swindon. Hawksworth had retired at the end of 1949, and at that time the organization of the locomotive department was completely changed. At the time of nationalization the

Great Western remained the only British railway to have retained the original organization that was once universal, in which the Locomotive Superintendent, or Chief Mechanical Engineer, as the office generally became known, not only designed, built and maintained the locomotive stud, but was also responsible for running them in traffic. All the drivers, firemen, cleaners, and running inspectors were on the pay-roll of the Chief Mechanical Engineer. Beginning on the Midland Railway in 1907 there had been a gradual breakaway from this old tradition, and the responsibility for 'running' was transferred, on one railway after another, to the traffic department. On some lines the Running Superintendent remained an independent officer, and on the LNER each of the three 'areas' had their own, reporting in each case to the Area General Manager.

On Hawksworth's retirement the previous CME organization was split into three: Mechanical and Electrical Engineering; Carriage and Wagon Engineering; and Locomotive Running. K. J. Cook, who had been Principal Assistant to the CME, became Mechanical and Electrical Engineer, but in a year's time there was another change, when Cook went to Doncaster to take charge of Mechanical and Electrical Engineering for both the Eastern and North Eastern Regions. In his place at Swindon came R. A. Smeddle, just as much an out-and-out North Eastern man as Cook was Great Western born and bred. The interchange proved of great benefit to both those historic locomotive centres. Smeddle, trained under Sir Vincent Raven, and winning his spurs under Gresley, was a man of immense drive and energy. Although no designer himself he was quick to appreciate the merit of the work in progress at Swindon, and from the very outset he backed Ell to the hilt. It became one of his major tasks in life to convince the 'doubting Thomases' in the traffic department at Paddington that Great Western engines with no more than the slightest alterations could do anything they liked to ask. A new spirit of enterprise and enthusiasm surged through Swindon works. From the disappointments and discouragements following nationalization Great Western men—and they still called themselves that!—

were prepared to 'lick the pants' off anybody. As for the chief, one of his delighted assistants once remarked to me: 'He's more "Great Western" than any of us!' Privately, for Alfred Smeddle and I were close friends, he had some pungent observations to make about the more hoary of Swindon traditions, and he shocked Hawksworth by hanging some very charming paintings of North Eastern engines of Raven design in the *sanctum sanctorum* which Dean, Churchward and Collett had occupied. His reply to Hawksworth was: 'Well you go up to Doncaster and see what Cook's hung in Gresley's old office!'

In modifying the draughting of the 'Kings' one of Churchward's specialities had to be discarded, namely the jumper ring on the blast pipe. This was designed to lift automatically when the going was heavy, and increase the area of the blastpipe exhaust nozzle, and so reduce the fierceness of the blast. When one was assured of a supply of first-class coal, and an engine was steaming continuously up to the 'sizzling point' of the safety valves the jumper ring was an admirable device for preventing excessive coal consumption. But in the 1950s reliable steaming in all conditions was more important than a few decimal points in the coal consumption per drawbar horsepower hour, and Ell found that to draught the engine for high output on indifferent coal he needed a plain blastpipe cap. The shape of the inner chimney was also changed, but taken together the alterations to blastpipe and chimney were very simply made, and in this alteration, which was finalized early in 1953, the outward appearance of those most elegant engines was unchanged. Connoisseurs could detect a very slight protrusion at the top of the copper cap, but to the ordinary observer a 'King' was still a 'King'. The experiments with new liveries were finished by that time, and the 'Kings' were back in their old Brunswick green.

In the spring of 1953 Smeddle invited me to go to Swindon to see engine No. 6001 *King Edward VII* on the stationary plant. Several times previously I had been to the works and beheld the fascinating spectacle of an engine with wheels and motion moving at express speed, but not moving an inch. Never before, however,

One of the 'WD' Austerity 2-10-0s, No. 73798 *North British*, with R. A. Riddles (left) and A. Black standing in front of the firebox.

The Ultimate from Swindon: 'King' Class 4-6-0 No. 6015 *King Richard III* rebuilt by R. A. Smeddle with twin blastpipe and chimney.

An Eastern 'A3' in its final form, with Kylchap exhaust arrangements, No. 60055 *Woolwinder*.

The GNSR 4-4-0 *Gordon Highlander* and the Highland Jones Goods 4-6-0, on a special excursion from Largs to Glasgow, leaving Ardrossan.

The LNER streamlined 'A4' No. 4498 *Sir Nigel Gresley* leaving Kingmoor yard Carlisle, on an enthusiasts special to Crewe, via the Settle and Carlisle line.

had I seen such a sight as this! For No. 6001 was going very nearly 'all out', at a road speed of 75 m.p.h., and at a steam rate which needed two firemen, working in turn, to keep the firebox replenished. Under nationalization the maximum rate at which a single fireman was expected to work continuously was 3,000 lb. of coal per hour; a tidy charge in itself, of more than 1¼ tons per hour, but No. 6001 developing over 2,000 horsepower in the cylinders needed more than that. It was not that she was extravagant—far from it—but with the modified draughting more coal was producing more steam, and the tests were gradually worked up until the boiler was practically at its limit. To say that I watched supremely fascinated would be an understatement. It was not only the performance of the engine that was so thrilling to observe on the various charts and gauges; but it was the evident pleasure and enthusiasm of all the young engineers involved that was so inspiriting. An older hand, a test engineer whose father had been an express driver, paused in his work and said to me: 'She's great now she's got one of Mr Ell's "Bob Martins" in her blastpipe!'

The performance on the test plant, once the initial thrill of sheer spectacle had been absorbed, was that of facts and figures, and still there were sceptics at Paddington. When it came to the interpretation of the results in terms of actual load haulage out on the line the ultimate performance reached almost sensational heights. On the test plant the *King Edward VII* had been steamed up to a maximum rate of 33,600 lb. per hour, and a controlled road test was planned with a steam rate of 30,000 lb. per hour. As these tests had been carried out primarily with the restoration of the pre-war 1¾-hour Bristol service it might have been imagined that the road test would have taken the form of a very fast run with a moderate load; but there is always the problem of getting a suitable timetable path, over the Western Region's busiest main line. Accordingly, all these controlled road tests were made on a schedule roughly in accordance with the fastest Bristol and South Wales expresses running at that time, involving a start-to-stop average between Reading and Stoke Gifford of about 55 m.p.h. To absorb the power developed from a steam rate of 30,000 lb. a load of *twenty-five* bogie corridor coaches was needed! Smeddle invited me to ride in the dynamometer car on one of these trips, and the trip proved the experience of a lifetime.

In the course of my ordinary business I was then travelling between Bath and Paddington every week, as I still am today, and I was familiar enough with ordinary express train standards, in which we would run at 65 to 70 m.p.h. on level track behind 'Castles' with loads of 350 to 400 tons, and with 'Kings' up to 450 or so. But here on this memorable day we were setting out from Reading with 795 tons behind the tender, and very soon we were running at much the same speed as that of the ordinary expresses. The numerous dials, instruments, and charts in the dynamometer car indicated just the same performance as I had witnessed on the stationary plant at Swindon; but here, in the open country, storming up the Vale of the White Horse, was a demonstration, vivid almost beyond imagination. of what it meant in plain terms of coaches, and 'miles per hour'. The modifications to the 'King' front-end devised by Ell and so vigorously sponsored by Smeddle were now proved brilliantly successful, and authority was given for all thirty engines of the class to be altered in readiness for the acceleration of the Bristolian which was planned for the late spring of 1954. Then there was to be a general acceleration of all expresses on the Bristol route, and a number of 'Castles' also received the 'Bob Martin' treatment at the front end.

The summer of 1954 was one of the most exciting I ever remember from the running viewpoint. In the very first week of the accelerations I clocked the Bristolian from Temple Meads to Paddington in 96 min.—9 min. under schedule—with the *King Richard III*; and with the ordinary expresses the 'Castles' were regularly running at 75 to 80 m.p.h. on the level, with 400-ton tarins. As to maximum speed, with the *King Henry VI* I clocked $102\frac{1}{2}$ m.p.h. at the foot of Dauntsey bank. During that summer it was a positive delight to travel to and fro between Bath, Chippenham and Paddington, and I filled notebook after notebook with details of innumerable first-class runs. Among many 'Castle' engines that served us so well in those days I must mention particularly *Bridgwater Castle*, *Farleigh Castle*, *Fairey Battle*—one of those renamed in wartime after aircraft—*Earl Baldwin*, *Earl Waldegrave*, and one of the very last 'Castles' to be built, No. 7034 *Ince Castle*. I must not dwell entirely upon Western Region exploits, welcome though they were after the doldrums through which Swindon affairs passed for a time. But I cannot refrain from adding that the exhilaration spread to the West of England line in 1955 and 1956 with the acceleration of the Cornish Riviera Express, the Torbay Express, and others to their old standards, and even better. I rode thousands of miles on the footplates of Great Western engines in those years, and several times more in the dynamometer car. They were great days on the 'Western'.

In the meantime things were happening elsewhere in Great Britain. In 1953, in honour of the Coronation of Her Majesty, the London–Edinburgh non-stop was named 'The Elizabethan' and accelerated to a run of $6\frac{3}{4}$ hours between Kings Cross and Waverley. No one thought, apparently, of putting a new Peppercorn 'A1' on to that most regal of trains; it was the 'A4s' every time—some of them were then nearing twenty years of age. I rode *Silver Fox*, one of the original 'silver' quartet of 1935 on the up train, and was fascinated and delighted with her immaculate performance. There was also a subtle difference in her going that I could not fail to notice. In Gresley's day we were all familiar with the characteristic 'ring' of the motion, particularly when coasting with steam off. *Silver Fox* was silent, and there was not the same syncopation in her beat that one could hear in earlier days. By that time Kenneth Cook had been at Doncaster for two years, and he was bringing some of the precision of Swindon works' methods to his new domain. As assistant works manager during the 1930s he had been closely associated with the introduction of optical methods of lining up engine frames and cylinders, and took great pride in the accuracy and thoroughness with which engines were repaired. He took the same methods to

Doncaster, and it was then possible to turn out repaired 'Pacifics' and other engines with tighter clearances than previously. They ran more quietly, and made longer mileages between visits to plant for overhaul.

The troubles with the Gresley conjugated valve gear, which influenced Edward Thompson so strongly to making such a campaign against it, were due to slogger developing from wear in the various pin joints. Cook was able to minimize slogger, by reducing the initial clearance needed. But he also increased the reliability of the Gresley three-cylinder engines by an alteration to the design of the inside big-end. Slogger in the pin joints of the conjugated valve gear led to over-running of the valve-spindle of the middle cylinder piston valve, and this, by giving much longer valve openings made the middle cylinder do an undue share of the work. This in turn put undue loading on the big-end, and in numerous instances caused over-heating, and in certain spectacular cases complete failure. Cook introduced a design of big-end based on that of the Great Western four-cylinder engines, which in turn was derived from the de Glehn four-cylinder compound 'Atlantics' imported from France in 1903-5. The adaptation of the big-end to suit the Gresley three-cylinder engines was very successful, and from 1954 onwards the 'A3' and 'A4' 'Pacifics', coming out of Doncaster plant after general overhaul ran like sewing machines, and moreover stayed like it. It was very pleasing that the interchange of Chief Mechanical Engineers between Doncaster and Swindon should have such beneficial effects, at both places.

At the same time I must add that despite his work at Doncaster Cook's heart still remained very much in the West Country. I shall always recall with amusement a fleeting incident that occurred at Grantham one evening. I had been at York on signalling business and was travelling south by 'The Heart of Midlothian', hauled by a Peppercorn 'A1'. When we stopped at Grantham I was in the dining car, and we had not been there more than a minute when the down Yorskhire Pullman, normally non-stop from Kings Cross to Doncaster, drew in and stopped.

There, at precisely the opposite Pullman window was Cook, travelling with his family. Windows were down in a moment, and in a brief conversation he told me their engine was short of steam. But the conversation was almost immediately cut short when we got the 'right-away'. Our engine was evidently on dead centre, for we had to set back a yard or so before getting properly under way. As we drew forward Cook had his top window drawn aside again, and as we passed he shouted across: 'Three cylinders don't start as well as four!'

Be that as it may, the condition of the 'A4s' was such that a further acceleration of the 'non-stop' was possible in 1954 to 6½ hours: 392·7 miles between Kings Cross and Waverley in 390 min. It was a magnificent achievement in itself, but the engines and their drivers could, and did, do a great deal better on many occasions. With them it became a point of honour that time should be kept, and I have seen as much as twenty-one minutes of lost time regained. Cook applied his modernization techniques to the non-streamlined 'A3' class also. Those engines not only had the motion and big-ends modified, but they were fitted with double-chimneys, and the full Kylchap arrangement of double-blastpipe and the series of petticoats to the chimneys that was originally fitted on the 'Cock o' the North' 2-8-2s and one isolated 'A3' in Gresley's time. As thus modernized the 'A3s' took a noble part in the blaze of excellent working that led me to title this chapter 'St Martin's Summer'. The last time I rode a steam locomotive in ordinary service on the East Coast route was in the late autumn of 1958, on the up 'Flying Scotsman' non-stop from Newcastle to Kings Cross; we had an 'A3', the *Pretty Polly*, and she gained seventeen minutes net, on a schedule of 286 min. for the 268·3 miles: an average of exactly 60 m.p.h. throughout.

Because I have dwelt rather upon the work of ex-Great Western and ex-LNER locomotives in this chapter it must not be imagined that the Southern and the LMSR were lagging behind. The Bulleid 'Pacifics' had to be rebuilt, removing the troublesome oil bath and chain-drive valve gear. At the same time the 'air-smoothed' casing was removed, and revealed the engines as very massive-looking things, though without any particular character—to my eyes at any rate. They did well enough afterwards though not surpassing the best of their achievements in their true Bulleid condition. All the 'Merchant Navy' class were rebuilt, but when the withdrawal of steam started in earnest not all the 'West Country' and 'Battle of Britain' class had been done. This is not a book about 'running', so beyond saying that those last years of steam found the old stalwarts still in great form there is nothing to add about the engines of the former LMSR.

By the late 1950s the death warrant of steam had been signed, and it was indeed ironical that those years witnessed some of the finest locomotive performance this country had ever known. Wherever one travelled it was the same: Cornish Riviera, South Wales, Bournemouth, Atlantic Coast—there is no need to go the rounds; it was all the same, except perhaps to mention especially the brilliant work being done by 'converted Royal Scots' on the Midland service between St Pancras and Manchester. Strange to look back and reflect that these were the tools we were so soon to throw away.

CHAPTER THIRTEEN

THE SLAUGHTER

AT the end of the year 1960 there were some 16,000 steam locomotives in service on British Railways; by the time this new
edition of *Steam Locomotive* is on sale there will be very few, if
any, left. The whole stud will have been scrapped within a space
of eight years. It is never pleasant to dwell upon the details of
executions, and this chapter will be brief, and I hope not too
provocative. The neophytes would have had us believe that those
16,000 engines were a lot of superannuated old crocks. It is certainly true that there were some considerable veterans amongst
them; but the great majority were good working units with an
excellent basic standard of performance, and with many years of
useful life yet remaining. Quite apart from the express passenger
'stars', such as those referred to in the previous chapter, there
were thousands of modern honest-to-goodness medium-powered
units like the Great Western 'Halls' and 'Granges', the Stanier
'Black-Fives' and the ex-LNER 'B1s', and the corresponding
2-8-0 freighters.

In the early days of nationalization, when the deficit kept
mounting year by year, it was rather pathetic to hear high officials
saying: 'Oh, we shall be all right once we get rid of steam.' I
need not make the obvious comment in respect of the last few
years! The true fact was that for main line service locomotives
of greater power than the existing Class '7' and Class '8' were
needed to provide accelerated service, and the diesels offered an
easy though very expensive way of getting it. Even today one
hears people talk as if there were some magic, inherent quality in
a diesel that steam does not possess, and which gives it a superior
performance. This, of course, is pure nonsense. The difference
between a 'Deltic' and an 'A4' is simply that the one has more
tractive effort. One would naturally expect a 'Deltic' to have the
edge on an 'A4', just as one would expect a 'Pacific' to do better

than an 'Atlantic'. I will not get myself involved in the thorny problem of relative costs, except to say that as far as I know there has never been published a full financial justification for the replacement of steam by diesel traction, nor for the use of imported fuel instead of our great source of indigenous mineral wealth.

One gains the unfortunate impression that the withdrawal has been hastened for reasons other than sound business. Less than eight years ago we were still building 'BR9' 2-10-0s: splendid engines, easy to work, economical in fuel, and having a high route availability, and yet it would be interesting to know how a commercial undertaking would justify scrapping them—more than 200 of them—after so short a life. One must not be too critical. The British Railways Board had a hard enough task without having to parry awkward comments from its friends outside the railway service. But when one has studied railway and locomotive history over the whole life of the steam locomotive, and one sees the axe come down with the fury and speed that it has done in the last few years it causes one inevitably to stop and think. I feel sure that future historians will be astonished at the summary methods used in what finally became a slaughter. And there I must leave it—16,000 steam locomotives scrapped in eight years.

CHAPTER FOURTEEN

THE SURVIVORS

AFTER the slaughter, what remains? The introduction of the steam locomotive was the greatest single factor in fostering the industrial and economical upsurge of Great Britain in the nineteenth century; in furthering the development and expansion of the British Empire, and of our export trade generally. The great advantages in manufacturing techniques of materials were in the first place very largely due to the needs of steam railways. The very first plant for production of Bessemer steel on a commercial basis was laid down at Crewe locomotive works. And this story of great engineering evolution and endeavour is now almost at an end. In the country that gave birth to the steam locomotive and suckled it to become one of the noblest of machines, what is being done to provide a permanent memorial to this shining page in our technical history? One is very much afraid that no clear answer can yet be given. Many historic locomotives have been saved from the scrapheap, and are housed in one or other of the museums at present under the care of the British Railways Board. The future of these exhibits is uncertain, while they remain a charge on a Government-owned organization the yearly deficit from which is constantly mounting.

Other retired veterans are in somewhat safer keeping, in the Science Museum in London, and in Municipal museums, at Birmingham, Glasgow, Leicester and Swindon. Other locomotives withdrawn in comparatively recent years from active service have been purchased by private individuals or societies. Some of these, like those bought by Sir William Butlin, have been for stationary display, while others have already been used as working units for hauling special trains on British Railways. It is largely because there has been no national plan for establishment of a permanent Railway Museum of appropriate size that so many individual enterprises have been launched. Even if the exhibits at

Clapham and York could be considered as permanent, and similarly that joint concern of British Railways and the Swindon Corporation, one could hardly regard as satisfactory a situation in which one found the Great Northern and North Eastern survivors at York; one Brighton and one London and North Western veteran also at York, and others at Clapham; some Midland engines at Leicester, and another one at Clapham; most of the Great Western engines at Swindon, but one of the most important exhibits of all at the Science Museum.

In the meantime every issue of every journal in the railway enthusiast press contains appeals for funds to preserve this or that locomotive, following the successful ventures to preserve and run certain great celebrities like the *Flying Scotsman*, the *Sir Nigel Gresley* and the *Pendennis Castle*. Interest in British locomotives is world-wide, and several have found what one hopes will be permanent homes in the United States of America. Others, saved from the scrapheap under a plan for preservation drawn up when R. A. Riddles was member of the Railway Executive responsible for mechanical and electrical engineering, are lying in retirement, just as they were taken from traffic, awaiting some attention if space for their exhibition is eventually found. It all amounts to a series of disjointed efforts. In the aggregate, the survivors total up to quite a considerable number; but scattered as they are, and in such diverse circumstances, it would need a pilgrimage of several weeks to pay a visit to them all.

If the present position is not satisfactory, that existing prior to World War II was even worse. Among the old railway companies only the London and North Eastern, as successor to the North Eastern Railway, seemed to have any official regard for its historical heritage. The Railway Museum at York was a splendid enterprise, and in addition to famous North Eastern engines restored to their original condition it came to include such alien celebrities as the Stirling 8-footer No. 1, the Brighton 0-4-2 *Gladstone* and the *City of Truro*. At that time the preservation of historical locomotives was a matter for individual appeal rather than a considered plan for preserving those with the greatest historic significance, and it is now, for example, the isolated and rather unrepresentative 4-2-2 No. 123 that represents the express passenger stud of the Caledonian Railway, rather than one of the world famous 'Dunalastairs'. Again the Great Eastern is represented at Clapham by one of the Holden mixed traffic 2-4-os, instead of the more obvious choice of a 'Claud Hamilton'.

Unfortunately, however, by the time some kind of policy for locomotive preservation was launched there was not a great deal of choice, in most cases, and a small-wheeled 2-4-0 restored to the gorgeous Royal Blue livery of the Great Eastern is better than nothing. Saddest of all is that there is no example whatever of twentieth-century London and North Western express passenger practice. If ever a locomotive class deserved a niche in the gallery of fame it was the *George the Fifth*, to stand beside its distinguished 4-4-0 contemporaries, the Midland compound, and the Great Central 'Director' that adorn the present collection at Clapham. But the LMSR, like the Great Western in Churchward's time, was not very preservation minded, and by October 1949, before the British Railways scheme for locomotive preservation had got under way, the last North Western express passenger engines had faced 'the firing squad'.

Perhaps the greatest misfortune of earlier days was Churchward's decision, in 1905, to scrap the two broad gauge veterans *North Star* and *Lord of the Isles*. It is true that the former engine had been much rebuilt from the 'elegant ornament' delivered from Robert Stephenson's works in 1837, and a replica using many of the original parts was constructed for the Great Western centenary celebrations in 1935. But of the two engines I consider the *Lord of the Isles* was the greater loss, because the 8-foot 4-2-2 singles fairly epitomized the broad gauge for the majority of travellers. *Lord of the Isles*, built in 1850, was sent new to the Great Exhibition of 1851, and went into traffic in 1852. She then did thirty-two years' service, and was withdrawn in 1884. William Dean refrained from scrapping her, and she was subsequently sent on exhibition to Edinburgh, in 1890, to Chicago in 1893, and finally to Earls Court. Then Churchward decided she was taking up valuable space at Swindon, and the outcome was dismissed in a single sentence in *The Locomotive Magazine* of March 15, 1906: 'Our readers will learn with regret that the two historic broad gauge veterans *North Star* and *Lord of the Isles* have recently been scrapped.' And that was that!

Scottish enthusiasts, and indeed all those who love the older locomotives of Great Britain, owe an immense debt of gratitude to James Ness, who while General Manager of Scottish Region arranged for the preservation of 4-4-0 locomotives of the North British and Great North of Scotland Railways, put them into first class running order and restored them to their original liveries. Furthermore, the two ex-LMSR veterans, the Caledonian 4-2-2 and the Highland 'Jones Goods' 4-6-0, which had lain in somewhat uncertain state at St Rollox, were similarly treated. These four restored engines, all 'in glorious technicolour', then proceeded to run special excursions in many parts of Scotland, and in this exhilarating period they were joined for a time by the Great Western *City of Truro*. The majority of these specials were double-headed, and it does need much imagination to picture the visual impact made by the green *Gordon Highlander*, and the yellow 'Jones Goods' in double harness, or the Caley 'single' piloting *Glen Douglas*. The visitor from Swindon was as brilliantly colourful as any of them, for when she was taken out of York Museum and put into running order she was decked in her original livery, that of Dean's day on the Great Western. The four Scottish veterans, joined by a Glasgow and South Western 'pug' and a Caley 0-6-0 and 0-4-4 tank, are now finally retired, secure, lovingly tended, and displayed in the Glasgow Municipal Museum.

The *City of Truro*, before she came finally to rest in the present railway museum at Swindon, had an eventful career. When that fiery Scots advocate Norman Doran Macdonald worked up such a furore of a campaign for the preservation of the Caledonian single No. 123, in 1931, and a similar campaign was waged by North Western enthusiasts on behalf of the 'Jumbo' No. 790 *Hardwicke*, its ultimate success gave the cue to Great Western supporters to do something similar for the *City of Truro*. The fate of the broad gauge *North Star* and of the *Lord of the Isles* was vividly recalled; but in the early 1930s space need not have been a problem. Providing the LNER were agreeable, there was space at York. A strong campaign was worked up, much to the disgust, I believe, of Mr. Collett; but *City of Truro* was saved, and she duly went to York. In company with the other preserved engines she was moved to a place of greater safety 'somewhere in Scotland' during the war years, and duly returned to York as a static exhibit afterwards.

In the meantime the museum was getting somewhat crowded. The LNER, with their traditional regard for historical relics, decided to preserve two 'Atlantics': the first-ever British engine of the type, H. A. Ivatt's small boilered 990, named *Henry Oakley*, and the pioneer large-boilered Great Northern 'Atlantic' No. 251. The former had been installed in the museum shortly before the war, and with the arrival of No. 251 in 1950 space was at a premium. At that time the lives of these engines that were preserved were regarded as finished. True there had been a glorious episode in 1938 when the 'Stirling' 8-footer No. 1 had run the rails once more. But railway enthusiasts in general were inclined to regard that as the brief intervention of a special providence, in the form of massive support from Sir Nigel Gresley. In 1938 he was such a power in the railway world that once an idea had his backing no practical difficulties would be allowed to stand in the way. And the difficulties that *did* supervene, from the time No. 1 was extracted from the museum until she took the road out of Kings Cross on June 30th, 1938 would almost fill a book of their own. In the early 1950s there was no Gresley, and the great engineers of the old railway companies were then retired.

Then another personality began to come into the picture, a Yorkshire business man, Alan F. Pegler, who had certain resources to back his unbounded enthusiasm for steam locomotives in general, and for Great Northern enginers in particular. The centenary of the opening of the Doncaster plant was approaching, and Pegler, mindful of what Gresley himself had done in 1938, put to the authorities one of the most elaborate programmes of living railway pageantry that had been conceived in this country since the Railway Centenary celebrations at Darlington in 1925. It was not enough that the 'Stirling' 8-footer should once again be brought out of York Museum. Both the 'Atlantics' must come too, and both of them should *run*. On two successive Sundays there should be a special train named 'The Plant Centenarian'— for in Doncaster no one talks of the railway 'works'. It was the 'plant' where the 'Stirling' 8-footers, the Ivatt 'Atlantics' and the Gresley 'Pacifics' were born. On the first Sunday the two Ivatt 'Atlantics', 990 and 251, were to double-head the down train from Kings Cross to Doncaster, and the pioneer Gresley streamlined 'A4' *Silver Link* was to work it back to London. On the following Sunday the special started from Leeds, headed by the two 'Atlantics', and returned in the most terrific style, behind *Silver Link*.

How this grand conception was successfully carried out is another long story. But done it was, and the idea of using the museum pieces for revenue-earning purposes on special trains was well and truly launched. Managerial opinion on such a daring enterprise was not entirely convinced by the end of the year 1953. To any Great Western enthusiast the year 1954 had a special significance, and I discussed with Alan Pegler the possibility of getting the *City of Truro* out of York in time to make a golden jubilee run from Plymouth on May 9, 1954. He took it up just as enthusiastically as the celebration of important anniversaries on his own East Coast route; but the Western Region authorities were not quite ready, and the Golden Jubilee of the famous Ocean Mail run passed by. But the seeds had been sown, and with a tremendous Great Western enthusiast in the chair at Paddington, in the person of R. F. Hanks—'Reggie' to his enormous circle of railway friends—*City of Truro* was extracted from York three years later. Not only was she put into magnificent running order but she was repainted in the Dean style, with light red underframes, the original lining, and the elaborate monogram, consisting of the letters GWR in scroll ingeniously intertwined. It is true that the engine, as restored, was something of an anachronism, having a superheater boiler, top feed, and a large Churchward copper-capped chimney. But while the perfervid purists shook their heads, the great majority of us were delighted.

As renovated *City of Truro* was such a splendid engine in traffic that there were quite serious thoughts of trying to repeat the classic feat of May 9, 1904, when she attained a maximum speed of 100 m.p.h.-plus in the descent of Wellington bank. I was on her footplate one Sunday evening in 1957 when Chief Inspector Andress and a very enthusiastic Bristol driver and fireman definitely set out to equal, if not to break, the fifty-three-year-old record. The odds were rather against us from the start, because we had a heavily loaded eight-coach corridor train of modern stock, 285 tons, whereas in 1904 the load of the Ocean Mail was one of only five postal vans, 148 tons. Nevertheless, that delightful museum piece reached 84 m.p.h. in the descent, and I have very little doubt that with an equivalent load to that of 1904 she would have topped the '100'. But the very circumstances that prevented her doing so in 1957 were in themselves a manifestation of the popularity such trips enjoyed. The train was crowded. Hardly a seat was vacant, and quite apart from giving so many people a Sunday trip to the sea the interest in the engine itself from ordinary travellers was intense.

From that time the practice of running special trips hauled by engines of historic interest rapidly spread. Many were organized by the Stephenson Locomotive Society, the Railway Correspondence and Travel Society, the Locomotive Club of Great Britain, and others. British Railways co-operated readily enough while steam was in general use, even to the extent of acceding to requests to run locomotives far beyond their normal haunts. Alan Pegler, for example, took the Gresley 'A4' *Mallard* to Blackpool, and a special organized excursion in connection with the annual air display at Farnborough was worked, as far south as Basingstoke, by a Great Northern 'Atlantic' and a Great Central 'Director' in double-harness. By that time the scrapping of steam had begun in earnest, and while some engines that were ear-marked museum pieces were restored to some of their former glory, as in the case of the Midland compound No. 1000, with others the ranks were thinning, and then once again Alan Pegler proved a pioneer. He purchased an engine outright, at the same time making a contract with the British Railways Board enabling him to have the engine serviced and stabled at appropriate running sheds, and to provide his engine to work special trips for enthusiasts and others. The engine he purchased was none other than the Gresley 'Pacific' No. 4472 *Flying Scotsman*. Since then that famous engine has worked specials crowded to capacity in nearly every case, to many parts of the British railway system far beyond the original sphere of activities of the Gresley 'Pacifics'.

Where Pegler pioneered others have followed, and today some very celebrated British express locomotives are in private hands, including the Great Western 4-6-0 *Pendennis Castle*; another 'Castle', built after nationalization and now equipped with twin orifice blast pipe and chimney, *Clun Castle*, and above all the hundredth 'Pacific' constructed at Doncaster, the 'A4' streamliner No. 4498 *Sir Nigel Gresley*. Another interesting and beautifully restored engine in private hands is the Gresley 'K4' 2-6-0, *The Great Marquess*. With the gradual elimination of steam on British Railways has followed, naturally, the gradual contraction of facilities for servicing and maintenance, and one feature in particular that has become an embarrassment to the running of the organization of special steam-hauled trips is the elimination of water columns. Pegler himself at once countered this difficulty by equipping *Flying Scotsman* with a second tender, and this made possible non-stop running between Kings Cross and Newcastle; but popular as steam-hauled specials were with enthusiast groups, the natural antipathy to steam by the higher ranks of the British Railways management began to show in more positive form, and despite the fact that each and every trip hauled by a veteran steam locomotive was a 'money-spinner', in the autumn of 1967 the edict went forth that there were to be no more.

It was, of course, well known that the management of British Railways was then in a very unhappy state, and since then two very senior personalities who were known to be implacably opposed to steam, on principle, have passed to other spheres of activity. It is to be hoped that ways will be found to recommence the running of special excursions that gave such an immense amount of pleasure, but were also sound revenue earners. At the same time one must emphasize once again that these activities are no more than a series of unconnected individual enterprises, when officialdom, it would seem, would be quite prepared to let the memory of the steam locomotive be completely effaced. There is, of course, not much fear of that, having regard to the numerous amateur societies now in existence, and to the activities of those who build and own model railways. It would nevertheless have been much pleasanter if the Government department responsible for the national museums had reacted to popular sentiment adequately and had instituted, under a centrally co-ordinated authority, the preservation and utilization of historical relics of the steam age. As it is the survivors of this great age of steam are scattered, harassed, and persecuted like the flying remnants of an army defeated on the field of battle.

It would, however, be completely wrong, and out of keeping with the spirit of the great-hearted men whose life's work forms the backbone of this book, to end on a depressing or defeatist note. The place of the steam locomotive in history is secure, and in what may prove a surprisingly short time those whose object is to denigrate or belittle will be forgotten, and the age of steam seen in perspective for the great age it truly was. This book has been concerned with the British home railways and their men. The locomotive building firms, which at one time made such a massive contribution to our export trade, have been mentioned no more than incidentally. In all but a few instances they have served the home railways purely as manufacturers, working to designs prepared in the railway drawing offices. There is nevertheless an equally great story to be told of the splendid engines built at Forth Bank works, at Hyde Park, at Gorton 'tank'

Atlas, Newton-le-Willows, Queens Park, and other famous establishments, that have taken the reputation of the British steam locomotive to the farthest corners of the earth. In that story the names of Charles Beyer, Henry Dübs, William Lorimer, and their successors in various fields would rank alongside the Ramsbottoms, the Kirtleys, and the Drummonds of the home railways. Some day there may be scope for a book about the locomotives we have exported. But so far as the British home railways are concerned I can only conclude by wishing long life to the survivors, and to the rest, peace to their scraps.

INDEX

Accelerations, 1932 onwards, 208
Accidents:
    Aisgill, MR, 1913, 145
    Box, GWR, Engine No. 8, 100
    Derby Junction LNWR, 99
    Penistone, MS&LR, 1884, 97
    Preston, LNWR 1896, 112
    Retford level crossing, 58
    Snowdon Mountain Rly, 1896, 117
Assoc. of Rly. Loco. Engineers, 170
Automatic Train Control, NER system, 115
Balancing, 27 et seq.
Battle of brakes, 71
Battle of gauges, 32
Boilers:
    On The Royal George, 13
    Multitubular type, 13
    Midfeathers, 59
    On Ivatt Atlantics, 125
    On 'Dunalastairs', CR, 120
    Churchward's designs, 148 et seq.
Cable Traction suggestions, 15
Compounding:
    F. W. Webb's system, 68
    GWR Tandem No. 8, 100
    W. M. Smith's system, 131
    The Midland type, 131, 143
    De Glehn system, 151
Corridor Tenders, 200
Crawl to the South, 113 et seq.
Design styles:
    Robert Stephenson's, 17
    Mid-Victorian trend, 74 et seq.
Dynamometer Cars, 247
Elizabethan, The, 255, 257
Engineers:
    Adams, W., 90 et seq.
    Allan, Alexander, 41, 61, 77
    Armstrong, Joseph, 53
    Aspinall, Sir John, 122 et seq.
    Baister, R., 115
    Beames, H. P. M., 178, 208
    Beattie, J., 64
    Bodmer, J. G., 28
    Bond, R. C., 197, 241
    Bowen-Cooke, C. J., 99, 154 et seq., 178, 238
    Braithwaite, J., 19, 27
    Brunel, I. K., 21 et seq., 30, 53
    Buddicom, W. B., 41, 43
    Bulleid, O. V. S., 226, 236
    Bury, E., 24 et seq., 38 et seq.
    Chambers, H., 196

Engineers: continued
    Churchward, G. J., 147 et seq., 170, 208
    Clayton, J., 170, 192
    Collett, C. B., 172
    Cook, K. J., 251, 255
    Cox, E. S., 241
    Crampton, T. R., 33, 37, 45, 56
    Cumming, C., 175
    Dean, W., 74, 93
    Deeley, R. M., 141 et seq.
    Dixon, John, 12, 19
    Drummond, Dugald, 76, 80, 88, 98, 119, 133, 162
    Drummond, Peter, 76, 80, 88, 163, 166
    Ell, S. O., 248
    Ericsson, 19
    Fairlie, R., 70
    Fernihough, W., 28, 39
    Fletcher, E., 49, 66 et seq., 130
    Fowler, Sir H., 143, 165, 170, 181
    Gooch, Sir D., 29, 32, 39, 46, 52 et seq., 76, 93
    Gray, John, 47
    Gresley, Sir H. N., 162, 170, 173, 234, 256
    Hackworth, Timothy, 12, 13, 19, 24
    Hawksworth, F. W., 226, 234, 251
    Holcroft, H., 176 et seq.
    Holden, James, 136
    Hughes, G., 170, 181
    Ivatt, H. A., 116, 122
    Ivatt, H. G., 228, 237
    Johnson, S. W., 82, 131
    Jones, David, 89
    Joy, David, 46 et seq., 65, 82
    Kendal, John, 51
    King, H. C., 149
    Kirtley, M., 49
    Locke, Joseph, 12, 38, 43, 77
    Longridge, M., 16
    Maunsell, R. E. L., 163, 170
    McConnell, J. E., 31 et seq., 41, 44, 60 et seq.
    McDonnell, A., 66 et seq., 130
    McIntosh, J. F., 116, 119, 134
    Paget, C., 141 et seq.
    Pettigrew, W., 91
    Ramsbottom, J., 61
    Raven, Sir Vincent, 115, 130, 165, 251
    Riddles, R. A., 236 et seq.
    Robinson, J. G., 127 et seq., 169, 173
    Sackfield, T., 161
    Sacré, C., 90, 97
    Smeddle, R. A., 251

Engineers: *continued*
  Smith, F. G., 162
  Smith, W. M., 130, 132
  Spooner, C. E., 70
  Stanier, Sir William, 208, 237
  Stephenson, G., 11, 14, 44
  Stephenson, R., 13 *et seq.*
  Stirling, James, 88
  Stirling, Matthew, 163
  Stirling, Patrick, 86 *et seq.*, 101,
109, 125
  Stroudley, W., 49, 76, 80, 82, 89
  Sturrock, A., 56 *et seq.*, 63, 87
  Surtees, R., 138
  Thompson, E., 226, 234, 256
  Trevithick, Francis, 41
  Wainwright, H. S., 138, 162
  Webb, F. W., 65, 68 *et seq.*, 72, 128
  Westinghouse, G., 71
  Whale, G., 96, 128
  Whitelegg, R. H., 139
  Whitelegg, T., 138, 139
  Worsdell, Wilson, 96, 107, 130, 132
  Worsdell, T. W., 92
Financiers, etc.:
  Hudson, G., 32, 38
  Background to the Mania, 37
Footplates, 107, 142
Framing (locomotives):
On the *Patentee*, 25
  On Forrester's 'Boxers., 26
French influence (1930), 212
Grouping (1923):
  CME's of the group, 172 *et seq.*
  LMS constituents, 180
  Loco's for 'The Royal Scot', 182
Highland 'River' case, 167
Institution of Mechanical Engineers, 44
Jellicoe Specials, 166
Lickey Incline, 34
Loco. Inspectors, 153
Loco. Trials:
  Rainhill, 17 *et seq.*
  Knight of St Patrick GWR, 152
  LNWR Interchange 1909, 155
  LNWR-*v*-GWR 1910, 156, 158
  Ralph Brocklebank LNWR, 160, 161
  First GNR Pacifics, 178
  Launceston Castle on LMS, 182
  Leeds-Carlisle, LMS, 185
  GWR *v* LNER 1925, 189
  British Railways, 1948, 238 *et seq.*
  BR Controlled road, 248 *et seq.*
  LNER 'V2' at Swindon, 249
  King Edward VII, 252 *et seq.*
Loco. Types and Designs:
  British Standard, 243 *et seq.*
  Evening Star, 246

Loco. Types and Designs: *continued*
  Early Examples
    Royal George, 13
    Lancashire Witch, 14
    Rocket, 18, 23
    Sans Pareil, 18, 23
    Novelty, 18, 27
    Liverpool, 23
    Stephenson's *Patentee*, 25, 33, 46
    Forrester's 'Boxers', 26, 42
    Stephenson's 'Long boiler', 35 *et seq.*
    Great 'A', 37
    Old Crewe types, 43, 77
    Jenny Lind, 46 *et seq.*
  Caledonian, 80, 120, 264
  Great Eastern, 83, 136
  Great Northern, 87, 122, 176, 265
  GWR types:
    Firefly, 33, 37
    Great Western, 46, 76
    'Iron Duke' class, 52, 263
    Dean 7 ft. 8 in. single, 74, 93
    'Atbara' class, 148
    'City' class, 148, 264, 266
    Albion (4-6-0), 151
    North Star (4-6-0), 152
    The Great Bear, 159
    'Castle' class, 187, 254, 268
    'King' class, 195, 251
    'Hall' class, 218
  Highland:
    'Small Ben' 4-4-0, 81, 118
    'Strath' 4-4-0, 89
    'Lock' 4-4-0, 89
    Jones Goods 4-6-0, 122, 264
    'River' 4-6-0, 167
    'Clan', 4-6-0, 175
  Lancashire and Yorkshire, 122
  London, Brighton & South Coast:
    'Gladstone', 79, 105
  LNWR types:
    The 'Bloomers', 60
    Lady of the Lake, 62
    Precedent type, 79, 84, 264
    Precursor, 128
    George the Fifth, 156, 263
    Sir Gilbert Claughton, 159
  London & South Western:
    'T9' 4-4-0, 81, 118
    Adams 4-4-0, 91
    'Paddlebox' 4-4-0, 135
    'The Bug', 135
  Manchester, Sheffield & Lincolnshire, 90
  Midland:
    Johnson types, 83, 85
    Compounds, 131, 143
  Railway Operating Division, 169
  South Eastern, 88

Loco. Types and Designs *continued*
  SE&CR:
    Borsig 4–4–0, 164
      E1 rebuild, 174
    LMS types:
      'Royal Scot' 4–6–0, 196
      Mixed Traffic 4–6–0, 218
      The Princess Royal, 220
      'Black Staniers', 219
      'Duchess' Class, 223
    LNER types:
      Enterprise (4–6–2), 198
      Flying Scotsman, 268
      Ivat-Gresley 'Atlantics', 210, 265
      Cock o' the North, 213
      Streamlined Pacific, 215, 267, 268
    L.N.E.R. types:
      'B1' 4–6–0, 227
    Southern types:
      'King Arthur' class, 191
      'Lord Nelson' class, 194
      'Schools' class, 202
      'Merchant Navy' class, 226, 236
      Bulleid Pacific rebuilt, 257
    War Dept., 2–8–0 & 2–10–0, 237
Manning of Locomotives, 104 *et seq.*
Museum pieces, 261 *et seq.*
Nationalization, 233 *et seq.*
  Regional situations, 234 *et seq.*
  Engine standardisation, 240 *et seq.*
Organization of Loco. Dept.:
  General, 39, 95, 98
  Midland Rly., 142
  Midland load limits, 144
Personalities:
  Booth, Henry, 12, 13
  Bowen-Cooke, Miss, 171
  Cockshott, F. P., 109
  Earle, Hardman, 12
  Elliott, John, 141
  Gibb, George S., 132
  Granet, Sir Guy, 141 *et seq.*, 179
  Hudson, G., 32
  Inglis, Sir J., 157
  Lardner, Dr D., 21
  Paget, Sir Ernest, 141
  Pease, Joseph, 16
  Pole, Sir Felix, 188, 195
  'Rathbone and Cropper', 12
  Walker, Sir Herbert, 162, 236
  Watkin, Sir E., 117
Plant Centenarian Express, 126
Races:
  London–Aberdeen, 108 *et seq.*
  Plymouth–London, 149

Railmotor Cars, 137
Railway Executive Committee, 165
Railway Operating Division, 165
Railways, Early:
  Brecon and Merthyr, 50
  Bristol and Birmingham, 31
  Eastern Counties, 27, 28
  Festiniog, 69
  Grand Junction, 39, 41
  Great Northern, 56
  Great Western, 30, 52
  Liverpool and Manchester, 12, 17 *et seq.*
  London and Birmingham, 22, 41
  London, Brighton & South Coast, 47
  London and North Western, 41, 43, 96
  Manchester, Sheffield & Lincolnshire, 117
  North Midland, 42, 49
  Nottingham and Grantham, 48
  Oxford, Worcester & Wolverhampton, 63
  Rhymney Railway, 51
  Snowdon Mountain, 117
  Stockton and Darlington, 11, 13, 24
  Tilbury, absorption by Midland, 139
  York and North Midland, 33
Riding of Locomotives, 36, 60, 102, 103, 105
Royal Trains, 96
Scrapping of steam, 259
Speed Records:
  London–Exeter, 1844, 33
  Ocean Mails, 1904, 94
  Newcastle–Edinburgh, 1895, 112
  Crewe–Carlisle, 1895, 112
  Victoria–Dover, 1896, 114
  London–Plymouth, 1903, 148
  Cheltenham Flyer, 203 *et seq.*
  London–Newcastle, 1935, 214
  Silver Jubilee, 215
  Mallard, 1938, 224
Sour-apple harvest, 228
Standardization schemes, 227, 240
Superheating, first applications, 155, 156
Swindon civic developments, 53 *et seq.*
Train wrecking: *Merlin*, 1956, 193
Valve gears:
  Stephenson link motion, 64
  Joy's radial gear, 65
  Conjugated, for 3 cyl, engines, 176, 234
  Improved gear on LNER, 197, 256
War services, 166 *et seq.*, 225 *et seq.*
Water troughs, 62

GEORGE ALLEN & UNWIN LTD
Head Office:
London: 40 Museum Street, W.C.1

Trade orders and enquiries:
Park Lane, Hemel Hempstead, Herts.

Auckland: P.O. Box 36013, Northcote Central, N.4
Barbados: P.O. Box 222, Bridgetown
Beirut: Deeb Building, Jeanne d'Arc Street
Bombay: 15 Graham Road, Ballard Estate, Bombay 1
Buenos Aires: Escritorio 454–459, Florida 165
Calcutta: 17 Chittaranjan Avenue, Calcutta 13
Cape Town: 68 Shortmarket Street
Hong Kong: 105 Wing On Mansion, 26 Hancow Road, Kowloon
Ibadan: P.O. Box 62
Karachi: Karachi Chambers, McLeod Road
Madras: Mohan Mansions, 38c Mount Road, Madras 6
Mexico: Villalongin 32 Mexico 5, D.F.
Nairobi: P.O. Box 30583
New Delhi: 13–14 Asaf Ali Road, New Delhi 1
Ontario: 81 Curlew Drive, Don Mills
Philippines: P.O. Box 4322, Manila
Rio de Janeiro: Caixa Postal 2537–Zc–00
Singapore: 36c Prinsep Street, Singapore 7
Sydney, N.S.W.: Bradbury House, 55 York Street
Tokyo: P.O. Box 26, Kamata

Hamilton Ellis

BRITISH RAILWAY HISTORY
1830-1876

'He must know Bradshaw by heart. He has turned his involved material
into a lucid and brilliantly entertaining story, written in fresh prose . . . so
well-written and readable a book as this is also an important contribution
to nineteenth-century English social history. Hamilton Ellis shows himself
to be not only a learned man with an eye for the picturesque and comic,
but also an historian capable of making a complicated subject clear and
relating railways to the life and habits of the people who used them.' JOHN
BETJEMAN in the *Daily Telegraph*

SOUTH WESTERN RAILWAY

Of the great British railways before 1923, the senior company was the
London and South Western, or, as it was generally called, the South Western.
Older than any of the big northern companies, older even than the Great
Western, its history was unbroken by amalgamation until it became the
major constituent of the Southern Railway.

Its mechanical history, with which the book is chiefly engaged, was outstanding; it was served by a succession of brilliant locomotive engineers;
it was a pioneer of automatic signalling; all-round quality distinguished its
train services and its rolling stock. Yet it had its foibles, and occasionally its
misfortunes, which add a tincture to its story. Stretching from London to
Plymouth and North Cornwall, serving Hardy's Wessex and Trollope's
'Barset', it was a lovely line.

THE BEAUTY OF OLD TRAINS

'This is a "must" for all railway-lovers—for the young so that they may
see for themselves the riches their fathers enjoyed; for the elders that they
may enjoy again the pleasures of bygone days.' *Birmingham Post*

GEORGE ALLEN & UNWIN LTD.